The Victorian Male Body

Edinburgh Critical Studies in Victorian Culture
Series Editor: Julian Wolfreys

Recent books in the series:

Rudyard Kipling's Fiction: Mapping Psychic Spaces
Lizzy Welby

The Decadent Image: The Poetry of Wilde, Symons and Dowson
Kostas Boyiopoulos

British India and Victorian Literary Culture
Máire ní Fhlathúin

Anthony Trollope's Late Style: Victorian Liberalism and Literary Form
Frederik Van Dam

Dark Paradise: Pacific Islands in the Nineteenth-Century British Imagination
Jenn Fuller

Twentieth-Century Victorian: Arthur Conan Doyle and the Strand Magazine, *1891–1930*
Jonathan Cranfield

The Lyric Poem and Aestheticism: Forms of Modernity
Marion Thain

Gender, Technology and the New Woman
Lena Wånggren

Self-Harm in New Woman Writing
Alexandra Gray

Suffragist Artists in Partnership: Gender, Word and Image
Lucy Ella Rose

Victorian Liberalism and Material Culture: Synergies of Thought and Place
Kevin A. Morrison

The Victorian Male Body
Joanne-Ella Parsons and Ruth Heholt

Nineteenth-Century Emigration in British Literature and Art
Fariha Shaikh

The Pre-Raphaelites and Orientalism
Eleonora Sasso

The Late-Victorian Little Magazine
Koenraad Claes

Coastal Cultures of the Long Nineteenth Century
Matthew Ingleby and Matt P. M. Kerr

Dickens and Demolition: Literary Allusion and Urban Change in the Mid-Nineteenth Century
Joanna Robinson

Forthcoming volumes:

Her Father's Name: Gender, Theatricality and Spiritualism in Florence Marryat's Fiction
Tatiana Kontou

The Sculptural Body in Victorian Literature: Encrypted Sexualities
Patricia Pulham

Olive Schreiner and the Politics of Print Culture, 1883–1920
Clare Gill

Dickens's Clowns: Charles Dickens, Joseph Grimaldi and the Pantomime of Life
Johnathan Buckmaster

Victorian Auto/Biography: Problems in Genre and Subject
Amber Regis

Victorian Poetry, Poetics and the Literary Periodical
Caley Ehnes

Culture and Identity in Fin-de-Siècle Scotland: Romance, Decadence and the Celtic Revival
Michael Shaw

Gissing, Shakespeare and the Life of Writing
Thomas Ue

The Victorian Actress in the Novel and on the Stage
Renata Kobetts Miller

For a complete list of titles published visit the Edinburgh Critical Studies in Victorian Culture web page at www.edinburghuniversitypress.com/series/ECVC

Also Available:
Victoriographies – A Journal of Nineteenth-Century Writing, 1790–1914, edited by Diane Piccitto and Patricia Pulham
ISSN: 2044-2416
www.eupjournals.com/vic

The Victorian Male Body

Edited by Joanne Ella Parsons and
Ruth Heholt

EDINBURGH
University Press

Edinburgh University Press is one of the leading university presses in the UK. We publish academic books and journals in our selected subject areas across the humanities and social sciences, combining cutting-edge scholarship with high editorial and production values to produce academic works of lasting importance. For more information visit our website: edinburghuniversitypress.com

© editorial matter and organisation Joanne Ella Parsons and Ruth Heholt, 2018
© the chapters their several authors, 2018

Edinburgh University Press Ltd
The Tun – Holyrood Road,
12(2f) Jackson's Entry,
Edinburgh EH8 8PJ

Typeset in 11/13 Adobe Sabon by
IDSUK (DataConnection) Ltd

A CIP record for this book is available from the British Library

ISBN 978 1 4744 2860 6 (hardback)
ISBN 978 1 4744 2862 0 (webready PDF)
ISBN 978 1 4744 2863 7 (epub)

The right of Joanne Ella Parsons and Ruth Heholt to be identified as the editors of this work has been asserted in accordance with the Copyright, Designs and Patents Act 1988, and the Copyright and Related Rights Regulations 2003 (SI No. 2498).

Contents

Series Editor's Preface — vii
Acknowledgements — ix

Introduction: Visible and Invisible Bodies — 1
Ruth Heholt and Joanne Ella Parsons

Part I. Constructed Bodies

1. Violent Play and Regular Discipline: The Abuses of the Schoolboy Body in Victorian Fiction — 25
   Alice Crossley

2. Punishing the Unregulated Manly Body and Emotions in Early Victorian England — 46
   Joanne Begiato

3. The New Man's Body in Ménie Muriel Dowie's *Gallia* — 65
   Tara MacDonald

Part II. Fractured and Fragmented Bodies

4. Pirates and Prosthetics: Manly Messages for Managing Limb Loss in Victorian and Edwardian Adventure Narratives — 87
   Ryan Sweet

5. Tuberculosis and Visionary Sensibility: The Consumptive Body as Masculine Dissent in George Eliot and Henry James — 108
   Meredith Miller

6. Monstrous Masculinities from the Macaroni to Mr Hyde: Reading the Gothic 'Gentleman' — 128
   Alison Younger

7. Visible yet Immaterial: The Phantom and the Male Body in Ghost Stories by Three Victorian Women Writers — 148
   Ruth Heholt

Part III. Unruly Bodies

8. Aesthetics of Deviance: George du Maurier's Representations of the Artist's Body for *Punch* as Discourse on Manliness, 1870–1880   171
   Françoise Baillet

9. Suffering, Asceticism and the Starving Male Body in *Mary Barton*   193
   Charlotte Boyce

10. Fosco's Fat: Transgressive Consumption and Bodily Control in Wilkie Collins' *The Woman in White*   215
    Joanne Ella Parsons

11. Sensationalising Otherness: The Italian Male Body in Mary Elizabeth Braddon's 'Olivia' and 'Garibaldi'   234
    Anne-Marie Beller

Contributors   251
Index   255

Series Editor's Preface

'Victorian' is a term, at once indicative of a strongly determined concept and an often notoriously vague notion, emptied of all meaningful content by the many journalistic misconceptions that persist about the inhabitants and cultures of the British Isles and Victoria's Empire in the nineteenth century. As such, it has become a by-word for the assumption of various, often contradictory habits of thought, belief, behaviour and perceptions. Victorian studies and studies in nineteenth-century literature and culture have, from their institutional inception, questioned narrowness of presumption, pushed at the limits of the nominal definition, and have sought to question the very grounds on which the unreflective perception of the so-called Victorian has been built; and so they continue to do. Victorian and nineteenth-century studies of literature and culture maintain a breadth and diversity of interest, of focus and inquiry, in an interrogative and intellectually open-minded and challenging manner, which are equal to the exploration and inquisitiveness of its subjects. Many of the questions asked by scholars and researchers of the innumerable productions of nineteenth-century society actively put into suspension the clichés and stereotypes of 'Victorianism', whether the approach has been sustained by historical, scientific, philosophical, empirical, ideological or theoretical concerns; indeed, it would be incorrect to assume that each of these approaches to the idea of the Victorian has been, or has remained, in the main exclusive, sealed off from the interests and engagements of other approaches. A vital interdisciplinarity has been pursued and embraced, for the most part, even as there has been contest and debate amongst Victorianists, pursued with as much fervour as the affirmative exploration between different disciplines and differing epistemologies put to work in the service of reading the nineteenth century.

Edinburgh Critical Studies in Victorian Culture aims to take up both the debates and the inventive approaches and departures from convention that studies in the nineteenth century have witnessed for the last half century at least. Aiming to maintain a 'Victorian' (in the most positive sense of that motif) spirit of inquiry, the series' purpose is to continue and augment the cross-fertilisation of interdisciplinary approaches, and to offer, in addition, a number of timely and untimely revisions of Victorian literature, culture, history and identity. At the same time, the series will ask questions concerning what has been missed or improperly received, misread, or not read at all, in order to present a multi-faceted and heterogeneous kaleidoscope of representations. Drawing on the most provocative, thoughtful and original research, the series will seek to prod at the notion of the 'Victorian', and in so doing, principally through theoretically and epistemologically sophisticated close readings of the historicity of literature and culture in the nineteenth century, to offer the reader provocative insights into a world that is at once overly familiar, and irreducibly different, other and strange. Working from original sources, primary documents and recent interdisciplinary theoretical models, Edinburgh Critical Studies in Victorian Culture seeks not simply to push at the boundaries of research in the nineteenth century, but also to inaugurate the persistent erasure and provisional, strategic redrawing of those borders.

Julian Wolfreys

Acknowledgements

Firstly, I would like to thank my co-editor, Dr Ruth Heholt, for her unfailing enthusiasm and drive. I also owe thanks to Dr Nadine Muller for her essential input at an earlier stage of this project. Much respect and thanks are also due to all of our wonderful contributors, not least because without their brilliant words this collection would not exist. Additionally, I would like to thank Dr Marie Mulvey-Roberts, Dr Sarah Chaney and Dr Paul Craddock for reading earlier versions of my chapter; their insightful comments have been invaluable. Finally, I would like to thank my husband, Chris, for his patience and support.

Joanne Ella Parsons

Thanks to Jo for her resilience and patience. Thanks also to Katia Bowers for reading my chapter and for her excellent suggestions. I would like to thank Nigel Kingcome for introducing me to masculinity theory many years ago. Thanks to William Hughes for support and friendship. And thanks to Frosk for support and proofreading.

Ruth Heholt

Both authors would like to thank Julian Wolfreys for his kind support of this project.

Introduction: Visible and Invisible Bodies

Ruth Heholt and Joanne Ella Parsons

The characteristics of the privileged group define the societal norm [. . .] The characteristics and attributes of those who are privileged group members are described as societal norms – as the way things are and as what is normal in society. This normalization of privilege means that members of society are judged, and succeed or fail, measured against the characteristics that are held by those privileged. The privileged characteristic is the norm; those who stand outside are the aberrant or 'alternative'. (Wildman and Davis 1995: 890)

While the male body has often served as a paradigm and metaphor for male-dominated culture and society, it has also served as a site for struggle. (Hall 1994: 6)

In *1895: Drama, Disaster and Disgrace in Late Victorian Britain*, Nicholas Freeman discusses the way that same-sex desire in men was viewed, arguing that surprisingly late in the nineteenth century, 'homosexuality had yet to be articulated in the bourgeois consciousness, and late-Victorian perceptions of it had not crystallized into the fatally neat syllogism, "he is not 'manly' therefore he may be an 'invert'"' (Freeman 2011: 13). Despite this lack of rigid categorisation in relation to homosexuality, simultaneously, the male body *was* being categorised, judged, and in the case of Oscar Wilde, eventually condemned. Throughout the Victorian era there were things that a white male body was not supposed to do; bodily acts that were not allowed to be performed, sexualities that were taboo, clothes that adorned the male body that were deemed inappropriate. The male body, in the nineteenth century was bound, constricted and limited in how it could express itself. Or so it would seem. In fact, the way that the white male body was seen and spoken about changed over the Victorian period, shifting from the rigid prescription of manliness to flamboyant and extrovert celebrations of otherness and sometimes back again. However there is no neat correlation between these extremes, and both were apparent (and many other bodily expressions and expectations in between) at various times in the nineteenth century. *The Victorian Male Body* examines the differing expressions and forms that the white male Victorian body represents and embodies, turning the spotlight onto one of the most ideologically important of all Victorian bodies. Exploring a wide variety of texts the essays in this collection follow feminist masculinity studies and examine the Victorian bastions of manliness and masculinity. *The Victorian Male Body* discusses the contradictions inherent in the ideological construction of the white, middle-class male body, foregrounding the importance of the white male body in the nineteenth century, in literature and other sorts of representations.

It is argued that it is imperative to look at the embodied reality of white masculinity as historically masculinity has *not* been a spectacle: everyone else has formed the spectacle and white men have been the invisible, or at least less visible, powerful surveyors. This argument, which began within feminist and postcolonial studies, was taken up enthusiastically by scholars from the newly emerging area of masculinity studies in the 1980s. Anthony Easthope argued this position in 1986 when he declared that 'masculinity has stayed pretty well concealed. This has always been its ruse in order to hold on to power [. . .] Masculinity tries to stay invisible by passing itself off as normal and universal' (Easthope 1986: 1). Concealment and invisibility are seen as a 'ruse' used by masculinity, and this 'ruse' was part of what enabled the masculine hold on power. If power cannot be seen, it cannot be resisted; if it is obscured it is less likely to be questioned, more likely to be taken-for-granted and left in place. As Chapman and Rutherford argued in 1988: 'masculinity remains the great unsaid. The contestation is over the bodies of black and gay people and women. Masculinity remains somehow removed' (Chapman and Rutherford 1988: 11). The materiality of the body is transcended, the particularity of the white male position is universalised, normalised and obscured. Although these theorists are discussing twentieth-century culture, Foucault talks of this as a historical (but still relatively new) phenomenon:

> Traditionally power was what was seen, what was shown [. . .] Discursive power, on the other hand, is exercised through its invisibility; at the same time it imposes on those whom it subjects a principle of compulsory

visibility. In discipline, it is the subjects who have to be seen. Their visibility assumes the hold of the power that is exercised over them. It is the fact of being constantly seen, of being able always to be seen, that maintains the disciplined individual in his [sic] subjection. (Foucault 1977: 187)

Discursive power is invisible and the disciplining and powerful gaze is turned outward, illuminating the marginalised, whilst itself remaining in the shadows: attention is diverted away from the centre.

John Rajchman, discussing Foucault, writes:

> Foucault's hypothesis was that there exists a sort of 'positive unconscious' of vision which determines not what is seen, but what *can* be seen. His idea is that not all ways of visualizing or rendering visible are possible at once. A period only lets some things be seen and not others. It 'illuminates' some things and so casts others in the shade. (Rajchman 1985: 391)

This idea that only certain things can be seen at one time leads to an anomaly in the theoretical discussions of vision that emanate from both the centre and the margins. In the discussion that cites white men and the white centre as invisible, this invisibility is predicated on the visibility of others. Fanon writing in 1952 gives cry to his distress at this enforced visibility:

> I am given no chance. I am overdetermined from without. I am the slave not of the 'idea' that others have of me but of my own appearance. I move slowly in the world, accustomed now to seek no longer for upheaval, I progress by crawling. And already I am being dissected by white eyes, the only real eyes. I am *fixed*. Having adjusted their microtomes, they objectively cut away slices of my reality. I am laid bare [. . .] Why, it's a Negro! (Fanon 1967: 116)

Fanon's visibility and overdetermination originate from *outside* himself, from 'without'. His self and his reality are sliced away from him – in this (white) discourse they are not important. He is laid bare; stripped and dissected until the part of him that *is* deemed important is irrevocably visible – he is down to only his skin. The white eye, the one that commits this act, is the only 'real' eye, because it is the one that holds the power. Fanon's own eye and way of seeing carry no hegemonic power, and therefore Fanon as an autonomous human being need not even be acknowledged by the white hegemony. It is only Fanon's body that is visible and that matters. In Fanon's case, the white power to see equates with the white power that controls the oppressed. However, within this equation there is another aspect to the visibility of the dominated, and that is the seemingly anomalous, often cited, *invisibility* of the oppressed. Where Fanon cites the compulsory visibility of black people, he himself also acknowledges their simultaneous invisibility, and bell hooks maintains that 'one mark of oppression was that black folks were compelled to assume the mantle of invisibility' (hooks 1992: 168). A closer look at this anomaly, though, means that it is resolved quite easily. Whilst Fanon's *body* is compelled into visibility, he is not allowed to *look*. He is denied the gaze himself, merely becoming the object of the white gaze. bell hooks claims that it is this denial of the gaze that itself leads to invisibility for those who are othered: 'to be fully an object then was to lack the capacity to see or recognize reality. Those looking relations were reinforced as whites cultivated the practice of denying the subjectivity of blacks (the better to dehumanize and oppress), of relegating them to the realm of the invisible' (ibid.: 168). Thus compulsory visibility for othered people slips quite easily into compelled invisibility. What is not seen is the humanity and agency of the other, partly through the very visibility and objectification of their bodies. If only certain things can be seen at once, in this case it is the bodies of the oppressed that are seen, whilst their individuality and agency are not.

In most discussions, it is this visibility that plays such a large part in the marginalisation and systematic disempowerment of the other. As David Levin concludes; 'the power to see, the power to make visible is the power to control' (Levin 1993: 7). White men have traditionally been related to the spirit – the mind – while those identified as 'other' were assumed to be subject to their biology and rooted in their bodies. Gail Ching-Liang Low argues that 'white' in racialised terms 'ex-nominates itself as a colour', and she quotes Victor Burgin, who says, 'To speak of colour of skin is to speak of a body. "People of colour" are embodied people. To have no colour is to have no body' (Low 1996: 196). White men are not embodied in the same way as colonised or oppressed people. And yet, even within colonial literature there is a sense of *another* point of view. People of colour and colonised people obviously look at white people and this has been carefully documented by people like Homi Bhabha, bell hooks and C. L. R. James among others.[1] In the press, the literature and art of the Victorian era, in various ways, white men also look at and scrutinise other white men as we shall see in some of the chapters to come. The power relations obviously differ, but ways of looking are complicated, ambiguous and often contradictory.

In very many literary and artistic representations, the white male body in its various forms is a vital marker for a variety of practices and discourses in the nineteenth century. Indeed the Victorian period saw a new physicality for the white male body. Kenneth R. Dutton explores the concept of the built body and argues that:

> Along with the invention of the camera, the awakening of interest in physical exercise in the second half of the nineteenth century was one of the chief focuses of the emerging fascination with the visual appearance of the actual human body, as distinct from the idealized and conventionalized bodies of traditional art. The body had now become an object of interest *in itself*, and the developed body was promoted as being within the reach of the ordinary citizen. (Dutton 1995: 101, emphasis in original)

In the mid-nineteenth century the cult of developing the male body arrived, building a white body that was meant to be looked at. In 1865 *The Handbook of Manly Exercises, Comprising Boxing, Walking, Running, Leaping, Vaulting, Etc.* was published by George Routledge and Sons. This book was just one in a range of texts offering advice about the best way to develop a muscular and strong body. Dutton argues that this was in part a result of anxieties about the softening of the male body: '[i]n a society where the effects of the Industrial Revolution were becoming evident in the creation of a more sedentary, less physically active workforce, the very biological need of the body for some form of vigorous exercise sought an outlet either in sporting activity or some other systematized form' (ibid.: 99). Bodily regimes predicated on scientific systems, self-discipline and regulation were part of what formed a manly character.

As the century progressed the spectacle of the muscular, white male body became an important signifier of a certain kind of masculinity. The epitome of this was the professional muscular showman Eugen Sandow. Dutton argues that by the beginning of the twentieth century Sandow 'was the possessor of the world's best known body' (ibid.: 124). Quite slight in stature (compared to a bodybuilder like Arnold Schwarzenegger), Sandow had a remarkable, sculpted body which he displayed to the public, making a fortune in the process. Dutton suggests that:

> [Sandow's] great innovation lay in the shifting of the audience's attention from the strength of the male physique to the look of the physique. By the use of poses, audience interest could be maintained for the duration of a stage act, and the scene was set for the development of muscular display as a mode of public entertainment [. . .]

> The developed body, henceforth, was no longer an object restricted to the context of artistic representation, at one remove from physical reality, or to less openly avowed or even clandestine (but essentially private) encounters. It was transposed into a new domain, to become a socially acceptable focus of aesthetic attention on the part of mass audiences. (ibid.: 122)

This is not, of course, an invisible male body as discussed above; it is a body built for display, worked on and celebrated. It is an intensely physical body. With an interesting turn of phrase David L. Chapman, writing in 1994, claims that, '[o]ur fathers and grandfathers considered Sandow the epitome of masculine beauty' (Chapman 1994: ix). 'Our' mothers and grandmothers are nowhere to be seen here, and Chapman uses the word 'beauty'. Sandow's was a body to be gazed upon; ostensibly, by white men themselves. However, this worked-upon/built body is the subject of self-discipline and sacrifice – both of which were requisites of Victorian masculinity. It is not a body that is biologically fixed and determined, it is a chosen body-type that displays strength of will and a negation of pain. Where Franz Fanon cites the fact that he is 'slave to his appearance', fixed within his racialised body by the racist view from outside, Sandow's body relates to Yvonne Tasker's discussion of the built bodies of the 1980s hard-men of the cinema. In these cases she argues, '[b]odybuilding is offered as a form of protection which speaks to insecurity. Within this discourse, the body itself functions as a sort of armour against the world' (Tasker 1993: 123). The fully muscular body is an impenetrable body; one that protects itself and excludes the possibility of otherness.

This enunciates the ideal of the white colonial body and it is evident in the colonial action novels that became so popular in the second half of the nineteenth century. Ten years before the year of drama and disaster that Freeman explores, in 1885, H. Rider Haggard wrote his story of high colonial adventure, *King Solomon's Mines*, a text, he boasts, in which 'there is not a *petticoat* in the whole history' (Haggard 1998: 9, emphasis in original). Dedicating it to 'all the big and little boys who read it' (ibid.: n.p.) Haggard presents a homosocial, colonial world of men: black as well as white. In many ways this late Victorian novel epitomises the paradoxes, pluralities and diversities associated with the white colonial body. The main characters are carefully described according to their physical attributes. The manly ideal is encapsulated in the figure of Sir Henry Curtis who, our narrator Allan Quatermain tells us, is 'about thirty

[. . .] one of the biggest-chested and longest-armed men I ever saw. He had yellow hair, a big yellow beard, clear-cut features, and large grey eyes set deep into his head. I never saw a finer-looking man' (ibid.: 11). His companion, John Good, is 'short, stout and dark, and of quite a different cut [. . .] He was broad, of medium height, dark, stout, and rather a curious man to look at' (ibid.: 12–13). The description of our hero, Allan Quatermain, comes with the novel of the same name set years later. Comparing himself to Sir Henry Curtis he tells us:

> I could not help thinking what a curious contrast my little dried-up self presented to his grand face and form. Imagine to yourself a small, withered, yellow-faced man of sixty-three, with thin hands, large brown eyes, a head of grizzled hair cut short and standing up like a half-worn scrubbing-brush – total weight in my clothes, nine stone six – and you will get a very fair idea of Allan Quatermain. (Haggard 1995: 7)

Haggard does not present the ideal of a manly man; in this 'ripping yarn' Quatermain, perhaps the ultimate hero of late Victorian colonial adventure narratives, is small, puny and ugly, and he draws attention to his less-than-perfect physicality. Of course, one of Quatermain's characteristics is self-deprecation. He speaks of himself as cowardly, bumbling and physically incapable. Yet, he always survives terrible hardship and danger and belongs in what he calls his 'native wilds' (ibid.: 12). Perhaps because his body is so physically tough he is able to ignore it, safe in the knowledge it will carry him through his hair-raising adventures in Africa. Quatermain's white, colonial body matters and does not at the same time.

The complexity of the colonial narrative in Haggard's work reflects the contradictions inherent in the imagining of imperial masculinity whereby '[m]en were expected to be strong, authoritative, decisive, disciplined and resourceful' (Beynon 2002: 30). In *King Solomon's Mines*, the adventurers walk into a village where the natives have not seen white men before. By some accident Good has his legs exposed and the native women admire his 'beautiful white legs' with a 'feeling of intense admiration' and '[t]hey fixed their dark eyes upon their snowy loveliness' (Haggard 1998: 129–30). Here (narrated with humour by Quatermain) it is Good's body that is visible; that is exposed and being looked at. This is reminiscent of a passage related by the traveller and explorer Mungo Park when he visited Africa in the late eighteenth century. Here he is given shelter in a village, but crowds come to see him:

> I found it rather a troublesome levee, for I was obliged to take off one of my stockings and show them my foot, and even to take off my jacket and waistcoat to show them how my clothes were put on and off [. . .] All this was to be repeated to every succeeding visitor, for such as had already seen these wonders insisted on their friends seeing the same, and in this manner I was employed, dressing and undressing, buttoning and unbuttoning from noon to night. (Park 2002: 113)

In both these passages, there is humour and recognition that this is an unusual position for a white man to occupy in a colonial setting. And neither fictional nor real traveller is fixed into this position or oppressed by it whether through body or mind. But while there is no question of this visibility forming any sort of oppressive self-identity, these bodies are undoubtedly on display.

The works of H. Rider Haggard are, in the main, *about* the white male body and its counterpart – the (most often magnificent) body of the colonised figure of the 'noble savage'. The imposing figure of the Zulu king Umbopa in *King Solomon's Mines* is compared to that of Sir Henry Curtis when they first meet. Alan Quatermain tells us:

> Sir Henry told me to ask him to stand up. Umbopa did so, at the same time slipping off the long military great coat he wore, and revealing himself naked except for the moocha round his centre and a necklace of lions' claws. He certainly was a magnificent-looking man; I never saw a finer native. Standing about six foot three high he was broad in proportion, and very shapely. In that light, too, his skin looked scarcely more than dark [. . .] Sir Henry walked up to him and looked into his proud, handsome face.
>
> 'They make a good pair, don't they?' said Good: 'one as big as the other.' (Haggard 1998: 49)

Quatermain scrutinises and deeply admires Umbopa's naked body, which is contrasted with Curtis' clothed white form. Umbopa disrobes, casting off his Westernised great coat to reveal his body and the necklace of lions' claws. Low argues that such moments in Haggard's work (and there are many), belong 'to the movement of the Orientalist gaze as both a disciplining and narcissistic eye/I. Its gaze which lingers on the physical surfaces of the black man's body is [. . .] also homoerotic' (Low 1996: 53). She claims that in this way the black male body is animalised and sexualised. Discussing Robert Baden-Powell's encounter with a Matabele warrior she says that the warrior's framing 'as animal becomes simply part of the landscape; his body framed by the conventions of high art' (ibid.: 54). The native body and the landscape are intermingled.

John Beynon suggests that, 'Haggard paints a mythopoetic pastoral idyll of masculinity through nature. The romance and grandeur of the great open spaces as the true home of men is celebrated, along with an imperialistic nostalgia for the lost tribes of Natal, the Transvaal and Zululand' (Beynon 2002: 38). Beynon argues that this hides the savage and violent colonial exploitation of the colonised other. However, in this schema, the wide open spaces allow the white man to stretch his body and test his physicality in a way that was not possible in industrialised 'tame' Britain. There is a separation of the heroic and stoic white male body and the African landscape. The coloniser conquers and names and categorises the colonised landscape, keeping a 'healthy' separation from it and the natives. This follows the tradition of the eighteenth-century Romantic view of the self and nature. In the Romantic schema the body, as it resides within the landscape, is seen as unimportant. The landscape – nature itself, is *used* to transcend the body in order for the mind to be able to contemplate the sublime, leading to an expansion of the spirit. The discourse posits the mind's transcendence and elevation from the body, its materiality and the landscape itself. The white coloniser is superior to both and the ideal is to overcome and conquer the materiality of body and nature. Originating with the Romantic poets such as Wordsworth, this view of the self as separate from nature in metaphysical terms, places the mind firmly above the body in the Kantian dichotomy of mind/body.

In colonial literature the body of the white male adventurer/hero is defined by the body of the native (such as Umbopo) but also pitted against the feminised landscape of the space that has been colonised. In much criticism this is also seen as one of the problems inherent in the colonial literature of the Victorian era. If it is the body of the colonised native subject that is to be displayed (without volition), then the landscape too is subject to conquest and exploitation by the white coloniser. Lynne Segal argues that in these colonial narratives:

> [j]ust as Africa itself is persistently depicted as 'female' (passive, inviting, wild, dangerous and deadly), so the language of the colonial narrative is one of sexual conquest [. . .] Africa itself [is] but the backdrop for the white man's testing of himself. The metaphor of the female object, to be opened up, penetrated, conquered, serves to underline the masculine features of the white man's testing of his 'virility'. 'There [in Africa]' as Somerset Maugham wrote, 'a man is really a man.' (Segal 1992: 173)

It is this feminine African landscape that the adventurers traverse in *King Solomon's Mines*. The treasure map details two large rounded mountains; 'Sheba's Breasts' and in a straight line down from the 'breasts', passing another landmark in the place of the 'naval', there, drawn as a triangle, we come to 'the mouth of the treasure cave' (Haggard 1998: 27). As Lindy Stiebel says, 'Haggard's map is a "body-scape" of Africa as woman' (Stiebel 2001: 14). The adventurers must traverse this body to gain their destination and fulfil their quest to the treasure cave. This is the cave that the explorers will penetrate deeply; to plunder the priceless jewels hidden there.

In order to be able to get to the treasures buried in the caves, the explorers must undergo intense physical hardship. Low suggests that in *King Solomon's Mines*,

> The landscape of difficulty provides the opportunity for a narrative of the heroic performance of the male body under pressure. Associated with physical prowess, achievement, self-control and a regime of bodily discipline, physical pain becomes the means by which these ideals may be attained, and a ritual process by which an exclusively male community is created. (Low 1996: 50)

The body is almost transcended as, in order to complete the quest, Quatermain and his group must exercise strict discipline and overcome pain and endure hardship, echoing the pain that must be undergone in order to build the muscular body. As Low says, '[a]cts of privation may be read as heroic acts necessary to effect the submission of the native land' (ibid.: 50). Here, the *will* of these white explorers overcomes both the body and the landscape. In this schema the mind/spirit is above (and superior to) the material. Yet this presupposes a particular view of landscape and the body; one that is being tested and rethought at the moment. This began with what has been termed the 'affective turn' whereby there is a re-turn to the emotions, the body, the material and experience (Clough and Halley 2007). From the point of view of affect theory the landscape is no longer seen as something 'over there'; a distant prospect which is external to the self and which can be represented in literature or art. In the newer conceptions coming from cultural geography and eco-criticism the centuries-old view of the landscape as 'scenery' is deemed to involve a false dichotomy, and any separation of self and place is, in fact, untrue. Berberich et al. claim that '[i]ncreasingly, [the] acceptance of the "immaterial" has extended beyond the "pictorial" and "representational" view of landscape to also include other modes of phenomenological experience and "bodily practices" through which we encounter, "read", relate and construct space' (Berberich et al. 2012: 22). The division between the landscape and the body is collapsed and what becomes important is the *experience* of landscape through and within the body. Indeed, in *King Solomon's Mines*, when Alan Quatermain encounters the feminised landscape of Africa depicted in the treasure map discussed above, his body takes over. The travellers have followed the map through the desert and at this point are nearly dying of thirst:

> Just at that moment the sun came up gloriously, and revealed so grand a sight to our astonished eyes that for a moment or two we even forgot our thirst.
>
> For there, not more than forty or fifty miles from us, glittering like silver in the early rays of the morning sun were Sheba's breasts [. . .] Now that I, sitting here, attempt to describe the extraordinary grandeur and beauty of that sight language seems to fail me. I am impotent even before its memory. (Haggard 1998: 85)

While it might be possible to argue that the sublime sight of the mountains allowed Quatermain to transcend his body (the raging thirst he feels), the emotion, the feeling beyond language and the failed impotence of his body all point to an affective response. The body is *never* separate from its environment and the white male body is as immersed in its surroundings/as much a part of them as any other type of body.

In a fascinating discussion William A. Cohen posits the idea that the body itself was *always* fully implicated in discussions about the spirit side of what is now termed mind/body 'split', claiming that for the Victorians '[t]his essence – whether called by traditional, religiously inflected names such as "soul" or "spirit" or identified with newer, psychologically oriented terms like "mind" and "self" – was almost always imagined as *interior* to the individual' (Cohen 2009: xi, our emphasis). From this point of view there is no binary or dichotomy and the spirit is part of an embodied state. This is an interesting idea and Cohen claims that in Victorian literature '[w]hat is human, these writers were excited and frightened to discover, is nothing more or less than the human body itself. Embodied experience was the solution that writers in a variety of styles and genres struck upon in response to contemporary questions about the nature, location, and plasticity of the human essence' (ibid.: xi). Cohen's hypothesis locates not just the 'soul' but the human body as well. And this idea of 'embodied experience' echoes contemporary theories of affect that are currently being applied to bodies, texts and experiences from all eras. As we have been arguing, the white male body in Victorian times was *not* removed, and indeed in colonial texts, representations and mythopoetic imaginings it was entirely rooted in nature and the landscape.

Although this idea of the white colonial body as immersed in its surroundings positions the discussion of the white coloniser differently, it does not negate the fact of colonial violence; in fact it can render it more immanent. White, middle-class men *embodied* the ideals of nation, empire and the physical superiority of those who were white, Western and not female. This involved an invasion of territory, the physical presence of the coloniser and the invasion of the psychic space of those colonised. In the colonies, white virtues were to be educated into, and imposed upon the colonial subject; through both body and mind. C. L. R. James documents a childhood in the West Indies educated via the white, English public school code which not only espoused but morally imposed the ideals of 'playing with the team', 'keeping a stiff upper lip' and 'playing with a straight bat' at least on the cricket pitch, where these codes were imbibed most fully (James 1963: 25). James talks about these colonial codes being naturalised and therefore unquestioned because '*everything* began from the basis that Britain was the source of all light and leading, and our business was to admire, wonder, imitate, learn; our criterion of success was to have succeeded in approaching that distant ideal' (ibid.: 30, emphasis in original). 'Success' in both Britain and the colonies depended on a bodily playing out of the codes of masculinity; 'the British reticence, the British self-discipline, the stiff upper-lips' (ibid.: 42). And all these were (and often still are) encoded within masculine sports and encapsulated the ideal of 'manliness' apparent in the Victorian and Edwardian eras. As Stephen Whitehead suggests, 'by the end of the nineteenth century an idealized version of masculinity – encompassing physicality, virility, morality and civility – had emerged to some prominence' (Whitehead 2002: 14). It was these codes, morals and ideals that were employed to limit and control both coloniser and colonial subject.

In this idealisation men moved and acted, fought and physically staved off corruption and degeneration, upholding Christian morality. Indeed it could be argued that the white, middle-class, male body in Victorian culture needed to be on display in order to uphold a conception of the normalised ideal. Donald Hall suggests that in the cult of Muscular Christianity, '[t]he male body appears as a metaphor for social, national, and religious bodies, while at the same time it attempts to enforce a particular construction of those bodies'(Hall 1994: 8). The white, male, physical body itself becomes a symbol of much wider ideological concerns and ideals. This conception of the male body as a metaphor has been put forward elsewhere. Dutton posits the following view:

> The human body [...] can be understood only in the context of the social construction of reality; indeed, the body itself is seen as a social construct, a means of social expression or performance by which our identity and value – for ourselves and others – are created, tested and validated. (Dutton 1995: 13)

One facet of this, he contends, is the 'view of the body as metaphor' (ibid.: 13). Donald Hall also posits the idea of the male body as a metaphor. Whilst we certainly do not dispute the concept of the body as a social construct (indeed this is examined in depth in the essays collected here), there may be more of a problem with the idea that the body is a metaphor. One of the consequences of viewing the male body as a metaphor may be that the actual embodied physicality of this body is negated and in danger of being ignored in favour of looking at its 'symbolic value' (ibid.: 13). There has been a long and important strain of cultural, feminist and postcolonial criticism that has examined how the ethnically marked body or the bodies of women have been made to 'stand in' for something else; given neither objective nor subjective agency in their own right. In this way the body of the 'other' is positioned against, or in opposition to the white male body, which is symbolically marked as the 'norm'. Yet if this 'norm' itself is discussed as a metaphor there seems nothing left to push back against. It becomes a phantom – a no-thing and a no-body. Perhaps too often in academic studies of masculinity it is examined as a 'myth' (and a destructive one at that), that needs to be demystified, de-essentialised, proved to be a social construction and dismantled.

Postcolonial studies examines oppression and the positioning and 'creation' of the oppressed by the dominant white colonists. It looks at the *experience* of people under colonial rule, at the twin points of power whereby people were subjugated: power and knowledge – especially the imperial 'knowledge' of other peoples and the historical impact that this has had on oppressed and marginalised people. Postcolonialism looks at the process that 'othered' and 'abnormalised' colonised people in relation to a dominant white ideal of the normal: a process that positioned them as 'different'. In contrast, masculinity studies looks at the creation of 'Imperial Man' and offers knowledge about the creation of this dominant and idealised persona. These are two different, although interrelated, emphases. Put simply, postcolonialism looks at the processes that oppressed people and at their experiences of that oppression. Masculinity studies looks at the processes that made white men dominant and at the experience of that position of dominance. Because of this two different projects are formulated, but they are projects that link at various points. Masculinity studies takes as its raison d'être the destruction of the idea of a privileged, normal masculinity. As Stephen Whitehead and Frank Barrett put it in the introduction to one of the definitive masculinity studies texts, *The Masculinities Reader*: 'what we are fighting against is a culture that privileges men and masculinity' (Whitehead and Barrett 2001: 13). However, where masculinity studies seems to involve a process of coming-into-non-being (the deconstruction of the white, privileged masculine norm), Ato Quayson cites postcolonialism as 'a process of coming-into-being' (Quayson 2000: 9). Thus, where masculinity studies advocates the deconstruction of what is largely its own position (white and middle class), postcolonialism is involved in a process of *reconstruction*; of subjectivity, position, history and agency. With this in view, *The Victorian Male Body* attempts a *re*construction as well as a *de*construction of the way in which white masculinity was represented in the nineteenth century. Thus, where Judith Butler notes 'the masculine privilege of the disembodied gaze, the gaze that has the power to produce bodies, but which is itself no body (Butler 1993: 136), the essays collected here examine this 'no body'. Scrutinising the hegemonic concept of the 'perfect' male body and also looking at what happens when greed, limb-loss, illness or death intervene, the book highlights the assumptions that were made about the embodiment of masculinity and manliness in a range of Victorian texts.

Overall the essays argue that the white, male body in Victorian times was in no way, and could never be, the unified, whole, perfect muscular and disciplined ideal upheld by colonial discourse. This questions the idea of this body as a (singular) metaphor and helps to begin to unpick and pluralise its symbolic value, exposing the fractures, imperfections and failures of the male body. Further, the ideal itself shifted and changed over the century, and there was in fact no singular concept of the perfect male body. Indeed, as the chapters in this volume examine, far from there being just one ideal body, plurality and flexibility were granted to many white men. As Richard Dyer notes in relation to whiteness, the fact that white people *can* be categorised as so many things *other* than 'white' provides much of the privilege of that (largely unseen) racialised position (Dyer 1997). In this way, in order for there to be flexibility, there has to be flexibility *from* something and we moot a plethora of 'silent' ideals from which other expressions of masculinity diverted. While we agree that there is, and never was, one, unified, complete, (perfect?) construction of a white male body, we argue that in Victorian society there existed a discourse around this ideal that had real and embodied consequences for women, people of colour, colonised subjects and white men themselves. Denying and deconstructing essentialist notions associated with race, class and gender are understandable (and important) reactions to discourses and notions that are very uncomfortable. However, this work should not be taken so far that the fact that essentialist notions existed in Victorian social and cultural representations – religion, family, the press, art and literature for example – is by-passed. We must not overlook the fact that power and privilege were much more likely to reside with those who were coded as the 'norm'. Thus while questioning the concept of a single ideal for the white male body, we also feel it is important to acknowledge that white men often benefited from and often occupied a more powerful and privileged position than was possible for women or people who were not white. Indeed only people possessing certain types of body were able even to approach an embodiment of these idealisations and expectations. There are delicate lines to traverse here, and there has to be a consideration of the embodied experience for those white men who were not so privileged. Another consideration has to be the fact that no-one can ever fully embody any sort of ideal position and there will always be gaps and cracks and failures. In order to examine this, *The Victorian Male Body* does not put forward a simple equation of white masculinity and crisis, instead what is explored are the ways in which white masculinity changes, adapts and survives.

Contents

The book is divided into three sections: 'Constructed Bodies', 'Fractured and Fragmented Bodies' and 'Unruly Bodies' with each section examining different aspects of Victorian masculinity and the body. Part I, 'Constructed Bodies', looks at issues relating to traditional, manly masculinity. Focusing on the way that manly bodies are forged, the chapters in this section explore the different ways to 'make' a man. We open the collection with Alice Crossley's discussion of the body of the Victorian schoolboy. This is a much abused body, and she argues that the ability to endure physical abuse for the schoolboy was 'a significant element in successful (or failed) masculine development'. Examining a range of texts, including work by

Dickens, Thackeray and Meredith, Crossley argues that violence, abuse and hardship formed part of a 'survival' narrative for boys. Thus harsh physical experience was an initiation or rite of passage that middle- and upper-class boys must endure in order for them eventually to become patriarchal leaders. However, Crossley points to other experiences that are highlighted in the texts she examines: sexual, feminised and the homosocial comfort of the bonds of friendship. There may be a lack of cohesion in the symbolism of abuse, corporal punishment and violence but, she argues, the Victorian fascination with the schoolboy figure and his physicality is apparent in much Victorian literature.

The second chapter in our collection is by Joanne Begiato, and she offers an illuminating discussion of the increased focus on the will through the nineteenth century and, in doing so, explores the various forms of self-restraint that early Victorian men were supposed to impose upon their bodies and minds. She provides an analysis of the denial of gratification in various forms, with an extensive consideration of diet, alcohol and sex. Begiato consults the archives of the Colney Hatch pauper lunatic asylum, to build on the current scholarship that considers the interplay between masculinity and madness in this era. Using the examples of General Paralysis of the Insane and intemperance, Begiato considers the gendered implications of such diagnoses.

Tara MacDonald then explores the 'social purity' movement of late Victorian culture, which she explains 'encouraged a focus on the male body as a symbol of English purity'. Amidst fears about degeneration, she argues that the figure of the 'New Man' emerges. Focusing on Ménie Muriel Dowie's novel *Gallia*, MacDonald examines the representation of the New Woman and her practice of deliberate and careful sexual selection. The question of choice for Victorian women when choosing the father for their children is not one that is often discussed and MacDonald's chapter offers a fascinating insight into a subject that looks at sex and gender 'aslant'. The result seems to be, however, that sexual and gender objectification shifts onto the figure of the New Man as he becomes 'a physical specimen and national symbol'.

Part II, 'Fractured and Fragmented Bodies', considers the incomplete, disabled, diseased or dead male body. What happens when the body itself is imperfect? The essays in this section interrogate how the discourse around masculinity changes in relation to the not-perfect white male body, uncovering subversion and dissent coming from some seemingly unlikely places. In the first chapter of this section, Ryan Sweet turns his attention to pirate narratives and the symbolism of limb loss: from 'peg legs' to hooks in place of hands. Looking at adventure narratives such as Robert Michael Ballantyne's *The Madman and the Pirate* (1883) as well as, of course, Robert Louis Stevenson's *Treasure Island* (1881) and J. M. Barry's *Peter Pan* (1904), Sweet applies some contemporary notions from disability studies to the texts. Revising the argument that Victorian pirate tales equate 'bodily loss with moral decrepitude' Sweet extends the discussion to suggest that there is also what he terms 'an alluring hyper-masculinity' with these disabled piratical characters. Examining some biographical details about Stevenson's own ill health, Sweet looks at the empowerment of the physically impaired characters evident in some of the most iconic Victorian pirate tales.

The next chapter, by Meredith Miller, discusses male characters who have tuberculosis, in the work of Henry James and George Eliot. Miller argues that TB has been seen as a female illness in Victorian culture, a disease which was seen as 'pathological', but which was also associated with the 'purifying expression of feminine virtue and gentleness'. Here, however, she traces the disease's signification for male consumptives, pointing to the often-overlooked representation of them as visionary, refusing robust, active expressions of masculinity. Miller suggests that the tubercular male body is a feeling body; a body from which the spirit has *almost* departed. In this refusal of more accepted notions of Victorian masculinity Miller argues that the consumptive body is one which juxtaposes 'visionary aestheticism and masculine dissent'.

Alison Younger's chapter is a foray into the world of Gothic masculinities and the spectacle of the monstrous body of the deviant male. Considering the notion of the adorned and fashioned body, Younger examines dandies and macaronis as the transgressive antitheses to the gentleman and she discusses how they reveal anxieties surrounding the manly figure of the gentleman and serve to reinforce dominant discourses of normative masculine values and codes. In this essay, Younger provides an illuminating discussion on the interplay between fear, as perceived through the lens of monstrosity, and the construction of the aberrant male form.

Ruth Heholt closes this section with her consideration of another type of aberrant male form; the ghostly male body in Victorian ghost stories. While previously, most criticism has focused on the body of the female ghost; this essay addresses the imbalance. Using work from three women writers – Catherine Crowe, Rhoda Broughton and Edith Nesbit – Heholt charts the trajectory of the ghost story and its engagement with changing notions of masculinity. Heholt presents the complicated and contradictory readings of the ghostly male body as she reveals that it can be variously constructed as a powerful reinforcement of manliness or a weak figure of broken masculinity. This chapter also provides a fascinating discussion of how 'real-life' ghost sightings and Spiritualism allowed a more powerful 'female gaze', which served to disrupt gendered boundaries.

Part III, 'Unruly Bodies', examines the male body that is excessive: too fat, too thin, too foreign, or too feminine. These bodies undermine notions of restraint and self-command. The chapters in this section argue that excess (of whatever sort) destabilises the notion of the ideal masculine mind holding perfect sway over the body. In the chapters are considerations of masturbation, bodily-health and well-being, the links made between a 'healthy body' and a 'healthy mind', diseased bodies, anxieties about infection, and there is discussion of over- and under-consumption and degeneration, and 'health benefits' manifested through various actions. In the first chapter in this section, Françoise Baillet explores illustrations of the artist in the satirical periodical paper *Punch*. Examining George Du Maurier's almost cartoon-like illustrations of the artist figure, Baillet contextualises them as being part of a wider debate around class and masculinity. Using stereotypes prevalent in the Victorian period of the artist as 'the dandy, the secluded poet, the decadent avant-gardist, the degenerate aesthete' Baillet argues that Du Maurier pits the artist's body against dominant constructions of masculinity as robust and active. Over-refined, languid and even ill, the figure of the avant-garde artist expresses decadence and embodies contemporary anxieties about national identity, class and gender. Reproducing some of the illustrations, Baillet's chapter provides an entertaining and informative romp through *Punch*'s satirical take on the masculine body.

The starving male body is the focus of Charlotte Boyce's chapter. Concentrating on *Mary Barton* by Elizabeth Gaskell, Boyce examines the significance of food, and more specifically the lack of it, in the novel. Appetite in various forms and manifestations was of concern in Victorian discourses about masculinity, and conceptions of 'hunger' were often used to connote a lack of control or animal-like impulses or compulsions. Firmly contextualising hunger within a class framework, Boyce looks at ideas of unruly and dangerous working-class masculinity, subject to ravening hunger and bestial instincts. Seemingly at odds with this she follows John Barton, whose journey begins with self-sacrifice and appetite control, but which morphs into excessive and nihilistic self-indulgence and deliberate starvation. Playing with notions of self-control and self-denial

Gaskell finally abjects John Barton, propelling him into the non-human. Boyce argues that by expelling Barton from the discourses of gender and class, Gaskell refuses to resolve the contradictions she herself has set up around class, appetite and masculinity.

Joanne Ella Parsons' essay examines the fat male body in the shape of Fosco from *The Woman in White*. Parsons argues that his fat is a 'performance' that has been gained from excessive self-control and will, which is in opposition to usual contemporary constructions of the corpulent body. Using both a medicalised reading, as well as an exploration of the gendered foodstuffs and consumption that have created his bulk, Parsons argues that the Count's body is a site of mystery and contradictions which blurs gender boundaries. Her argument extends into a discussion of the extent of the Count's transgressive power, which is variously revealed and hidden by his form.

The focus of Anne-Marie Beller's chapter is the well-known sensation fiction writer, Mary Elizabeth Braddon. Beller chooses two of her poems, 'Olivia' and 'Garibaldi', in order to argue that Braddon uses the Italian male body as a lens through which to reveal British anxieties and tensions surrounding questions of manliness and nationhood. In her essay, Beller contextualises her discussion by examining Victorian attitudes towards Italy, revealing similarities in their imposed negative (feminine) gendered readings of the country and its peoples, to the construction of Orientalism. Beller asserts that while Italy and the Italians seem to provide a binary opposition to the perceived 'character' of England and the English, Braddon, as a woman writer, is in a position to interrogate this. Therefore, Beller argues, Braddon challenges contemporary stereotypical views of Italians in her poems and creates, instead, a more complex construction of Italian masculinity in order to destabilise the fixed binaried otherness usually imposed upon the Italian body.

In examining and scrutinising the male body we have an ethical concern with deconstructing a norm that oppressed and repressed others. By bringing it to light and giving it centre stage in a sustained critical discussion *The Victorian Male Body* re-evaluates the way that this body was written about and represented at the time, revealing that the 'ideal' in fact manifests as a variety of 'ideals', sometimes competing, sometimes cohering, that make up a fascinating site of exploration. *The Victorian Male Body* opens up new avenues for scholarly enquiry and innovative ways of thinking about this most problematic and, arguably, most ideologically compelling of forms.

Note

1. See Homi K. Bhabha (1994), *The Location of Culture*, London: Routledge; bel hooks (1992), *Black Looks: Race and Representation*, Boston: South End Press; and C. L. R. James (1963/1994), *Beyond a Boundary*, London: Serpent's Tail.

Works Cited

Berberich, C., N. Campbell and R. Hudson (eds) (2012), *Land and Identity: Theory, Memory, and Practice*, Amsterdam: Rodopi.
Beynon, J. (2002), *Masculinities and Culture*, Philadelphia: Open University Press.
Bhabha, H. K. (1994), *The Location of Culture*, London: Routledge.
Butler, J. (1993), *Gender Trouble*, New York: Routledge.
Chapman, D. L. (1994), *Sandow the Magnificent: Eugen Sandow and the Beginning of Body Building*, Urbana: University of Illinois Press.
Chapman R. and J. Rutherford (1988), *Male Order: Unwrapping Masculinity*, London: Lawrence Wishart.
Clough, P. and J. Halley (eds) (2007), *The Affective Turn: Theorizing the Social*, Durham, NC: Duke University Press.
Cohen, W. (2009), *Embodied: Victorian Literature and the Senses*, Minneapolis: University of Minnesota Press.
Dutton, K. R. (1995), *The Perfectible Body: The Western Ideal of Male Physical Development*, New York: Continuum.
Dyer, R. (1997), *White: Essays on Race and Culture*, London: Routledge.
Easthope, A. (1986), *What a Man's Gotta Do: The Masculine Myth in Popular Culture*, New York; London: Routledge.
Fanon, F. [1952] (1967), *Black Skin, White Masks*, New York: Grove Press.
Foucault, M. [1977] (1994), *Discipline and Punish: The Birth of the Prison*, New York: Vintage Press.
Freeman, N. (2011), *1895: Drama, Disaster and Disgrace in Late Victorian Britain*, Edinburgh: Edinburgh University Press.
Haggard, H. R. [1887] (1995), *Allan Quatermain*, Oxford: Oxford University Press.
Haggard, H. R. [1885] (1998), *King Solomon's Mines*, Oxford: Oxford University Press.
Hall, D. E. (ed.) (1994), *Muscular Christianity: Embodying the Victorian Age*, Cambridge: Cambridge University Press.
hooks, b. (1992), *Black Looks: Race and Representation*, Boston, MA: South End Press.
James, C. L. R. (1963), *Beyond a Boundary*, London: Serpent's Tail.
Levin, D. (ed.) (1993), *Modernity and the Hegemony of Vision*, Berkeley: University of California Press.

Low, G. C. (1996), *White Skins/Black Masks: Representation and Colonialism*, London: Routledge.
Otter, C. (2008), *The Victorian Eye: A Political History of Light and Vision in Britain, 1800–1910*, Chicago: The University of Chicago Press.
Park, M. [1779] (2002), *Travels into the Interior of Africa*, Ware: Wordsworth.
Quayson, A. (2000), *Postcolonialism: Theory, Practice of Process*, Cambridge: Polity Press.
Rajchman, J. (1985), *Michel Foucault: The Freedom of Philosophy*, New York: Columbia University Press.
Segal, L. (1992), *Slow Motion: Changing Masculinities, Changing Men*, London: Virago Press.
Stiebel, L. (2001), *Imagining Africa: Landscape in H. Rider Haggard*, Westport, CT: Greenwood Press.
Tasker, Y. (1993), *Spectacular Bodies: Gender, Genre and the Action Cinema*, London: Routledge.
The Handbook of Manly Exercises, Comprising Boxing, Walking, Running, Leaping, Vaulting, Etc., (1883), available at: https://books.google.co.uk/books?id=4btNAQAAMAAJ (last accessed 30 May 2017).
Whitehead, S. (2002), *Men and Masculinities*, Cambridge: Polity Press.
Whitehead, S. and F. Barrett (2001), *The Masculinities Reader*, Cambridge: Polity Press.
Wildman, S. M. and A. D. Davis (1995), 'Language and Silence: Making Systems of Privilege Visible', *Santa Clara Law Review*, 35: 3, pp. 881–906.

Part I

Constructed Bodies

Chapter 1

Violent Play and Regular Discipline: The Abuses of the Schoolboy Body in Victorian Fiction

Alice Crossley

Boys' school stories from the Victorian period engage persistently with debates about masculinity, and fictional representations of school life provide provocative commentary on what might constitute manly behaviour. School (both the private variety and, more tenaciously, the public school) was recognised by many authors in this period as the embodiment of a set of social values associated with patriarchal dominance and elitism, but also as a crucible to forge the masculinity of its young male brethren. In Victorian fiction, educational adventures primarily examine moments of school life that take place beyond any form of detailed academic accomplishment, to focus more on the individual's moral development, socialisation, reputation, the forging and testing of friendships, the perils of temptation, and physical prowess. They therefore recount the potential to explore both moral and somatic forms of progress outside of the classroom, making school a significant element in successful (or failed) masculine development.

Rather than centre solely on the psychological and moral aspects of school life, this essay takes as its focus the ways in which such moments are experienced by the youthful male body and, in particular, the texts examined here illustrate some of the abuses to which the schoolboy body is subject in Victorian fiction. Physical, tactile interaction between boys (or boys and their teachers) emerges as a way of reading both individual and collective experiences at school. The essay isolates examples from the work of Charles Dickens and George Meredith to highlight the ways in which corporal punishment was used to illustrate the lack of agency possessed by the vulnerable schoolboy body. The lasting impression of pain and indignity associated with flogging or caning, however, is also shown to inspire a kind of fraternal bonding in these episodes, experienced through the boys' shared physical suffering and sympathy. In a more competitive strain, bullying and fighting, recounted in the satirical work of W. M. Thackeray, shows how the young male body becomes a tool for displays of dominance and the coveted popularity among peers. Lastly, the essay interrogates the ways in which the schoolboy body becomes sexualised in these fictions, through analyses of two of the more famous Victorian boys' school stories: Thomas Hughes' *Tom Brown's Schooldays* (1857) and Frederic W. Farrar's *Eric, or Little by Little* (1858). Physical experiences, and especially those inflicted on the body by external forces, are therefore a crucial part of the ways in which schooldays are imagined in Victorian fiction to prepare boys for their adult afterlives in wider society. In these texts, however, even abusive or violent forms of physical ritual and performance can also demonstrate how the youthful male protagonists become equipped to survive and even flourish in the dormitory, classroom, sports pitch and playground. In doing so, several of these texts suggest, they are provided with the opportunities at school to emerge as respectable patriarchal leaders endowed with physical and mental strength – if they are able to survive the rigours of the experience.

As several of the essays in this volume demonstrate, strenuous, yet often bewildered efforts to clarify appropriate forms of manliness, and to prescribe codes for manly behaviour, inform the work of many authors at mid-century. Amidst competing discourses of muscular Christianity or athleticism, politeness and civility, or self-help and educational reform – all of which contributed different, often conflicting points of emphasis – fictional writing about the public school as a crucial bastion of upper middle-class patriarchal values gathered impetus in this period. John Tosh has briefly drawn attention to the role of school in a boy's progress towards manhood at this time, observing that for the prosperous middle and upper classes 'public school had become the defining initiation into manhood' (Tosh 2005: 112). As Tosh explains, a school's role as the moment of 'defining initiation' for a boy is limited to certain social strata, yet the notion of school as a means of propagating codes of manliness finds repeated broadcast in the literature of the day. For many fictional young boys, whether in the Bildungsroman of Charles Dickens and W. M. Thackeray or popular school stories such as Hughes' *Tom Brown's Schooldays*, Farrar's *Eric* (1858), or, later, Rudyard Kipling's *Stalky & Co.*, schooldays (whether halcyon or turbulent) mark an integral stage of male socialisation and maturation.

Although the premise of sexual difference could distinguish manliness from femininity, the mid-century in particular constituted a shift in the encoding of perceived manly qualities. These were increasingly viewed in opposition to the demonstrably virile male who had previously dominated as an ideal, to encompass and legitimise less aggressive (yet still not effeminate) forms of masculinity. In fiction from the middle of the nineteenth century, displays of virtuous manly behaviour could be set against an inherited, more traditional brand of manliness, in which physical assertiveness and even aggression could be celebrated. The emerging concept of moral manliness emphasised instead sincerity, self-discipline, industry and authenticity. The shift in pressure to conform to these less physical forms of masculine performance, however, was by no means complete; factors such as class, occupation, religious faith and involvement in the project of imperialism obscured even further any acceptance of moral manliness as a cultural norm. Discourses of gender were and are, of course, rarely if ever absolute. In fiction, though, the vision of a boy's school – as both a site, and as representative of a recognisable, discrete period of child or adolescent development – offered the opportunity for writers to focus their attention on the dialogues between alternating, often simultaneously-experienced versions of masculinity. In tracing the modification of a boy's sense of identity, initially cultivated by the feminised domestic home, to a markedly male homosocial environment both paternalistic and combative, the school functions as a recognised forum for male development and identification.

In particular, the young male body provides a specific focus for the narration of schoolboy experience in Victorian fiction. The chapters dealing with Salem House in Charles Dickens' *David Copperfield* (1850) and Rippenger's School in George Meredith's *The Adventures of Harry Richmond* (1871), as well as W. M. Thackeray's short stories 'Dr Birch and his Young Friends' (1848) or 'Mr and Mrs Frank Berry' (1843), are not only invested in youth's scholastic years as integral to middle-class socialisation or as preparation for adulthood; these years are evaluated through the extremities of physical pain and pleasure that they seem to engender almost simultaneously. Significant moments of stress, distress and delight become closely associated with physical sensitivity or corporal abuse, drawing the reader's gaze to the juvenile body. David Copperfield's entrance and attendance at Salem House provides an especially memorable account of the physical mistreatment of schoolboys. However, as William Cohen has observed in his provocative work *Embodied: Victorian Literature and the Senses*, bodily interactions and tactile experience are crucial to David's early years, before he even enters Mr Creakle's establishment:

> Like other children in Dickens's work, the young David Copperfield encounters the world primarily through his mouth: he kisses his mother, bites his stepfather, and is alternately stuffed and starved by the adults who care for him. (Cohen 2008: 35)

Physical, sensory impressions inform the boy about the nature of the world, and of the other people around him. This extends into his school life. David's time at Salem House, however, is initially determined not by his voluntary physical engagement with his new surroundings; his introduction at the school is dominated by a literal and humiliating reminder of the boy's physicality, as he is made to wear a placard 'on [his] shoulders like a knapsack' reading '*Take care of him. He bites*' (Dickens 1981: 75; 74). David is thus forced to signal his physical presence and supposed animal tendencies, to the point where this description begins to infect his own sense of self: 'I recollect that I positively began to have a dread of myself, as a kind of wild boy who did bite' (ibid.: 75). For the child this statement about his supposedly aggressive tendency, ascribed to him by the placard, engenders an acute feeling of shame. The anxiety experienced by David is evident in his dreams, in which his appearance and physical presence make 'people scream and stare' because he envisions himself wearing 'nothing [. . .] but my little nightshirt, and that placard' (ibid.: 76). Both the imagined state of undress and the pasteboard message reveal to his young mind the potentially uncivilised creature beneath. David's introduction to the other boys at the school is made under similar circumstances, defined by the placard:

> Some of them certainly did dance about me like wild Indians, and the greater part could not resist the temptation of pretending that I was a dog, and patting and soothing me, lest I should bite, and saying, 'Lie down, sir!' and calling me Towzer. This was naturally confusing, among so many strangers, and cost me some tears, but on the whole it was much better than I had anticipated. (ibid.: 80)

By making a joke of David's humiliation, however, his degradation is somewhat lessened. The pretend treatment of the child as a dog is viewed as an initiation substitute, and the 'patting and soothing' are 'naturally confusing' but not such an ordeal as he had feared.[1] The emphasis of the placard's words on the animal nature of the boy and his physical potential for actively violent behaviour also draws attention to the neglect and abuse that he continues to endure at the hands of others. From the bullying of his stepfather Mr Murdstone to Mr Creakle's brutal sphere of influence at the school David Copperfield is emphatically not 'Take[n] care of'. The edict 'Take care of him' is therefore ironic, highlighting the deliberate mistreatment (as opposed to adequate 'care') that he receives from both parties.[2]

David's experience at Salem House draws further attention to the lack of bodily agency allowed to the child in this period, by inclusion of physical abuse in the form of corporal punishment. As one of many schoolboys who attend the private institution, David is absorbed into the wider body of students and subsequently treated in the same brutal manner. On the first day of lessons, the reader is informed, '[h]alf the establishment was writhing and crying' in demonstration of the canings that they receive (Dickens 1981: 85). Mr Creakle demands silence in the schoolroom, although as soon as he enters, 'the boys were struck speechless and motionless'. The headmaster is eager to inflict punishment, however, despite the boys' obedience: 'It will be of no use your rubbing yourselves; you won't rub the marks out that I shall give you' (ibid.: 85). These threats of indelible marks that cannot be erased from the skin underscore the impact of the school experience on the child's submissive body. The cane in Salem House, however, is not employed as a means to maintain discipline over unruly or disobedient youths. The boys remain passive and have no choice but to witness Mr Creakle's repeated attacks on their small figures. Their inert silence is grotesquely transformed into 'writhing and crying' following the teacher's ministrations, so that 'they were too much troubled and knocked about to learn' (ibid.: 90). A lack of agency, reinforced through corporal discipline, produces an intensely affective state for the boys in the schoolroom. Through the marks inflicted on their reluctant bodies, the children are unwillingly propelled from frightened silence and stasis to vigorous sound and movement in response to the pain that has been imposed upon them.

This experience of a harsh and brutal master who wields power and strength over his charges accords with Dickens' own remembered time at school. In an essay for *Household Words* in 1851, he wrote of his memories of William Jones, his own tyrannical schoolmaster:

> The only branches of education with which he showed the least acquaintance, were, ruling, and corporally punishing. He was always ruling ciphering-books with a bloated mahogany ruler, or smiting the palms

> of offenders with the same diabolical instrument, or viciously drawing a pair of pantaloons tight with one of his large hands, and caning the wearer with the other.
>
> We have no doubt whatever that this occupation was the principle solace of his existence. (Dickens 1851: 49–50)

Dickens' autobiographical reminiscence reveals the bitterness towards the man whose 'solace of his existence' was found through the wanton practice of corporal chastisement. Mr Creakle, a fictional parallel of Dickens' old schoolmaster, evinces the same perverse glee in caning his young charges:

> He had a delight in cutting at the boys, which was like the satisfaction of a craving appetite. I am confident that he couldn't resist a chubby boy, especially; that there was a fascination in such a subject, which made him restless in his mind, until he had scored and marked him for the day. (Dickens 1981: 85)

The boys' flesh is testament, at Salem House, to the sadistic pleasures of the perverse adult male to whose care they have been entrusted. Such passages expose both the predatory and vicious tendencies of men like Creakle and Jones, and also render a pitiful portrayal of contemporary school practices prior to educational reform, in which flagellation emerges as a widely adopted means of discipline.

Dr Middleton, in George Meredith's novel *The Egoist* (1879), emerges as another advocate for 'Busby' and 'the birch!', recommending that, in his education of the lad he has in his ward, Sir Willoughby Patterne should '[h]orse him and birch him if Crossjay runs from his books' (Meredith 1987: 116). Such punishments are understood to cultivate manliness in the youth, through the process of humiliation, which promotes resilience and self-sufficiency. Dr Middleton assures Willoughby, '[b]oys of spirit commonly turn into solid men, and the solider the men the more surely they do vote for Busby [. . .] We English beat the world because we take a licking well' (ibid.: 116).[3] Flogging, in Middleton's view, has a tempering effect on boys, who learn 'to take rough and smooth as they come', and therefore become useful, manly specimens (ibid.). The experience of flogging at school is conceived in such representations as a rite of passage, and a practice that strengthens the characters of boys as they mature. In the short fictional story 'Ushers', appearing in *Household Words* (1856), the speaker reflects flippantly on such attitudes, exemplified by his own headmaster:

> The hideous pleasure of inflicting pain upon unoffending and defenceless objects did not seem to be considered cowardly, immoral, or unchristian; but the restraint of it, on the contrary, as milksoppy, nonsensical, and (settler of all controversy!) un-English. The indolence of the preceptor is backed by the heartlessness and folly of those who entrust their children to him [. . .] 'Beat the nonsense out of them;' 'Let them rough it a little;' 'let them find their own level;' 'nothing like a little wholesome bullying;' 'boys will be boys', are thrown from all sides at the educational reformer. (Payn 1856: 98)

The set of maxims here, promoting the ethos of corporal punishment in schools as having nothing to do with being 'cowardly, immoral, or unchristian', is interrogated, drawing attention to the imperial mission of colonisation with which this form of manliness could be associated. This is set against the unmasculine 'milksoppy [. . .] un-English' attitudes of those who branded such treatment of children cruel, malicious and outdated.

Natalie Rose has proposed that, in *David Copperfield* in particular, 'flogging is an important node in the social circulation of fascination as Dickens implicates the punishment in the evisceration of the will of both the flogger and his victim' (Rose 2005: 519). Her argument indicates that men like Creakle, in exerting their despotic power over young boys, also exert a kind of psychic influence or seductive fascination over susceptible children such as David.[4] This 'evisceration of the will' provides a contrast with Victorian justifications for whipping and caning at schools, which are premised on the assumption that such physical punishment can effect a conversion from undisciplined boyhood to adult male agency and self-restraint. Unsolicited methods of physical chastisement, however, could also be a system of discipline reinforced by the schoolboys themselves. Both fictional and autobiographical accounts in the period refer to the tacit acceptance and even promotion of corporal punishment, which could be viewed in the light of a school tradition that boys were proud to uphold. W. M. Thackeray pokes fun at such boys, who seem foolishly complicit in their own subjugation, in the following passage from his *Irish Sketch Book* (1842):

> There are at this present writing five hundred boys at Eton, kicked, and licked, and bullied by another hundred—scrubbing shoes, running errands, making false concords, and (as if that were a natural consequence!) putting their posteriors on a block for Dr Hawtrey to lash at; and still calling it education. They are proud of it—good heavens!—absolutely vain of it; as what dull barbarians are not proud of their dulness and barbarism? [. . .] it's the good old English system; every boy fights for himself—hardens 'em, eh, Jack? (Thackeray 1857: 348)

The 'bull[ying]' and 'lash[ing]' that these hypothetical Etonians 'call [. . .] education' is humorously depicted by Thackeray as a brand of 'dulness and barbarism', of which they are proud in their continuation of 'the good old English system'. William Collins Watterson has suggested, however, that this 'system' of birching and flogging at public schools like Eton is effectively converted into a ritualised, aristocratic means of mutual definition, as he acknowledges that 'boys recognised the rod as both phallic and potent', functioning as an iconographic reminder of the patriarchal, dynastic elite who formed the body of the schoolboys (Watterson 1996: 100). Schoolboys engage in the '"consensual ritual" of the rod', he argues, which bonded boys together within the discrete scholastic community, and also a 'differentiating ritual' which distinguishes them from average schoolboys at lower-class establishments (ibid.: 99). Watterson's thesis about 'consensual ritual' is partly visible in novels such as Meredith's Bildungsroman *The Adventures of Harry Richmond* (1871), in which the school idol's brutal beating becomes a signal moment of intense solidarity felt by the rest of the boys who witness the event: 'we had no sense of our hero [Heriot] suffering shame' (Meredith 2009: 44). Instead, the impact of this public flogging of the school favourite cements the feeling of shared spirit among the boys: 'Far from dreading the rod, now that Heriot and Temple had tasted it, I thought of punishment as a mad pleasure' (ibid.: 46). Even young Harry perversely views the experience as quasi-honourable, so that he and his friends begin to see their 'stripes as a neo-feudal badge [. . .] of valour' (Watterson 1996: 99).

In work by writers such as Dickens and Thackeray, however, there is little recognition of the potential for flagellation to produce a particularly beneficial environment to foster positive models of masculinity.[5] Instead, in novels like *David Copperfield*, the pliant schoolboy body is seen to become little more than fleshly material, beaten for an adult man's sadistic personal pleasure. After running away from London, on a route that deliberately takes in his old school (thereby refining his acute sense of isolation from his peers within its walls), David's young body is taken advantage of even further, and its lack of healthy vigour exacerbated by those he meets on the road. Before reaching Dover and his Aunt Trotwood, David comes across trampers, who hurl stones at the child, and a tinker, who threatens that he will 'rip your young body open' and who, stealing the boy's handkerchief, used such 'roughness' that he 'threw me away like a feather' (Dickens 1981: 180; 181). David's observations that the tinker's female companion was treated even worse than he – she has a black eye, and is knocked down into the road bleeding during this altercation over the handkerchief – align his body with that of the disenfranchised, poverty-stricken woman habitually molested by this vagrant, as they both lack power and will. Even before this episode, David's encounter with the old man in Chatham, who cheats David out of his jacket, strikes a menacing note that references the fragility of the child's body – particularly David's frame, which is underfed and underclothed: '"Oh, my eyes and limbs [. . .] Oh, my lungs and liver" [. . .] he screwed out of himself, with an energy that made his eyes start in his head' (ibid.: 178). The man's sinister exclamations refer to the internal biological organisation of the human body, which emphasises David's pitiful condition and the fragility of his body when subject to violent external forces. The boy's body is once more implicitly reduced to component parts, which could be dismembered, rather than a sentient being.

This lack of recognition of a boy's individual feelings and conscious sensibilities was, of course, one accusation made about the callous treatment of boys in schools in the period, where ritual bullying and frequent flogging or caning were the norm. David's early experiences, at Salem House and just afterwards, provide a clear comparison with Doctor Strong's school in Canterbury:

> Doctor Strong's was an excellent school; as different from Mr Creakle's as good is from evil. It was very gravely and decorously ordered, and on a sound system; with an appeal, in everything, to the honour and good faith of the boys, and an avowed intention to rely on their possession of those qualities unless they proved themselves unworthy of it, which worked wonders. We all felt that we had a part in the management of the place, and in sustaining its character and dignity. Hence, we soon became warmly attached to it. (ibid.: 231)

Whereas at Salem House David and his fellow inmates had been grouped together indiscriminately, forming a community inadvertently through the parity of their experiences forged by pain and discomfort, at Doctor Strong's there is 'order' and a 'system', of which the boys are proud to form a cohesive part. This sense of unity creates pride and attachment in the boys, rather than the reluctant peer-identification of the incarcerated boys evident in Salem House, where Mr Creakle is figured 'like a giant in a story-book surveying his captives' (ibid.: 84).

In viewing schoolboys as a collective body, and therefore encouraging a group dynamic rather than emphasising the individual physicality of each child, these Victorian stories of schooldays draw attention to the potential for mutual bodily engagement, which is often figured through moments of rough games, competitive play and bullying. Myriad bodies are put on display, against which others can be compared, their strength tried, stamina evaluated, and the possibilities of tactile experience examined, all in this forum for specifically male maturation. The physical community of school is noted in Charlotte Yonge's *The Heir of Redclyffe* (1853), in which Philip Morville defends the public education system in England through his statement that most men 'have been rounded into uniformity like marbles, their sharp angles rubbed off against each other at school' (Yonge 1853: 58). Having 'sharp angles rubbed off against each other' accords largely with many popular accounts of school, and this indicates the language typical of such descriptions, gesturing towards a mutual, physical friction designed to create coherence and manly 'uniformity'.

There are certain features of school that recur frequently in this period, in both novels and short stories. Bullying is a repetitive characteristic in fictions detailing school experience and, in particular, the treatment by elder boys of their younger peers through the fagging system draws attention to some of the unsavoury ways in which the male body could be regulated at school. There are also, however, more amicable ways in which such texts focus on the representation of the schoolboy body. In Victorian school stories the pleasures of food, the logic of community created through opposition to figures of authority, and the thrill of being out of bounds without permission are all employed to indicate solidarity among schoolboys. In work by W. M. Thackeray, physical satisfaction is often achieved through companionable consumption of good things, but some of the most memorable school episodes in his work are built around physical altercation and fighting, rather than the more naive pleasures of food. 'Mr and Mrs Frank Berry', in *Men's Wives*, for example, details a particularly energetic bout of pugilism, lasting 102 rounds. In this fight between Biggs, a scholar or gown-boy and 'second cock' of the school, and eponymous Frank Berry, the narrator recounts 'the most tremendous combat ever known' (Thackeray 2013: 87). This mock-heroic 'combat' takes place at Slaughter House School (a fictional incarnation of Thackeray's own school Charterhouse), and is recalled with an emphasis on boxing cant: 'Claret drawn in profusion from the gown-boy's grogshop [. . .] 15th round. Chancery. Fibbing [. . .] The men both dreadfully punished [. . .] The gown-boy's face hardly to be recognised, swollen and streaming with blood' (ibid.: 91). Such metropolitan slang gestures towards some of the most famous accounts of pugilism of the early nineteenth century, from Hazlitt's description of 'The Fight' (1822) to the popular work of Pierce Egan in his *Boxiana* series (1813–29). In doing so, it emphasises the school playground as a legitimate site for the display of competitive manliness and physical prowess. In Thackeray's novel *Vanity Fair* (1847) he explains to his readers that:

> there was everyday life before honest William; and a big boy beating a little one without cause [. . .] Don't be horrified, ladies, every boy at a public school has done it. Your children will do so and be done by, in all probability [. . .] Torture in a public school is as much licensed as the knout in Russia. It would be ungentlemanlike (in a manner) to resist it. (Thackeray 1983: 52)

Not only is 'beating', fighting and bullying or 'torture' conceived as everyday behaviour at school, but it also indicates a kind of peer-regulation which solidifies community. In fact, Thackeray claims, acceptance of this type of aggressive behaviour assumes a brand of respectability and elegant manliness. He also suggests that there is satisfaction to be found in this uniformity of repeated experience: 'Little boys always like to see a little companion of their own soundly beaten', which exercises sympathy for their fellow as well as implying temporary dominance over another child (Thackeray 2013: 87).

As well as enabling a form of parity and of solidarity between the pupils, fighting can also provide a means of regulating hierarchies within the establishment. At Slaughter House, for instance, the narrator of 'Mr and Mrs Frank Berry' admits the tacit existence of 'the sacred privilege that an upper boy at a public school always has of beating a junior' (ibid.: 87). Fights at school, therefore, become an important form of spectacle or entertainment, but also a way of rearranging existing hierarchies based on physical criteria. Schoolboy boxing matches often initiate subsequent close bonds of friendship between the boys who, having shared a unique and physically intimate attempt to enforce bodily dominance over one another, find that their conflict has transmuted into a relationship on another plane, and an alliance is forged instead from this display of pugnacious aggression. In these demonstrations of virile strength and resilience, however, there is also opportunity for the idolisation of those schoolboy heroes who triumph in a fight. The symbolically named George Champion, of *Doctor Birch and his Young Friends*, is described in particularly glowing terms as a 'lion', an 'Apollo in a flannel jacket', and 'invictus', whose strength and solidity inspire 'awe' (Thackeray 1891: 89; 90). This is also true to an extent in *Vanity Fair*, when Dobbin's fight with the bully Cuff results in his subsequent friendship with George Osborne, although, conversely, it is the victor, Dobbin, who idolises the younger child on whose behalf he fought. Thackeray's own scholastic years at Charterhouse inform his subsequent writing about the potential of a playground fight to impact on a boy's relationships with his peers. Gordon N. Ray in his biography of the writer asserts that, 'In unreformed Charterhouse, boxing was the chief entertainment, and a boy's position among his fellows depended largely upon his pugilistic strength and skill' (Ray 1955: 85).[6] The apparent ubiquity of these altercations demonstrates one of the reasons why they feature so prominently in contemporary accounts of school experience in Victorian fiction. However, as 'legends of combats are preserved fondly in schools', such physical contests also cast an aura of elitist mystique over those who could emerge victorious in these bouts or performances of male physicality (Thackeray 1891: 89).

While there are certain aspects of school life typically recounted in its fictional reconstruction, such as the schoolyard fight or the indignities of the flogging block, what often also emerges is an awareness of the peculiar intensity of the collegiate experience. This passion, exhilaration, or antipathy for the cloistered alma mater – produced by an environment estranged from the easy affection of the familial home – provokes a strong reaction as the young boy must assimilate into the often ritualised routine and cabal of private (grammar or public) education. The prospect of attendance at school might occasion a narrative pause in the Victorian novel to examine the experience and its impact on the juvenile mind at varied length. In Benjamin Disraeli's *Coningsby; or, the New Generation* (1844) for example, Henry Coningsby hears from his grandfather Lord Monmouth that he is to attend Eton College:

> This was the first great epoch of his life. There never was a youth who entered into that wonderful little world with more eager zest than Coningsby. Nor was it marvellous [. . .] the stirring multitude, the energetic groups, the individual mind that leads, conquers, controls; the emulation and the affection; the noble strife and the tender sentiment; the daring exploit and the dashing scrape; the passion that pervades our life, and breathes in everything, from the aspiring study to the inspiring sport: oh! what hereafter can spur the brain and touch the heart like this; can give us a world so deeply and variously interesting; a life so full of quick and bright excitement, passed in a scene so fair? (Disraeli 1911: 11)

This provides Disraeli with the opportunity to explain the 'eager zest' and anticipation felt by the boy. Eton in particular, but school more generally, enables the fictional adult speaker to reminisce with an almost electric fervour about 'the stirring multitude' of schoolboys, of whom he presumably numbered one once, and the 'tender sentiment' and 'dashing scrape' that they will experience. The emphasis here is on community, solidarity and the implied parity of experience felt by others who have shared this 'scene' or 'world' of intimate bonding through 'emulation and affection' which will 'touch the heart'. School life is not figured as one of isolation or seclusion. For many young boys, as with Coningsby, this landmark transition from a domestic home life to the social environment of school engendered pride, and an investment in the patrilineal traditions associated with the heritage of his newfound school.

This is particularly true of Tom Brown's experience. In a book written partly for fathers to read with their sons, and based also on the author's own experiences at Rugby school under the educational reformer Thomas Arnold, Thomas Hughes' *Tom Brown's Schooldays* (1857) recounts the feelings of its eponymous hero who is all afire to join his peers at that noble institution. Tom is swift to 'luxuriate in the realised ambition of being a public-school boy at last' and, making friends with Harry East within minutes, he 'began sucking in all his ways and prejudices, as fast as he could understand them' (Hughes 1999: 91). Tom's experience is figured as one of very deliberate integration, imbibing the values and 'prejudices' of fictionalised Rugby from the mouth of his new friend, whose words are 'suck[ed]' from him in a self-conscious process of acculturation by Tom. Hughes presents his young hero as a fervent acolyte, 'athirst for knowledge' about the school and his new situation, and Tom's level of engagement with the school and his peers is represented largely through physical exertion, rough play, and other moments of bodily emphasis (ibid.: 96). Tom is witnessed by the reader physically engaging with the other boys in the school by playing rugby football, running at Hare-and-Hounds, being tossed (thrown in the air in a blanket), fighting, fagging, and being 'roasted' by the bully Flashman.

Tom's mutual engagement with his peers through his body is carefully and explicitly gendered by Hughes, and the boy becomes representative of an active, vigorous, strongly heterosexual brand of juvenile masculinity, which nonetheless seeks to establish itself in opposition to – and as superior to – others whose style of manliness is apparently more equivocal. Both Donald Hall and Maureen Martin have drawn attention to Tom's defensive masculinity in a text which, according to Hall, represents both tenderness and brutal misogyny as key elements of youthful manliness at school. In particular, this tension is evident in Tom's protection and cultivation of a younger boy: 'Certainly Tom works to masculinize Arthur by taking him on swimming and fishing expeditions [. . .] But while doing so, Tom in effect becomes a surrogate mother' (Hall 1996: 133; 138). Tom's maternal efforts and intimacy with the spiritual young boy in his care dispense with the need for women in this all-male, cloistered world of school, although he is teased for his newfound sense of responsibility, being called a 'dry-nurse' by other boys, and accused of 'coddling' Arthur and 'keeping him under [his] skirts' (Hughes 1999: 231; 232). This feminisation of their relationship reveals a maternal instinct in Tom, but also potentially eroticises their friendship by figuring the saintly Arthur as 'a practice wife' (Martin 2002: 488). That their companionship is potentially a version of homosexual attachment is made evident in the episode when Tom and East catch and beat another boy, 'one of the miserable little pretty white-handed curly-headed boys, petted and pampered by some of the big fellows, who [. . .] did all they could to spoil them for everything in this world and the next' (Hughes 1999: 233). Martin suggests that although there is some parallel implied here between Arthur's friendship with Tom and the clearly homoerotic practices between this 'miserable little pretty' boy and the more senior boys who have taken him up, Tom and East's disgust at the pretty fag serves to distance them from any such deviant inclinations, ennobling and elevating Tom's association with Arthur instead (Martin 2002: 490–3). Martin indicates that the boundary between the homosocial and homosexual was less rigid in such an environment.[7] Tom's emotional investment in and connection to Arthur, therefore, promotes their erotic attachment, in comparison with the 'pretty' boy who is viewed as a base sneak and sycophant, effectively prostituting his honour and consenting to being 'pett[ed]' in exchange for protection and preferential treatment (Hughes 1999: 235). The distinction may seem somewhat artificially imposed, but it forms an important part of the discourse of masculinity in schoolboy fictions.

Martin indicates that 'love between boys can serve as a stepping stone to the mandatory heterosexuality of adult manhood', although Jenny Holt has suggested that, despite the opportunities afforded in school fiction of the period (in which the fagging system in particular could function as a form of social and gendered role play), writers like Hughes are responding to 'a crisis in male identity politics' so that 'the panic results in the rooting out and stigmatization of homosexual boys' (Martin 2002: 495; Holt 2008: 70). Although both Carolyn Steedman and Claudia Nelson observe that childhood in the nineteenth century tended to be associated with femininity, boys' school stories in particular engage in contemporary debates about both gender and sexuality, and schoolboys come to provide a focal point for 'male identity politics' (Steedman 1995: 9; Nelson 1991: 2). In writing of Victorian schoolboy experiences in fiction, however, the use of explicitly feminine names is often recurrent, albeit for varied purposes, from highlighting the young boy's capacity for sensitivity, to making him feel unmanly and humiliated. In Harriet Martineau's *The Crofton Boys* (1841), Hugh Proctor is horrified to learn that 'little boys are looked upon as girls in a school till they show that they are little men [. . .] they are called Bettys', suggesting that this forced method of cross-gendering is designed to shame and emasculate (Martineau 1841: 99). In *David Copperfield* Steerforth teases Traddles for being a coward, labelling him 'Polly', but, conversely, his decision to name David 'Daisy' is more complex, as the affectionate appellation references David's naive timidity and susceptibility to influence, while nonetheless also gesturing towards the homoerotic friendship that develops between the two as David idolises the handsome older boy. Steerforth's erotic interest in his 'Daisy' is made particularly suggestive in his query about David's imaginary sister: 'If you had had [a sister], I should think she would have been a pretty, timid, little bright-eyed sort of girl. I would have liked to know her' (Dickens 1981: 84). In *Tom Brown*, East's anxiety that Arthur might be 'called Molly, or Jenny, or some derogatory feminine nickname' indicates, according to Holt, 'that the boys are aware of the existence of queer subcultures' (Hughes 1999: 218; Holt 2008: 70). The name 'Molly' in particular may allude to a molly-house (a male brothel, or a meeting place for men), and the name Molly could be used to signify an effeminate man or a sodomite during the eighteenth and nineteenth centuries.[8] John Addington Symonds, in his private memoirs of Harrow in the 1850s, legitimises the implied connections here between a boy's feminisation and homosexual culture in the Victorian public school, reflecting that 'every boy of good looks had a female name, and was recognized either as a public prostitute or as some bigger boy's "bitch"' (Symonds 1984: 94). In several of the novels examined here, the feminisation of boys is usually discontinued as they mature, thereby idealising (and normalising) adult heterosexuality. However, these texts simultaneously illustrate the benefits of tactile male bonding and affective ties between the boys while they are at school, through hugging, kissing, stroking and petting, all of which still possess the capacity for an erotic valence. The exploration of this kind of attachment between schoolboys is often perceived as a virtue, so homoeroticism is then viewed equivocally, while behaviours viewed as homosexual remain unmanly and dangerous in school fictions of this period. Despite the rituals of emasculation that seem so popular in these stories therefore (for example through the use of girls' names), such gender subversion is often adopted as a sort of initiation designed to instil eventual fortitude and moral fibre – cultural ideals of manliness – in the boy. As both Nelson and Robson suggest, such fluid and ambivalent sexual tendency tends to be resolved into a more vigorous heterosexual masculinity by the end of the narrative, as is the case with Tom Brown and David 'Daisy' Copperfield.

Martin, however, in her analysis of the labile and fluid sexuality of the schoolboy, points out the way in which the boundaries between male/male erotic bonding and the autoerotic impulse were apt to become blurred in Victorian accounts of juvenile sexual practice: 'school administrators of the period tended to associate sex between boys with masturbatory isolation rather than with heterosexual union' (Martin 2002: 494). Rather than viewing homosexual inclination as an alternative to 'heterosexual union', then, the dialogue about such behaviour parallels the language and discourses of onanism, which became a subject for debate in medical circles and were part of the context of school reform. This is evident in Symonds' account of his schooldays, in which both masturbation and homosexual activity are viewed as equivalent deeds: 'Here and there one could not avoid seeing acts of onanism, mutual masturbation, [and] the sport of naked boys in bed together' (Symonds 1984: 94). While homoerotic attachment in fictional school episodes of the period may have been permissible as a means of fostering emotional bonding, masturbation incites definite fears about moral and physical purity. Discourses about masturbation often view it as a contagion, or a disease that is passed on between friends, an attitude evident in Henry Silver's report that 'Thackeray says one of the first orders he recd. [at Charterhouse] was "Come & frig me"' (Silver, in Ray 1955: 452n). Such claims indicate that schoolboy masturbation appears as both a form of collective, as well as autoerotic, behaviour. This private anecdote reveals the way in which the boy's body may lack integrity and individuality when at school. It can become difficult to distinguish one body from the communal body, and a youth like Thackeray – together with figures like David Copperfield, or the 'pretty' young fag for whom Tom Brown displays such scorn – becomes a facilitator of both his own physical abuse and the erotic satisfaction of others.

The dangerous allure of sexual pleasure at school, and warnings about the deleterious effect it was supposed to have on a boy's physique and constitution, was a running theme taken up in medical texts and advice literature in the Victorian period. Eminent specialist physicians such as François Lallemand and William Carpenter wrote about the horrors of masturbation and the impact it was thought to have, causing listlessness and weakness, madness, impotence and even death. Such was his anxiety on the topic that William Acton, in his *Functions and Diseases of the Reproductive Organs* (1857), included a letter from a man who had experience of the practice at public and private schools, stating to the physician the shameful extent to which 'the secret indulgence of the vice, [and] the communication of this habit from one boy to another', would inevitably occur 'wherever boys are gathered together' (Acton 1857: 107). The letter was reproduced in Acton's text to serve as a warning about the way in which the 'vice' was communicated between boys, particularly when living in close quarters such as dormitories.

It is unsurprising that schoolboy episodes in Victorian fiction alluded to the perils of masturbation, although they often did so obliquely, through reference to nameless temptation, immoral behaviour, and impurity or tainted physical and moral virtue. One such example is Frederic W. Farrar's popular school novel, *Eric, or Little by Little* (1858). Through the depiction of a series of typical scrapes, adventures, accidents and moral lessons provided by the text, the novel follows the downfall and eventual death of a young boy led astray at school. In one of the chapters, the topic of masturbation, described as 'the most fatal curse which could ever become rife in a public school', is raised (Farrar 1858: 70). Discussion of the topic is brought up by a new boy, perhaps aptly named 'Ball', who speaks in the dormitory to the other boys about 'his guilty experience', and 'advanced iniquity', with 'vile words' in the dark before they go to sleep (ibid.: 65; 67). Eric's simultaneous fascination and repulsion at Ball's temptation is experienced physically by the boy. Having listened to Ball speak, Eric 'felt himself blushing to the roots of his hair [. . .] then growing pale again, while a hot dew was left on his forehead' (ibid.: 66). Such physiological symptoms of the sin are also experienced when he awakes the next morning, which finds him 'restless and feverish', indicating the kind of disturbed sleep and agitation that medical writers ascribed to the habitual masturbator (ibid.: 67).

This episode, couched in terms of the 'vile' talk of the dormitory, illustrates that the physical and spiritual menace of masturbation, while typically conceived as a solitary vice, was nonetheless part of a collective experience between boys in stories of school life.

The school environment in the narratives drawn on here forms an affective community in which a boy's development of his masculine identity is fostered and regulated both by his peers and by his seniors. There is an emphasis in each text on physical demonstrations and bodily rituals as means to maintain the patriarchal, masculine values and traditions of the school. In novels and stories such as *Tom Brown* and 'Mr and Mrs Frank Berry', a pugnacious muscularity can become emblematic of vigorous manliness. The schoolboy body, however, does not always engage equally in the contests and performances of masculine display; in *David Copperfield*, for example, the child's fragility is figured on his body, which is repeatedly abused and beaten by more powerful adults. At the same time, he is also unwittingly, if timidly, fascinated by his handsome friend Steerforth, although David remains in a subjugated relation to the older boy, who makes a pet of him. At times, too, these texts also invite the reader to observe in these fictional boys an appropriation of explicitly feminine qualities, particularly at moments when the juvenile body is erotically charged. The reader's gaze is therefore drawn repeatedly to the schoolboy body, which is variously realised as passive and externally-regulated, or as potentially aggressive and combative. The schoolboy bodies examined here reveal a lack of symbolic cohesion, although the ways in which these fictional children negotiate the more extreme excesses of physical abuse – corporal punishment, fighting and violent play, and sexual initiation – demonstrate a repeated fascination with the schoolboy figure. In returning so frequently to the somatic impact of school life on maturation and male physicality, each account of the schoolboy experience provides an index for juvenile masculinity from fragile sensitivity to overt displays of manly assertiveness.

Notes

1. The inoffensive 'patting and soothing' that form David Copperfield's ritual initiation on his arrival at school, of course, also echo a more clearly sexualised 'patting and soothing', to which David's relief that 'it was much better than I had anticipated' might also refer. Although not directly referenced here, the problem of mutual masturbation at public schools is raised later in this essay.

2. Galia Benziman (2012) highlights this aspect of Dickensian childhood in her work *Narratives of Child Neglect in Romantic and Victorian Culture*.
3. 'Busby' here refers to Dr Richard Busby, a former headmaster of Westminster, who had a reputation for excessive use of the rod on his pupils.
4. Rose indicates, however, that men like Creakle could also be subject to their own involuntary process of attraction, which is evident in Dickens' description of his desire to flog a 'chubby boy' as 'like the satisfaction of a craving appetite' (Dickens 1981: 85), and an impetus beyond his own control or understanding.
5. Thackeray in particular associated school with corporal punishment, as evidenced by the names of his fictional teachers: Dr Swishtail, or Dr Birch.
6. Ray also recounts the infamous incident in 1822 when Thackeray got into a fight with schoolfellow George Stovin Venables, who broke Thackeray's nose. Nonetheless, the two stayed in touch after their time together at Charterhouse.
7. Isabel Quigly (1982) has similarly noted that 'the *pattern* [of public school] was homosexual: masculine values and company were enough; women were irrelevant to it', drawing attention to the fagging system as particularly emblematic of this (Quigly 1982: 7). Claudia Nelson (1991) has also observed that 'the effect of fagging was to create a gendered hierarchy within a single-sex society' (Nelson 1991: 65).
8. It is significant the names Polly, Molly, Jenny and Betty are all associated with the working class, or at least were often names attributed to servants and maids in nineteenth-century fiction.

Works Cited

Acton, W. (1857), *The Functions and Disorders of the Reproductive Organs in Youth, in Adult Age, and in Advanced Life. Considered in the Physiological, Social, and Psychological Relations*, London: John Churchill.

Adams, J. E. (1995), *Dandies and Desert Saints: Styles of Victorian Manhood*, Ithaca: Cornell University Press.

Benziman, G. (2012), *Narratives of Child Neglect in Romantic and Victorian Culture*, Basingstoke: Palgrave Macmillan.

Boyd, K. (2003), *Manliness and the Boys' Story Paper in Britain: A Cultural History, 1855–1940*, Basingstoke: Palgrave Macmillan.

Buckton, O. S. (1997), '"The Reader Whom I Love": Homoerotic Secrets in *David Copperfield*', *ELH*, 64: 1, pp. 189–222.

Cohen, W. A. (2008), *Embodied: Victorian Literature and the Senses*, Minneapolis and London: University of Minnesota Press.

Crossley, A. (2012), 'Youth in History: Masculine Development in Victorian Literature and Culture', *Peer English*, 7, pp. 9–23.

Danahay, M. (2005), *Gender at Work in Victorian Culture: Literature, Art and Masculinity*, Aldershot: Ashgate.

Dickens, C. (1851), 'Our School', *Household Words*, 4: 81 (11 October), pp. 49–52.

Dickens, C. [1850] (1981), *David Copperfield*, ed. Nina Burgis, int. Andrew Sanders, Oxford: Oxford University Press.

Disraeli, B. (1911), *Coningsby*, London: J. M. Dent.

Farrar, F. W. (1858), *Eric, or Little by Little*, Marston Gate: Leopold Classic Library.

Good, M. (2009), *Sentimental Masculinity and the Rise of History, 1790–1890*, Cambridge and New York: Cambridge University Press.

Hall, D. E. (1996), *Fixing Patriarchy: Feminism and Mid-Victorian Male Novelists*, Basingstoke: Macmillan.

Hewlett, J. T. J. (1841), *Peter Priggins, the College Scout*, ed. Theodore Hook, in *Collection of Ancient and Modern Authors*, vol. 311, Paris: Baudry's European Library.

Holt, J. (2008), *Public School Literature, Civic Education and the Politics of Male Adolescence*, Farnham: Ashgate.

Hughes, T. [1857] (1999), *Tom Brown's Schooldays*, ed. Andrew Sanders, Oxford: Oxford University Press.

Martin, M. M. (2002), '"Boys Who Will Be Men": Desire in *Tom Brown's Schooldays*', *Victorian Literature and Culture*, 30: 2, pp. 483–502.

Martineau, H. (1841), *The Crofton Boys*, London: William Clowes.

Mason, D. (2008), *The Secret Vice: Masturbation in Victorian Fiction and Medical Culture*, Manchester and New York: Manchester University Press.

Meredith, G. (1970), *Letters*, ed. C. L. Cline, Oxford: Clarendon Press.

Meredith, G. (1987), *The Egoist, a Comedy in Narrative*, ed. George Woodcock, London: Penguin.

Meredith, G. (2009), *The Adventures of Harry Richmond*, Teddington: Echo Library.

Nelson, C. (1991), *Boys Will Be Girls: The Feminine Ethic and British Children's Fiction, 1857–1917*, New Brunswick, NJ and London: Rutgers University Press.

Payn, J. (1856), 'Ushers', *Household Words*, 14: 334 (16 August), pp. 97–102.

Quigly, I. (1982), *The Heirs of Tom Brown: The English School Story*, London: Chatto and Windus.

Ray, G. N. (1955), *Thackeray: The Uses of Adversity, 1811–1846*, London: Oxford University Press.

Reed, J. R. (1974), 'The Public Schools in Victorian Literature', *Nineteenth-Century Fiction*, 29: 1, pp. 58–76.

Rose, N. (2005), 'Flogging and Fascination: Dickens and the Fragile Will', *Victorian Studies*, 47: 4, pp. 505–33.

Steedman, C. (1995), *Strange Dislocations: Childhood and the Idea of Human Interiority, 1780–1930*, Cambridge, MA: Harvard University Press.

Symonds, John A. (1984), *The Memoirs of John Addington Symonds*, ed. Phyllis Grosskurth, London: Hutchinson.
Thackeray, W. M. (1857), *The Irish Sketch-Book, by M.A. Titmarsh*, London: Chapman and Hall.
Thackeray, W. M. (1891), *Doctor Birch and his Young Friends*, in *The Works of William Makepeace Thackeray, in Thirteen Volumes*, vol. 12, London: Smith, Elder and Co.
Thackeray, W. M. [1848] (1983), *Vanity Fair*, ed. John Sutherland, Oxford: Oxford University Press.
Thackeray, W. M. [1852] (2013), *Men's Wives*, Marston Gate: CreateSpace.
Tosh, J. (2002), 'Gentlemanly Politeness and Manly Simplicity in Victorian England', *Transactions of the Royal Historical Society*, 6th series, 12, pp. 455–72.
Tosh, J. (2005), *Manliness and Masculinities in Nineteenth-Century Britain: Essays on Gender, Family and Empire*, Harlow: Pearson Education.
Watterson, W. C. (1996), '"Chips off the Old Block": Birching, Social Class, and the English Public Schools', *Nineteenth-Century Studies*, 10, pp. 93–110.
Yonge, C. M. (1853), *The Heir of Redclyffe*, London: Macmillan.

Chapter 2

Punishing the Unregulated Manly Body and Emotions in Early Victorian England

Joanne Begiato

In *Manliness: A Lecture* (1858), the minister Hugh Stowell Brown explained in great detail what constituted true manliness:

> I, virtue, I am manliness. I alone am manliness; without me you may be a fool, you may be a brute, you may be a demon, but you cannot be a man. I must be enthroned in your heart; I must have the absolute government of your physical, intellectual, moral being; I must regulate your life; I must direct you in your going out and your coming in; I must have the control of your thoughts, feelings, words and deeds; on such conditions only is it possible for you to be manly! (Brown 1858: n.p.)

Brown spelled out that 'virtue and manliness are identical', telling his working-class audience that manliness 'stands in strong and eternal antagonism to every form of Licentiousness' (ibid.). To be 'manly' was an ideal and an aspiration for men of all social ranks in the nineteenth century; the adjective conveyed prized masculine values to society including virtue, piety, courage, endurance, honesty and directness.

As Brown explains, to be manly, nineteenth-century men were required to manage their bodies and emotions; left unregulated, they could severely undermine manliness. Thus, physical and emotional self-control were essential to achieving manly qualities. Historians of masculinity demonstrate that Victorian men's character was forged in independence and self-discipline (Tosh 2005: 75). These were more than abstract values, however, since their attainment depended upon hard work and a pious mind and heart. As such, manliness was not predominantly cerebral but depended upon a man controlling his body and managing his feelings. Increasingly, historians recognise the importance of both bodies and emotions in the formulation of gender ideals. Christopher Forth, for example, demonstrates that dietary practices were considered materially as well as symbolically to construct the eighteenth- and nineteenth-century Western European male body; commentators envisaged food as impacting on nervous, digestive and reproductive systems, thereby to craft the materiality of manhood (Forth 2009: 582). Manliness from 1880 to 1914, Stephanie Olsen concludes, 'represented a cluster of carefully honed, controlled and directed emotions that were to ensure the embodiment, the emotional constitution of morality' (Olsen 2014: 13; 14; 166). This chapter positions itself within these historical approaches by tracing the relationship between the regulated male body and being manly in the early Victorian era, with particular emphasis on the meanings and consequences of the failure to manage appetites and emotions (ibid.: 3).

This perspective is useful because little scholarship focuses on how far adult men were rewarded for being manly and penalised for being unmanly. When the penalties imposed on men deemed unmanly are discussed, the attention is largely upon accusations of effeminacy as the forfeit for failing to conform to gender norms. John Tosh, for example, argues that men were faced with a 'stark binary form of manliness against effeminacy, self-indulgence against self-discipline – or vice against virtue' (Tosh 2005: 73). Thus, domesticity and intensive time spent with wives and daughters were considered to risk effeminising a man by undermining his vigour and authority (ibid.: 70). This chapter proposes that effeminacy was not the sole antithesis of manliness or its main threat (Ellis and Meyer 2009). To be unmanly could also indicate a variety of bodily and emotional failings, which were not necessarily equated with being feminine, including certain types of physical weakness, bodily excess or incapacity, and uncontrolled and unmanaged feelings. As Brown insisted in his lecture, 'there is no manliness in sin of any kind' and this relationship is considered in the first half of this chapter (Brown 1858). The chapter then turns to the penalties imposed for bodily and emotional excesses, demonstrating that they could have harsher consequences than the undermining of a man's masculine reputation, even extending to physical repercussions. It does so by examining the most extreme form of penalty incurred by the breakdown of male self-control over the passions: the categorisation of insanity. It analyses the case notes of a sample of 180 male patients admitted in 1851 and 1854 to Colney Hatch, the second pauper lunatic asylum for the County of Middlesex, which opened at Friern Barnet in July 1851 (Hunter and MacAlpine 1974).

Regulating the Manly Body: Self-Control and Bodily Appetites

Desirable standards of manliness required adult men to attain a high level of emotional and bodily management. Self-mastery over sexuality, food and drink was critical to becoming manly; how a man lived was as important as possessing a male body (Forth 2009: 579; 583). Physical moderation and abstinence were motivated by religion, health, morals and a modernising lifestyle. Christopher Forth argues that muscular ideals about masculinity came into being across Europe once modern lifestyles were perceived to be more luxurious and sedentary. Modernity was imagined to soften the body causing obesity, laziness, masturbation and sodomy (Forth 2009: 580–1; Calvert 2013: 39). As such, masculine character and body were both intended to be built through a simple diet, which would enable men to develop a harder body, resistant to the temptations of sexual excess (Begiato 2017: 181–4).

Elite boys and youths were trained in forms of manliness through schooling, religious organisations and engagement with sport (Rothery and French 2012: 17). Manliness and self-control were also demanded of low-ranking men nonetheless: even convicts. In 1861, for example, a prison governor reported to parliament on a commission into convict prisons in Ireland, explaining his regime for the convicts:

> I endeavour to inspire them with self-dependence and self respect – to generate in their hearts a repugnance to theft – to implant in their minds thoughts of true manliness – to encourage habits of temperance and honest, independent industry – to wean and win them from their past evil ways – to breathe into them the duty which they owe to their fellows, and place before them, clearly and patently, how they themselves can heal and eradicate their own mental and moral diseases, when assisted by a merciful and forgiving Providence. (Parliamentary Papers 1861: 78)

One of the most famous proponents of a disciplined lifestyle was Samuel Smiles who made it a crucial component of his doctrine of self-improvement in *Self Help* (1859). Smiles informed his working-class male readers that the highest object of life was 'to form a manly character, and to work out the best development possible, of body and spirit, – of mind, conscience, heart, and soul' (Smiles 1859: 150).

Self-control was critical in this endeavour. Smiles explained that his motivation for writing the book was the success of a talk to young northern working-class men in which he gave examples of successful men to show the audience that

> their happiness and well-being as individuals in afterlife, must necessarily depend mainly upon themselves, – upon their own diligent self-culture, self-discipline, and self-control, – and, above all, on that honest and upright performance of individual duty, which is the glory of manly character. (ibid.: 6)

For Smiles, manly character was sustained by not giving in to physical desire, whether for sexual gratification or food and alcohol, by controlling inappropriate passions and feelings such as anger and fear, and by physical hard work. Thus he advised his working-class reader to be frugal with money and diet. In his chapter 'Money, – Use and Abuse' he recommended that the provident man should not just plan for the future, 'he must also be a temperate man, and exercise the virtue of self-denial, than which nothing is so much calculated to give strength to the character' (ibid.: 137). By this date self-denial was in and of itself a virtue that supplied 'strength to the character' (ibid.: 137). Mastering temptation raised men's status; its lack produced discontented, poor men who suffered from 'weakness, self-indulgence, and perverseness' (ibid.: 139). Succumbing to temptation even stripped middle-class men of their manliness. He disparaged their 'ambition to bring up boys as gentlemen, or rather "genteel" men' through which they 'acquire a taste for dress, style, luxuries, and amusements, which can never form any solid foundation for manly or gentlemanly character' (ibid.: 143).

While the link between unmanaged passions and unmanliness was a feature of the Georgian and Victorian eras, arguably more was demanded of men's will-power in the latter. It is helpful to focus on the changing emphasis in dietary and alcohol restraint from moderation to abstinence to illustrate this. Restricted diet increasingly took on a more extreme form, for example, in abstention from meat. Vegetarianism was often considered a higher form of restraint in the Victorian period and was often adopted by those in the temperance movement (Calvert 2013: 20; 56). This non-denominational movement began with attempts to make milder beverages available, and from 1828 targeted spirit drinks. Teetotal societies were formed from the 1830s, which sought total abstinence from all alcoholic drinks (ibid.: 55; 99). Typically, they linked succumbing to temptation to the undermining of gendered bodies and minds. The temperance organisation, the Band of Hope, founded 1847, for example, issued an instructors' guide which observed that '[t]he youth who is under the influence of strong drink is at the mercy of his passions and has no resistance to temptation' and therefore unmanly (Olsen 2014: 108).

The dangers of uncontrolled habits were often delineated through gender conventions. Warnings of the dangers of drunkenness often focused on the gin-sodden woman consigned to prostitution thanks to her drinking. Moreover, many visual and textual Victorian temperance narratives centred on the decline of the respectable family man, depicting his fall as one of status in class, character and masculinity (Murray 2012: 291). In 'road to ruin' accounts, the man travelled a ruinous journey from decency to drunken degradation thanks to excessive consumption of alcohol. One of the most popular was George Cruikshank's series *The Bottle* (1847), which sold 100,000 copies and was visible to many more eyes since it was displayed in shop windows. These melodramatic, haunting images depict a respectable man succumbing to the temptation of alcohol, his decline illustrated through his diminishing masculine attributes. In the first plate he introduces alcohol to his comfortable home and family, by the second he is no longer the male provider, having been discharged from employment for drunkenness. Thus the room is cosy no more, denuded by the pawning of its comforts in exchange for more alcohol. The plates that follow show the family begging on the streets and the death of their youngest child. Next the man falls to the level of wife-beater, engaging in 'fearful quarrels, and brutal violence' until he murders his wife with a bottle. The remaining plates vividly depict the consequences of excessive alcohol consumption: the husband a 'hopeless maniac' in a cell, the children reduced to vice via the gin-palace and beer-shop; the daughter dead by her own hand; the son transported for robbery (Murray 2012: 296; 297; 301; 302). Here was a man utterly unmanned by failing to control his appetites and therefore his passions, the result being destruction of job, reputation, family and sanity.

The degrading physical losses of manliness caused by a descent into drunkenness were still powerful in temperance campaigns at the end of the century. For example, campaigns to make the Royal Navy teetotal used the connection in publicity. Agnes Weston's materials aimed at naval men made it clear that their inability to resist alcohol emasculated them. In one article she declared that 'the fine, manly, stalwart form of a man-o'-war's man reeling up the street, all his manliness gone, and the kindly, pleasant-spoken fellow turned either into a drivelling idiot or a rough swearing bully, is a spectacle sad enough to make men and angels weep' (quoted in Conley 1999: 9). What is striking in all these depictions is that the unmanly man is driven to insanity by his inability to resist bodily temptation. The fate of Cruikshank's drunkard is Bedlam and the drunken sailor becomes an 'idiot'. The final section of this chapter explores the associations between the failure of will to control the passions, definitions of insanity, and loss of manliness.

The Unregulated Manly body: Passions and Insanity

Given the social importance placed upon male self-control, there was a variety of social, economic and cultural penalties associated with unrestrained male behaviour, which affected men from all social classes. These had long been in place. Early modernists have shown that unregulated, intemperate, or violent behaviour undermined middling-sort men's reputations in communities linked through credit. Similarly, work on the sexual double-standard indicates that adulterous middle-class married men lost public honour in the eighteenth century (Bailey (Begiato) 2003; Capp 1999; Turner 2002). Class and gender historians have also revealed the role that gender played in constructing class identity in the first half of the nineteenth century when respectable, self-controlled, masculine behaviour was integral to middle-class identity, implying that failure to achieve this damaged social as well as gender status. In this era adopting such a manly persona was also part of working-class men's attempt to attain political and civic voices and social mobility, by demonstrating the capacity to manage their bodies and feelings (Davidoff and Hall 1987; Clark 1995). The lack of such manly characteristics therefore risked downward social mobility for many men.

Demonstrating lack of self-restraint became more risky in the nineteenth century because persistent and extreme lack of control over passions, bodies, bodily appetites and feelings was increasingly pathologised as a cause of insanity. In the early modern period, failure to control bodily appetites and the passions was seen as the road to crime and sin, punishment, and, eventually, redemption (Wiltenburg 2004). During the nineteenth century, emotions were understood differently as morally neutral, non-intellectual states, so that men's self-control needed to be a habituated state, more an inner instinct than a reasoned response (Dixon 2011: 304). Changing understandings of the medical aspects of passions meant that passions were less likely to be seen as a cause or symptom of organic disease and reconceptualised as the manias and phobias of mental illness (ibid.: 305–6; Dixon 2012: 341). Thus while there was consistency over time in the idea that succumbing to temptation escalated vice and undermined masculine identity, additionally it was considered to fuel a descent into madness, tainting the body through progressive loss of strength and constitution of the mind through mania.

Bodies and emotions were central to explanations for insanity. For medical practitioners the body also represented its owner's physical circumstances and moral standing (Wallis 2015: 99). Forth observes that nineteenth-century health manuals related good health with aesthetic, physical and moral traits. A man whose body was attractive and whose temperament was calm would therefore possess internal organs that functioned efficiently and harmoniously (Forth 2009: 583). From the 1790s to 1850s it was understood that madness lay in disordered nerves and minds, caused by factors like poverty, stress and emotional problems (Porter 2003: 305–19; Shepherd 2014: 116). Samuel Tuke set out the causes of the main forms of insanity in his *Description of the Retreat* (1813), a Quaker-family mental asylum established in 1796:

> The approach of a maniacal paroxysm, is generally marked by an uncommon flow of spirits, and great warmth of the passions. For a time, these are not unusually kept in considerable subjection; but the mind, in this state, seeks for situations unfavourable to its calmness. The mental excitement of some, leads them to form indiscreet and hasty attachments [what he calls disappointed affections], which, leading to disappointment, hastens or perhaps induces the complete development of the disorder. (Tuke 1818: 131)

Bodily appetites were critical too. Tuke noted that '[i]ntemperance is another very prevalent, and less ambiguous cause of insanity' (ibid.: 133). William Black, physician to Bethlem, added venereal causes to his list, published in *A Dissertation on Insanity* (1811) (Tuke 1818: 133; Goodman 2015: 152–3). Masturbation is a particularly representative example (Goodman 2015: 158–9). Lesley Hall observes that although the Victorian medical profession held varying views on the level of risk of masturbation, all saw it as having physical as well as moral consequences (Hall 1992: 365–87). Self-gratification facilitated and rooted sensual self-indulgence in men and made them unable to resist other temptations, leading to bodily disease and, in some views, insanity (ibid.: 373; 374; 382). In 'An Inquiry into a Frequent Cause of Insanity in Young Men', published in *The Lancet* in 1861, Robert Ritchie claimed '[t]hat insanity is a consequence of this habit [masturbation], is now beyond doubt' (quoted in Acton 1867: 95).

These same causes of insanity continued to be applied through the nineteenth century. For example, from 1867 to the end of the century the Surrey mental asylums Brookwood (a county asylum) and Holloway (a private sanatorium) identified as causes of insanity, mental worry, domestic trouble (including bereavement), adverse circumstances like business worries, love affairs, and 'physical' causes which included intemperance and bodily disease (Shepherd 2014: 124–5). In the 1890s the Board of Commissioners in Lunacy still applied six different categories for non-hereditary causes of insanity, which encompassed problematic circumstances, emotions and bodies; domestic trouble; adverse circumstances; mental anxiety and overwork; religious excitement; love affairs; and fright and nervous shock (Goodman 2015: 154).

In order to explore the penalties for men of failure to control bodily and emotional appetites, the next section is based on a sample of male case notes from Colney Hatch Asylum (later known as Friern Hospital). The series of case books from the male side of Colney Hatch are held at the London Metropolitan Archives and a sample of the case notes therein was transcribed from the years 1851 and 1854 to allow a survey of patient notes from the first years of the asylum's history. In the case books, asylum medical officers recorded various details about patients from their admission until their discharge or death, namely their medical condition, appearance, habits and behaviour (Andrews 1998). The case notes offer insights into medical officers' perceptions of their male patients and the links between failure of self-control, diminution of manliness, and insanity. The discussion focuses on those physical and moral causes (often the most numerous) which were related to the passions and self-control: General Paralysis of the Insane (GPI) and intemperance.[1]

The notes typically record more than one cause of insanity. This is because a previous medical diagnosis or family opinion is first stated on the notes, and then added to by the Colney Hatch medical officer following observation.[2] In cases where men remained in the asylum for long periods new symptoms appeared or were identified over time. Thus although thirty-seven men were identified as having features of GPI this was more often diagnosed after the men's admittance rather than as the primary cause, since it was 'generally conceived of as a progressive deterioration of the whole mental and physical personality' (Wallis 2011: n.p.). In some cases GPI was noted as incipient with descriptions of quivering of lips, tremor of facial muscles, difficulties in speaking, and unsteady gait, in others simply as abject or hopeless General Paralysis. It was not unequivocally established until the twentieth century that GPI was the final stage of untreated syphilis. In the mid-nineteenth century alienists had reached no consensus about its links with venereal disease, but understood it to be linked to alcoholic and sexual excess (ibid.: 100–1).

Indeed intemperance was also frequently recorded separately or as a possible contributor to the patient's condition alongside another stated cause. An intemperate lifestyle was mentioned in twenty-seven men's case notes. This category included drunkenness, usually addiction to spirits and beer, as well as a more general vicious lifestyle. Typically, men's strength and constitution was understood to be broken down by intemperance, their muscles rendered flaccid, and their bodies subject to impotency, trembling and mental derangement (Makras 2015: 137–8; 139–40). In several case notes, the reference to intemperance was an opinion given by the medical officer assessing the man; for example, James Fidler: 'Recurrent attack, of about 6 weeks duration – cause unknown – (probably intemperance)' (London Metropolitan Archive [LMA] 1854). In Charles Langley's case: 'There is a vagueness and difficulty about him which is suggestive of a fear of his having led a very irregular life' (LMA 1854). In some cases drunkenness was seen as exacerbating a prior cause of insanity. In John Costey, it worsened an accident:

> Instead of resting after this accident he went to work next day and was in the habit of drinking hard. Almost every day for twelve months previously he was intoxicated. He continued this habit until his admission to Peckham Asylum. He would drink beer, rum, and brandy on the same day and at the same sitting at the bar of public houses. (LMA 1854)

Intemperance was not restricted to alcoholism, and descriptions associated it with unrestrained sexuality and anger too.

In other cases it was the lifestyle itself which led to insanity. Some men seem to have identified this about themselves. Dwigne Leopold's own account of his troubles were recorded in his case notes in 1851: 'that when on his way from Ireland to visit France, passing through London he was mixed up with very bad company – and became intemperate – his brain was attacked and he became maniacal' (LMA 1851). Thomas West also attributed his condition to his lifestyle. His case notes recorded: 'He states that he is a native of Warwick and has been 17 months in London and that he has succumbed to the vices and temptations of the metropolis' (LMA 1854).

Vice included a number of 'immoral' practices. In two cases masturbation was identified as the cause of insanity. About James Fitzgerald, for example:

> His friends say that until seven years since he was a sharp active lad of regular habits – intelligent and very respectable – about that time it was noticed that he absented himself shutting himself in his room and gave way to the habits of masturbator under which evil practices his mind seemed entirely to break down. (LMA 1851)

This parallels Ritchie's 'premonitory symptoms' of the typical masturbatory inmate in the insane asylum, in which the youth gradually altered from being 'quiet and studious', of good behaviour and abilities, to an isolated, slovenly, apathetic, unmanageable character. Ritchie states that in the asylum such a patient was marked out by his unsociability, pale colouring, emaciated slouching frame, and flaccid muscles (Acton 1867: 95–7). Clearly, masturbation was seen as unmanning in a very physical way.

As well as recording state of health, the case notes commented when a male patient was 'dirty in habits'. In the vast majority of cases the disparaging term, 'dirty' or 'filthy' simply described incontinence and occasionally was used more diagnostically as a manifestation of insanity in which the patient handled his own urine or excrement. In two cases, however, the term dirtiness was extended to the man's moral behaviour. John Leslie's dirty habits included his uncovering himself (LMA 1854). William Phipps was 'reported as dangerous, (although hemiplegic) but not suicidal or Epileptic and as labouring under various Delusions and being dirty and indecent in his habits and as having used indecent language and threatened the lives of his wife and others' (LMA 1854). As Phipps' notes demonstrate, physical and moral causes and symptoms of insanity often made up a package of attributes which were rooted in lack of self-control of bodily appetites and passions.

Indeed, failure to control passions was itself referred to by patients and their families as a significant factor in the men's downfall. Lewis Aaron was admitted on 22 August 1851. Aged 35, married and a clothes salesman he was described as:

> A Jew with very marked features of that persuasion. He has been married about two years previous to which time he had a very Debauched life which evidently has caused the maniacal attack that he at present labours under. He has had two or three Epileptic Fits. His health is good and

> he affirms there only to have been fits of passion over which he had no control. His wife says that his passion and tempers are so ungovernable that it is impossible to live with him. His conversation is rational, though excessive and he complains bitterly of the confinement. (LMA 1851)

Bernard Fitzpatrick, aged 50, married and formerly a soldier, and more recently a hawker, was admitted for a third time to Colney Hatch in June 1854, having been last discharged as recovered in February that year (LMA 1854). He had recently been jailed for assaulting his wife and the police, and while in prison had used abusive and threatening language and shown 'much excitement' at times (LMA 1854). On admission the case notes recorded that,

> he is prone to excitement and rambles in his conversation. He says he might have been excited by passions and broke the windows of his lodging house and then struck the police who entered the house 'not with the foot of the bed-stead, I am more of a man than that'. (LMA 1854)

Like Aaron, Fitzpatrick clearly saw his passions as uncontrollable and leading to violence. He defined his manliness, however, by the means he used to strike the police. To be a man required a fair fight, with each man relying on fists alone (Newell 2017: 127–34.). The failure in both men to restrain passions was attributed to their previously debauched or intemperate lives. Fitzpatrick had served in the army from 1827 until he was pensioned out in 1839 having succumbed to yellow fever in the West Indies, which was identified as causing his insanity. Nevertheless, it was Fitzpatrick's questionable lifestyle and problematic self-restraint which was noted. Since the attack of fever he had been prone to insanity 'which has been excited by drinking beer' (LMA 1854). Moreover: 'Before his commitment to the House of Correction 6th May 1854 he has been drinking with some of his countrymen [. . .] when he showed violence and broke windows' (LMA 1854).

The importance of lack of self-control as a cause of male insanity is reinforced by practitioners' focus on rebuilding it to aid recovery and manliness. As Roy Porter observed, 'new psychiatric techniques of mastering madness, aimed at overpowering the delinquent will and passions' (Porter 2003: 314). Rather than trying to treat insanity through physical treatments, 'moral therapy' was introduced which focused on the restoration of self-control as enabling recovery from insanity. In England, this was initially a lay treatment influenced by continental models, most famously deployed by the Quaker Tuke family at their private asylum, the Retreat in York, established in 1796. The therapy reacted against coercive discipline previously use d in asylums, proposing that treatment removed the afflicted individual from the damaging environment into the asylum where the patient could regain control of emotions and learn self-regulation. Samuel Tuke remarked: 'most insane persons, have a considerable degree of self command; and [. . .] the employment and cultivation of this remaining power, is found to be attended with the most salutary effects' (Shepherd 2014: 116; Tuke 1818: 89). As Louis Charland observes, this philosophy was profoundly shaped by ideas about sensibility and benevolence but was not kindness for kindness' sake, 'it was kindness administered for a specific ethical goal: instilling discipline and self-control' (Charland 2007: 72). He describes it as 'ultimately a therapy of the passions. It worked on the passions, through the passions' (ibid.: 72). Such belief in the moralised value of will was shared in broader discourses of self-control. In 1857 the *North British Review* commented on drunkards: '[t]he great object in their treatment is to keep them from stimulants, and to train their moral feelings as to accustom them to bridle and overcome their morbid propensities' (quoted in Makras 2015: 141).

Though moral treatment rejected the use of restraint, confinement might be deployed by asylums to train men to control violence and bodily habits. Samuel Tuke explained that the Retreat included an apartment furnished with a bed, securely fastened to the floor in which a (male) violent patient could be temporarily confined, 'by way of punishment, for any very offensive acts, which it is thought the patient had the power to restrain' (Tuke 1818: 64–5). Tuke suggested that the room was not in high demand, presumably because moral treatment was successful. It is likely that the 'offensive acts' Tuke described were masturbation. In some asylums blisters would be applied to the necks or even genitals of men who masturbated as a counter-irritant to divert their mind from the dangerous bodily excess (Shepherd 2014: 137). In others the patient was segregated until able to master his own behaviour (ibid.: 133).

Moral treatment of the insane was widely used throughout the nineteenth century; it was adopted by the medical superintendents of new county pauper asylums from the mid-century. As Louise Hide observes about the period 1890–1914, asylums still aimed to use kindness and pedagogy to alleviate the patients' distress and to use reward and punishment to enable them to accept the consequences of their behaviour (Hide 2014: 91–120). However, with the vast growth in size of asylums from the mid-nineteenth century, such ambitions became impracticable and 'moral management' took over. This used the asylum buildings, material culture, exercise and amusement, and religious instruction to the same ends, rather than a specifically personalised approach (Charland 2007: 66; Porter 2013: 318; Shepherd 2014: 116–17, 125; Hide 2014: Chap. 4). While some aspects of the causes, diagnostic criteria, concepts of recovery, and treatment of insanity were applied to both sexes, they were also influenced by what society considered suitable gendered behaviour for the sexes (Shepherd 2014: 118).

The Paradoxes and Penalties of Being Unmanly

Until recently, most scholarly attention was paid to women and femininity, with the thesis that the representative cultural stereotype of madness in the nineteenth century was female (Makras 2015: 135–7). Current scholarship, however, addresses the 'forgotten madman' too, exploring how male insanity was equally influenced by ideas of masculinity (Makras 2015: 137; Hide 2014). Helen Goodman argues that nineteenth-century male mad doctors found it difficult to reconcile mental illness with men because madness was seen as a feminine condition (Goodman 2015: 149–50; 158; 160). Men displaying hysterical symptoms, therefore, demonstrated effeminacy because they were failing to perform the male virtues of strength, decisiveness and authority. In his *Treatise on the Nervous Diseases of Women* (1840), for instance, Thomas Laycock opined that hysterical male patients lacked self-control, and engaged in emasculating 'vicious habits' as a consequence, resulting in their blood being reduced to the state of a hysterical female (Goodman 2015: 161; 162). In Goodman's view, new causes of insanity were therefore conceived to assimilate men deemed insane into existing gender categories; namely adverse circumstances due to business and financial difficulties, and mental anxiety and overwork. These were appropriate causes of male insanity since they matched men's gender roles as breadwinners and workers (ibid.: 152; 155–7). Kostas Makras shows that medical, temperance and literary texts viewed the drunkard as emasculated because his body and mind were weakened by his habits, which rendered him unable to work and provide for his family (Makras 2015: 139–40; 143; 146). The corporeal symptoms of General Paralysis Insanity in male sufferers were particularly linked with compromised gendered characteristics. Jennifer Wallis observes that the features of GPI marked out men as the antithesis of idealised masculinity. Using medical descriptions and photographic evidence from the second half of the nineteenth century she shows that GPI's features of bodily atrophy and flaccidness implied for medical practitioners lives of male apathy, laziness and cowardice that contrasted with the ideal of bodily hardness and self-control (Wallis 2015: 102; 110).

This chapter builds on this exciting scholarship to pursue the relationship between insanity and masculinity further. The analyses outlined above either categorise the insane man as effeminate, which in the period studied tended to mean 'like-a-woman', or as the antithesis of ideal masculinity. While the stigma of effeminacy was certainly one way in which hegemonic masculinity was maintained, it is important to recognise that there were inferior models of male behaviour beyond being like a woman. Hegemonic masculinity was a set of norms imposed on subordinate groups of men as well as women in order to uphold its dominance, and therefore used effeminacy as one of its weapons of authority. However, as John Tosh points out in his reassessment of the thesis of hegemonic masculinity, several masculine values were not related to the maintenance of patriarchal control and were related instead to peer-group standing. In these instances, those who failed were less than men (Tosh 2004: 49; 51; 54). While intemperance, vice and GPI were characteristics of the most unmanly of men who failed to exercise self-control, this was a form of unmanliness that indicated inferior forms of masculine behaviour; in their worst form they indicated bestiality rather than effeminacy (Ellis and Meyer 2009). Working-class men who succumbed to drink or anger, for example, were frequently described as beasts (Makras 2015: 145). Failure to subdue passions and to exert control over bodily appetites made a man inferior because he allowed his unconstrained masculine traits (his passions and his bodily appetites) to dominate.

Furthermore, the intemperate or uncontrolled man who became insane was not simply the antithesis of ideal manliness. This is demonstrated in the apparently paradoxical views of men who displayed its symptoms in the second half of the nineteenth century. Juliet Hurn's study of GPI describes one strand of thought, influenced by French opinion, that the disease predominantly affected lower-class men who had been intemperate. Other British alienists, like John Connelly and Harrington Tuke associated GPI with middle-class men who had been struck down when successful, having 'lived hard' previously (Hurn 1998: 77). Hurn suggests that some discerned 'admirable aspects' within GPI sufferers because it betokened former virility and strength; indeed in one line of thought, such as that expressed by a naval doctor in *The Lancet* in 1868, sexual excess was a symptom rather than a cause (ibid.: 85). Thus, by the last decade of the nineteenth century, the standard GPI narrative recognised the critical role of intemperance and sexuality, but balanced such traits with positive counterparts because strong and vigorous men were perceived as most likely to be guilty of excess (ibid.: 75–86).

This is not so anomalous when situated in the broader paradox at the heart of the construction of masculinities. A major tension for men in constructing and maintaining masculine identity was its inherent ambiguities. For example, some of the attributes considered unmanly, namely excessive drinking, smoking, eating and womanising were also less respectable means by which masculinity was constructed and sustained among peers. All these activities were, after all, rooted in conviviality and virility. They were partially tolerated in youths and adult men when they might be seen as a passing phase before maturity was reached, or as an appropriate behaviour within a specific space or group (Davison 2014). Alex Shepard also argues that from the seventeenth century these behaviours were increasingly adopted by those who could not attain the normative version of manhood, as part of an anti-patriarchal masculine sub-culture (Shepard 2005). Given that these excessive forms of behaviour had disorderly repercussions including deviant behaviour, inter-personal violence, damage to property, and waste of earnings, there was considerable emphasis upon their management by the eighteenth and nineteenth centuries. In short, debauchery and intemperance were therefore seen to be natural forms of behaviour of the male body and temperament. In order to achieve manliness, the dominant form of masculinity in the period studied, these qualities therefore needed to be rigorously controlled. Nevertheless, alternative forms of masculinity continued which permitted and approved hard drinking and sexual virility. In many ways, the acknowledgement that male bodily collapse and insanity could be caused by such intemperate habits reinforced the cause of hegemonic masculinity by making the penalties of being unmanly shockingly clear.

Perhaps ironically, the moral treatment and moral management implemented in insane asylums exacerbated the unmanliness of men whose self-control over their passions and bodies had abjectly failed. These regimes did not punish in coercive or disciplinarian ways. Instead, they further undermined the men's manliness, at least temporarily, because such men were denied the very will and agency that defined them as manly. Although treatment sought to restore their self-control, male patients were placed in a childlike and dependent state. As Samuel Tuke commented about moral therapy:

> There is much analogy between the judicious treatment of children, and that of insane persons [...] even with regard to the more violent and vociferous maniacs, a very different mode is found successful; and they are best approached with soft and mild persuasion. (Tuke 1818: 95; 96)

Conclusion

To be a manly man required more than a programme of education and training to acquire the prized attributes that we still associate with the concept. To be unmanly was a very risky business that undermined one's place in society, community and family. Much was therefore invested in male self-control and the regulation of bodily appetites and passions. Failure to master the passions resulted in an inferior man, but not a man who was like a woman. While lack of self-control risked effeminacy, in the sense of being woman-like, it was more often associated with being unmanly because it diminished the male body, making it beast-like or child-like. Being unmanly not only incurred penalties through loss of public reputation, for, as definitions of insanity surely reminded them, when men failed to exert their will to master their own passions, they also lost bodily, emotional and mental integrity.

My thanks to Michael Brown for reading this chapter and sharing with me his expertise in the histories of medicine and masculinities, and to Jennifer Wynter for her advice on scholarship on the history of insanity.

Notes

1. Accounts of illnesses such as epilepsy or congenital learning difficulties are not included here.
2. In twenty cases the patient was recorded as entering with a diagnosis of cause unknown, or not assigned, and would then have his state assessed at Colney Hatch. Such a patient therefore might have cause unknown and a cause assigned in this analysis.

Works Cited

Acton, W. (1867), *The Functions and Disorders of the Reproductive Organs*, Philadelphia: Lindsay and Blakiston.

Andrews, J. (1998), 'Case Notes, Case Histories, and the Patient's Experience of Insanity at Gartnavel Royal Asylum, Glasgow, in the Nineteenth Century', *Social History of Medicine*, 11: 2, pp. 255–81.

Bailey (Begiato), J. (2003), *Unquiet Lives: Marriage and Marriage Breakdown*, Cambridge: Cambridge University Press.

Begiato, J. (2017), 'Celibacy, "Conjugal Chastity", and Moral Restraint', in J. Begiato and W. Gibson, *Sex and the Church in the Long Eighteenth Century: Religion, Enlightenment and the Sexual Revolution*, London: I. B. Tauris, pp. 167–94.

Brown, H. S. (1858), 'Manliness, a Lecture by Rev. Hugh Stowell Brown of Liverpool', in *Lectures Delivered before the Young Men's Christian Association*, London (unpaginated).

Calvert, S. J. (2013), 'Eden's Diet: Christianity and Vegetarianism 1809–2009', unpublished PhD thesis, University of Birmingham.

Capp, B. (1999), 'The Double Standard Revisited: Plebeian Women and Male Sexual Reputation in Early Modern England', *Past and Present* 162: 1, pp. 70–100.

Charland, L. C. (2007), 'Benevolent Theory: Moral Treatment at the York Retreat', *History of Psychiatry*, 18: 1, pp. 61–80.

Clark, A. (1995), *The Struggle for the Breeches: Gender and the Making of the British Working Class*, Berkeley: University of California Press.

Conley, M. (1999), '"You Don't Make a Torpedo Gunner out of a Drunkard": Agnes Weston, Temperance, and the British Navy', *The Northern Mariner/ Le Marin du nord*, IX, p. 19.

Davidoff, L. and C. Hall (1987), *Family Fortunes: Men and Women of the English Middle Class, 1780–1850*, Chicago: University of Chicago Press.

Davison, K. (2014), 'Occasional Politeness and Gentlemen's Laughter in 18th-century England', *The Historical Journal*, 57: 4, pp. 921–45.

Dixon, T. (2011), 'Revolting Passions', *Modern Theology*, 27: 2, pp. 298–312.

Dixon, T. (2012), '"Emotion": The History of a Keyword in Crisis', *Emotion Review October*, 4: 4, pp. 338–44.

Ellis, H. and J. Meyer (2009), *Masculinity and the Other: Historical Perspectives*, Newcastle-upon-Tyne: Cambridge Scholars Publishing.

Forth, C. (2009), 'Manhood Incorporated: Diet and the Embodiment of "Civilized" Masculinity', *Men and Masculinities*, 11: 5, pp. 578–601.

Goodman, H. (2015), '"Madness and Masculinity": Male Patients in London Asylums and Victorian Culture', in T. Knowles and S. Trowbridge (eds), *Insanity and the Lunatic Asylum in the Nineteenth Century*, London: Pickering and Chatto Limited, pp. 149–66.

Hall, L. (1992), 'Forbidden by God, Despised by Men: Masturbation, Medical Warnings, Moral Panic, and Manhood in Great Britain, 1850–1950', *Journal of the History of Sexuality in Modern Europe*, 2: 3, pp. 365–87.

Hide, L. (2014), *Gender & Class in English Asylums 1890–1914*, Basingstoke and New York: Palgrave Macmillan.

Hunter, R. and I. MacAlpine (1974), *Psychiatry for the Poor, 1851 Colney Hatch Asylum, Friern Hospital 1973, A Medical and Social History*, London: Dawsons of Pall Mall.

Hurn, J. (1998), 'The History of General Paralysis of the Insane in Britain, 1830–1950', unpublished PhD thesis, University of London.

London Metropolitan Archive (LMA) H12/CH/B13/1 Middlesex County Lunatic Aslyum Colney Hatch. Case Book, Male Side. No. 1, 1851; H12/CH/B13/4 Middlesex County Lunatic Aslyum Colney Hatch. Case Book, Male Side. No. 1, 1854.

Makras, K. (2015), '"The Poison that Upsets My Reason": Men, Madness and Drunkenness in the Victorian Period', in T. Knowles and S. Trowbridge (eds), *Insanity and the Lunatic Asylum in the Nineteenth Century*, London: Pickering and Chatto Limited, pp. 135–48.

Murray, F. (2012), 'Picturing the "Road to Ruin": Visual Representations of a Standard Temperance Narrative, 1830–1855', *Visual Resources: An International Journal of Documentation*, 28: 4, pp. 290–308.

Newell, D. (2017), 'Masculinity and the Plebeian Honour Fight: Dispute Resolution in Georgian England', unpublished PhD thesis, Oxford Brookes University.

Olsen, S. (2014), *Juvenile Nation: Youth, Emotions and the Making of the Modern British Citizen, 1880–1914*, New York: Bloomsbury Academic.

Parliamentary Papers (1861), *Eighth Annual Report of the Directors of Convict Prisons in Ireland, for the Year Ended 31st December, 1861*.

Porter, R. (2003), *Flesh in the Age of Reason: The Modern Foundations of Body and Soul*. New York: W. W. Norton.

Rothery, M. and H. French (eds) (2012), *Making Men. The Formation of Elite Male Identities in England c. 1660–1900: Sourcebook*, Basingstoke: Palgrave Macmillan.

Shepard, A. (2005), 'From Anxious Patriarchs to Refined Gentlemen? Manhood in Britain, circa 1500–1700', *The Journal of British Studies*, 44: 2, pp. 281–95.

Shepherd, A. (2014), *Institutionalizing the Insane in Nineteenth-Century England*, London: Pickering and Chatto Limited.

Smiles, S. (1859), *Self Help; with Illustrations of Character and Conduct*, Boston, MA [accessed at Online Library of Liberty website http://oll.libertyfund.org].

The Bottle and the Drunkard's Children, in Sixteen Plates Designed and Etched by George Cruikshank (1906), London and Glasgow [accessed at http://www.archive.org/details/bottledrunkardsc00crui]

Tosh, J. (2004), 'Hegemonic Masculinity and the History of Gender', in S. Dudink, K. Hagemann and J. Tosh (eds), *Masculinities in Politics and War: Gendering Modern History*, Manchester: Manchester University Press, pp. 41–60.

Tosh, J. (2005), 'The Old Adam and the New Man: Emerging Themes in the History of English Masculinities, 1750–1850', in *Manliness and Masculinities in Nineteenth-Century Britain*, Harlow: Pearson Education, pp. 61–82.

Tuke, S. (1818), *Description of the Retreat, an Institution near York for insane persons of the Society of Friends containing an account of its origins and progress, the modes of treatment and a statement of cases*.

Turner, D. (2002), *Fashioning Adultery: Gender, Sex and Civility in England, 1660–1740*, Cambridge: Cambridge University Press.

Wallis, J. (2011), 'General Paralysis of the Insane: The "Darkest Africa" of Psychopathology', Wellcome Trust Blog, http://blog.wellcome.ac.uk/2011/09/21/general-paralysis-of-the-insane-the-%E2%80%98darkest-africa%E2%80%99-of-psychopathology/ [accessed 31 March 2015].

Wallis, J. (2015), '"Atrophied", "Engorged", "Debauched": Degenerative Processes and Moral Worth in the General Paralytic Body', in T. Knowles and S. Trowbridge (eds), *Insanity and the Lunatic Asylum in the Nineteenth Century*, London: Pickering and Chatto Limited, pp. 99–113.

Wiltenburg, J. (2004), 'True Crime: The Origins of Modern Sensationalism', *American Historical Review*, 109, p. 5.

Chapter 3

The New Man's Body in Ménie Muriel Dowie's *Gallia*

Tara MacDonald

There was perhaps no more celebrated male body in the Victorian period than that of Eugen Sandow. Born in Prussia, Sandow worked as a circus and music hall performer before moving to London in 1889, where he eventually became the world's first modern celebrity bodybuilder. As his recent biographer David Waller notes, Sandow's appearance could solicit hysterical reactions from adoring crowds of women. An audience member at an 1890 music hall performance records that when Sandow appeared on stage, 'Those at the back of the room leapt on the chairs: paraquet-like ejaculations, irrepressible, resounded right and left; tiny palms beat till [. . .] gloves burst at their wearer's energy' (qtd in Waller 2011: 9). Sandow's sculpted physique extended beyond the boundaries of popular entertainment and erotic desire. The Natural History Museum moulded a plaster cast from his body to represent the ideal form of European manhood and Thomas Edison recorded him in one of the first films ever made (ibid.: 9). Artist E. Aubrey Hunt 'discovered' Sandow when he spotted him walking along the Lido in Venice in his bathing suit, after which he hired him to be the model for his portrait of a Roman gladiator. It was also Hunt who told Sandow about a strongman competition in London, which earned him the title of strongest man on earth and catapulted him to fame.[1]

Though not an Englishman, Sandow's physically fit body and disciplined exercise regime made him the perfect antidote for late-Victorian anxieties about national degeneration and male effeminacy. For instance, in an 1894 article entitled 'The Man of the Moment', New Woman author Sarah Grand expresses the concern, shared by many, that 'the physique of the race is deteriorating' (Grand 1894: 622). Grand attributes this 'national deterioration' specifically to the male of the species, finding men less energetic, less productive, and in need of guidance from women (ibid.: 625). She complains that while the 'girls are up and doing in the morning [...] the young men, indolent and nerveless, lie long in bed. Idleness and luxury are making men flabby' (ibid.: 626). Sandow, with his sculpted muscles and regime of physical fitness, presented a corrective to this lazy and flabby manhood, as well as an ideal that British men could themselves adopt. Constance Crompton further argues that Sandow's 'muscled masculinity soothed fin-de-siècle concerns about gender variance by wresting the meaning of men's corporeal beauty from the aesthetes' (Crompton 2011: 38). Though he posed nearly nude – typically only with a fig-leaf ensuring his decency – and presented himself as an object for display, Sandow's self-discipline and 'manly' work in maintaining his body ensured that he conformed to, rather than challenged, late-Victorian dictates of ideal manliness and beauty.

Despite his savvy ability to position himself as both a paragon of masculinity and an active promoter of his own brand, Eugen Sandow's success must be situated within the late-nineteenth-century emphasis on the male body as an object of national, sexual and scientific scrutiny. Sandow's rise occurred alongside various other cultural movements in late-Victorian England – such as the development of the social purity movement and the related repeal of the Contagious Diseases Acts – which encouraged a focus on the male body as a symbol of English purity. Furthermore, fears of degeneration in this period were linked with the emerging science of eugenics, first coined in English in 1883 by Francis Galton, Darwin's first cousin. Late-Victorian eugenics preached the improvement of the race by encouraging 'fitter' reproductive pairings and discouraging others deemed 'unfit' (Ruddick 2004: 24). The 'pure' English male body (or Prussian in the case of Sandow, an irony that seemed lost on many late-Victorians) was most fully embodied in the vision of the 'New Man'. As imagined by many New Women of the period, this was a man who practised, in Grand's words, 'virtue and self denial' as he adopted a female-inspired model of sexual continence and rejected 'degenerate' behaviour (Grand 1894: 622). Grand explains that the New Woman's ideal 'is a man whom she can reverence and respect [...] especially in regard to his relations with her own sex' (ibid.: 622). The New Man's sexual reserve made him the foil to the dandy and his relationship with New Woman was, in ideal terms, one of equality and shared political and artistic goals. New Woman writer Olive Schreiner saw the New Woman and New Man as creating a union that was a 'fellowship of comrades', explaining that the modern man departs from his predecessors in finding 'in woman active companionship and co-operation rather than passive submission' (Schreiner 1911: 256).

Though Schreiner focused primarily on the New Man's mental differences from earlier masculine models – understanding the relationship between the New Man and New Woman to be 'more largely psychic and intellectual than crudely and purely physical' – she nonetheless remarked on his role as a father and 'producer' of the future British race:

> If the New Woman's conception of parenthood differs from the old in the greater sense of the gravity and obligation resting on those who are responsible for the production of the individual life, making her attitude toward the production of her race widely unlike the reckless, unreasoning, maternal reproduction of the woman of the past, the most typical male tends to feel in at least the same degree the moral and social obligation entailed by awakening lifehood. (ibid.: 256)

Implied in such a movement away from 'reckless' reproduction is the notion that both men and women should look for a partner whose mental and bodily capacities make him or her an ideal parent. As utopian constructions of identity, the New Man and New Woman could thus weed out the 'Old' men and women, producing healthier, stronger stock. Though I have elsewhere focused largely on the New Man as the romantic partner and intellectual equal to the New Woman, I here explore the ways in which discourses about the ideal New Man intersected with the late-Victorian interest in physical fitness and emerging eugenic beliefs.[2] Though emphasis on the New Man as an embodiment of ideal masculinity took many forms, Ménie Muriel Dowie's novel *Gallia* (1895) presents a radical response to the objectification of the male body at the late century and what Angelique Richardson has termed 'eugenic feminism', the careful sexual selection practised by a number of New Women at the end of the century (Richardson 1999: 228).[3]

Before the publication of *Gallia*, Dowie was best known as the author of *A Girl in the Karpathians* (1892), a travel narrative about her journey on horseback through the Carpathian Mountains. Her first work of fiction was published in *The Yellow Book* in January 1895 and *Gallia* appeared in February of that year. It is typical of New Woman fiction, as Jane Eldridge Miller explains, in that it places 'women's consciousness as the center of the novel', a technique which allowed New Women authors 'to place a great deal of feminist argument in the mouths of their heroines' (Eldridge Miller 1994: 18). Indeed, the heroine Gallia Hamesthwaite is figured as a mouthpiece for feminist thought, but her specific focus on motherhood as the way for the New Woman to influence society distinguishes the novel from many others of this genre. Gallia chooses her future husband,

Mark Gurdon, based purely on his physical fitness and ability to create healthy offspring. Strikingly, Gallia is not distressed at Mark's past sexual indiscretions; in fact, she is pleased to hear of his mistress (and the woman's pregnancy), implying that this will make him a virile, 'fit' husband. As Gail Cunningham – one of the few critics to discuss this novel – claims, Gallia thus rejects the custom in which women condemn premarital sex, instead selecting her husband 'not *despite* but *because* of his sexual history' (Cunningham 2001: 99). In this novel, then, the New Man's body outweighs the purity of his mind, just as his role as a future father outweighs his role as a husband, as Dowie makes clear that Gallia will never love Mark. The novel is unusually explicit in its eugenic plotline: it is more common to find the New Woman stuck with a sexually deviant husband who is implicitly unfit for procreation. In fact, *Gallia* is atypical in imagining a conciliatory ending for the New Woman and New Man.

Yet, the novel is ambiguous about Gallia's decision to marry for the purposes of reproduction only, leaving her character's future development and the suitability of such a union in question. What is clear is that Gallia's objectification of the male body becomes a vehicle by which Dowie can dismantle the romantic plot of the late-Victorian novel and its related gendered hierarchies. Gallia's decision to marry Mark for his eugenic potential alone is marked not as a heroic or sacrificial act but simply as an attempt to control the course of her own life. She admits, 'I look at it like the women who marry for position and money – as a price [. . .] If I were living fifty years hence, I should not probably have to marry at all. But our yoke is the ignorance of our day' (Dowie 1895: 131). The novel's ambiguous eugenic plotline is also a result of Gallia's feelings for another man. She falls in love with 'Dark' Essex but he does not return her love (though he seems to change his mind as the narrative unfolds). His rejection of her frees Gallia from the burden of romantic love and she resolves, spurred on by her own mother's death, to throw herself into responsible motherhood.

In distinguishing between Gallia's love for Essex and her choice of Mark, the novel establishes a clear contrast between bodily passion and rational choice. Gallia in fact realises that if she were to fall in love again, 'it might be with someone quite unsuitable to be the father of my child', someone whose body would unfit him for fatherhood (ibid.: 129). In an article on the treatment of soldiers' bodies in *The Strand Magazine*, J. L. Cranfield argues that 'it is crucial to understand the different ways in which average British bodies held up under the considerable strain of the ideological baggage that was heaped upon them during this period' (Cranfield 2012: 550). Gallia is cognisant of the 'baggage' attached to both men's and women's bodies at the late century; her decision to marry Mark is one of feminist boldness, even as it demands her acceptance of her own body as a 'breeding machine' (Ledger 1997: 70). In what follows, I chart the novel's engagement with models of physical fitness and male beauty, the New Woman's understanding of her own body, and, finally, the way in which imagining the New Man as a eugenic ideal transforms him into the New Father.

The 'Old Hercules' and the Male Body

Gallia opens with the following statements: 'A little thought will usually show where a story begins. Gurdon considered very rightly that his began with a visit he paid to old Mrs Leighton in Cornwall gardens' (Dowie 1895: 3). The first chapter focuses not on Gallia, the character through whom much of the novel is focalised, but on Mark, as he visits his friend's mother. The story 'begins' with this moment since his visit 'usher[s] in an incident': Mrs. Leighton asks him to check on her son, Robbie, in Paris and during this trip Mark meets Robbie's Parisian mistress and also determines to 'get on' with his political career (ibid.: 3). His ambition is realised through a fortuitous meeting with an artist's model, a man whose income comes through exhibiting his body. Mark realises, to his surprise, that this man's origins as a government employee mirror his own and he seems to confront a vision of his possible future self. The opening chapters in Paris thus introduce the novel's emphasis on the objectification of the male body and the possibility that even highly educated men can be reduced to physical specimens.

When Mark first arrives in Robbie Leighton's Parisian studio, the narrator details their differing appearances. When the young men had last met at Oxford, they were nearly indistinguishable from the various other well dressed, if generic, university men. Now, Robbie's attire and carelessness marks him as a bohemian:

> Leighton's fair hair was four inches long where it had been barely half an inch, he had a weird beard of rough tow-coloured stuff which partially covered his white throat. He was extremely *décolleté*. A horrid rag of a tie disappeared into a stained blue waistcoat front, and a grey jacket with gaping side pockets modelled his muscles effectively with its greasy shine. Gurdon? Well, Gurdon looked exactly as one would have expected [. . .] There was about him that suggestion of bath and shaves and tailors and general precision, of which one is ashamed to feel a little tired because it is in itself so admirable. (ibid.: 7–8, emphasis in original)

Gurdon's 'manly qualities', as Cunningham notes, mark him as distinct in this bohemian world of 'gender ambiguity' (Cunningham 2001: 97). Yet, the focus soon shifts from Gurdon's 'admirable' appearance to that of Lemuel, Robbie's model. Upon noticing the man, Gurdon notes approvingly that he has a '[m]agnificent chest and shoulders' (ibid.: 8). Lemuel, the 'old Hercules', is bolstered by Gurdon's compliment and in response he 'stiffen[s] proudly; the muscles in his right arm swelled, and the strong old fingers grasping the wooden spear contracted a trifle more firmly' (ibid.). Lemuel admits that he has served as a model for various portraits: he posed for Zeus in 'Munkacszy's design for the ceiling of an audience hall at the Champ de Mars' and for 'Laurent's fresco at the Panthéon' (ibid.: 25). Like Sandow, Lemuel derives pleasure (and success) from his performance of ideal masculinity.

The next time that Mark meets Lemuel, he finds the man lifting weights – 'a couple of big iron bars' – for crowds of students outside the studios (ibid.: 24). Lemuel preaches the importance of exercise, telling Mark, 'You must make the muscles when they're young, sir, and they'll never quite disappear. Boxing made mine, when I was at the University' (ibid.: 26). Mark admits that he boxes three times a week, which keeps him 'wonderfully fit' and is a welcome contrast to his 'sedentary life' in government (ibid.). This encourages Lemuel's confession that he too began life as a government employee, one who quickly became disillusioned with the job. He tells Mark, 'Who knows, you may be sitting in the same seat' (ibid.). This possibility unnerves Mark; that Lemuel should possess 'a background which, in a tray full of human experiences, could not be distinguished from his own, was sufficiently disquieting' (ibid.). Though this moment stirs Mark's ambition, the irony, as Cunningham points out, is of course that he, like Lemuel, will also be prized for his body (Cunningham 2001: 97). For Mark, this confrontation is disconcerting and even uncanny. When Robbie enters into the room and interrupts their discussion, Mark feels that the whole conversation suddenly seemed 'unreal and shadowy. It was to be remembered often at other times' (Dowie 1895: 29). To further cement this as a prophetic moment, betraying the novel's emphasis on the male body as aesthetic object, Robbie announces that his female model is 'too vile' and instead, he asks Mark if he will model for him, telling him, 'There's a line in your jaw that I like rather' (ibid.: 29).

Anne-Sophie Leluan-Pinker reads the novel as offering a criticism of the Victorian male artist's idealisation of women, an artistic pose that silences women and encourages a '"sentimental" conception of femininity' (Leluan-Pinker 2007: n.p.). Indeed, both Mark and Robbie (and even her brother, Dark Essex) idealise Margaret Essex in this way, with Mark actually painting her portrait. Leluan-Pinker argues that these three main male characters systematically construct women as 'nothing but objects of the male gaze (a trend often resulting in a desire to frame women within the reassuring limits of a painting)' (ibid.). While I certainly agree with Leluan-Pinker that the novel demands a new, feminist 'way of seeing' that defies traditional sex roles, the novel's emphasis on the idealised, framed *male* body is an important way in which this aesthetic and gendered critique is mounted. Though Dowie details the way in which Gallia sizes up Mark's body, it is worth noting that these early chapters also see the men evaluating one another's bodies, as Mark compliments Lemuel's torso and Robbie admires Mark's jawline. The fact that the men trade physical compliments seems to demonstrate an environment in which male characters realise the importance of their appearance as an indicator of social and marital success. Brent Shannon has traced the growing importance of male fashion in late-Victorian England, a shift due to changing masculine identities as well as, more practically, the rise in the department store, the development of mass-produced clothing, and advertising innovations (Shannon 2006: 2). The novel, however, focuses not so much on clothing as on the men's bodies and their athletic and aesthetic regimens, as in Mark's 'admirable' grooming. But it also remains attentive to the way in which late-Victorian society continued to weigh down women's bodies with significant political and national meaning.

Prostitutes, Mothers, and the New Woman's Body

The first scene in which Gallia appears sees a return to London and a movement away from the artistic to the political, as Gallia mentions the Contagious Diseases Acts and the state regulation of bodies, a topic that has bearing on her still nascent eugenic views. When her aunt and mother ask her what has piqued her interest in the newspaper she is reading, Gallia responds, 'an agitation about the State regulation of vice' (Dowie 1895: 33). The Acts to which Gallia refers had been instituted in 1864, 1866 and 1869 by parliament in an attempt to control the increase of venereal disease amongst the armed forces. They were motivated by public anxiety relating to both prostitution and the spread of disease, and the Act of 1864 was introduced in parliament without public or parliamentary debate (McHugh 1980: 37).[4] Under the Acts, which covered eighteen military districts throughout

England, any woman suspected of being a prostitute could be forced to undergo medical examination. If surgeons found the woman to be infected, she could be confined to a Lock Hospital for three months; the maximum stay was increased to nine months in the 1869 Act (Walkowitz 1980: 76; 86). They therefore reflected the social assumption that a woman's body served 'as the site where a contaminating sexuality becomes visible' (Anderson 1993: 104). Social purist feminists, led by reformers such as Josephine Butler and Ellice Hopkins, eventually helped to repeal the Acts in 1886. They challenged the notion that the female body was responsible for social degeneration; instead, they argued, it was male sexuality that needed controlling (Ledger 1997: 112).

Gallia's candidness and interest in the Contagious Diseases Acts reveal her to be a New Woman. Her aunt chides her for discussing such a topic – *not* because it is an unfit subject for her to read about, but because it is a waste of time to consider 'for the simple reason that you are unable to assist its settlement one way or the other!' (Dowie 1895: 34). Despite not having the ability to vote or sit in parliament, Gallia insists that she 'must read about and think about it, because it is a question that only girls can settle ultimately' (ibid.: 34). This moment thus introduces Gallia's resolve that she – and all women – must possess knowledge and control over their own bodies. She also insists that she wants to understand her indebtedness to prostitutes, to 'that class of society which assures my class a good deal of its immunity' (ibid.: 34). This shocks her mother, a woman who has 'striven to play [her] part of wife and mother well'; and while Gallia apologises for offending her, she does not relinquish her point that middle-class women can only 'play' those parts because prostitutes also perform their social role (ibid.: 35). This relationship between prostitutes and middle- to upper-class women, both of whom consort with the same groups of men, is underscored when Gallia chooses Mark as a husband with full knowledge of his sexual indiscretions with Cara Lemuel, the model's daughter. Yet, in this case, his body – and that of his young mistress – figures as a measure not of disease but fertility.

Jill Rappoport points out that Gallia's understanding of the connection between prostitutes and women of her class echoes the social movement against the Contagious Diseases Acts, which sought to unite 'middle-class and working-class interests against sexual double standards' (Rappoport 2012: 146). Indeed, the movement was unique in consolidating cross-class female activism, as middle-class women fought for the rights of prostitutes. Yet Rappoport also contends that

Gallia's language distances her from prostitutes as it locates them in distinct classes. In fact, while Gallia wants to understand her indebtedness to these women, we might find that her act of locating Mark's fertility in the body of Cara actually serves to replicate the language of the Contagious Diseases Acts. Though Gallia wants to understand the role of the prostitute within the 'social state', her eugenic beliefs mean that she must necessarily understand a wide gap between 'fit' and 'unfit' women and men. Later in the novel, the narrator remarks that there are some women simply fitted for 'the oldest of all professions for women' and they cannot make good wives or mothers, a belief that Gallia herself seems to hold (Dowie 1895: 85). While she is initially set up in opposition to her conservative mother, Gallia's interest in social purity – which can be understood as a precursor to the eugenic movement – translates into a tangible interest in the role that mothers have in regulating the social body.

Implicated in the social purity movement was what Angelique Richardson terms 'civic motherhood' (Richardson 1999: 228). Many women who practised eugenic feminism envisioned their roles as wives and mothers as acts of citizenship. That is, to be a 'civic mother' entailed loving not one's husband but the community or the nation. Richardson explains, 'In eugenic love, the flesh should submit to the spirit in order to contribute to racial progress; pleasure is overshadowed and undercut by the imperative of (re)production' (ibid.: 230). So, the New Woman, like the New Man, should practise self-denial and self-sacrifice for the betterment of the nation. Richardson records that thinkers like Karl Pearson, a follower of Galton and founder of biometrics, argued that maternity should be 'considered essentially as citizen-making in the first place, and not as the accidental result of the private relation to an individual', and Frances Russell, wife of the former prime minister John Russell, encouraged young mothers to take an interest in evolution, 'where they may assist Nature almost as much perhaps as does the gardener in the development of his vegetable creation' (qtd in Richardson 1999: 230; 236). Reframing love as a eugenic pursuit gave women an active role in strengthening the nation and in evaluating what kind of man would make a suitably fit husband.

Richardson does not analyse Dowie's novel in depth, likely because it does not cohere to the typical model of eugenic feminism in that Gallia, unlike Sarah Grand's heroines, avoids linking her eugenic interests to the interests of the nation. Her interests are at once more personal and less sacrificial. It is her mother's death that forces Gallia to consider the social responsibility of motherhood. Gallia complicates the celebratory language of civic motherhood by understanding motherhood as *both* a sacrifice and a selfish, personal act. She explains that mothers perform 'a sort of self-sacrifice, which I have always thought the most subtle kind of selfishness in the world' since a woman 'gets a good deal out of motherhood; more than she does out of marriage' (Dowie 1895: 91–2). Gallia thus begins to construct motherhood as a more satisfying role for the New Woman than marriage – and to understand it not as an identity borne out of the marital union but as independent from it. Her desire to separate motherhood from marriage is what, in turn, allows her to de-romanticise her relationship with Mark and to look at him 'rather as a dealer might notice the points in a horse than as a lady might perceive a young man's claims to handsomeness' (ibid.: 121).

Gallia first clearly articulates these ideas in a conversation with her friends Gertrude Janion and Margaret Essex. Through this exchange, Dowie allows her heroine space to fully articulate her views but also relates the admittedly shocked responses of her friends: in registering the other women's alarm, Dowie demonstrates her heroine's militant perspective even as she situates her as the defiant mouthpiece of this new feminism. Gallia first explains her expectation that all men seeking a wife should ideally be 'well-grown and healthy and sound – in wind, limb, and temper' (ibid.: 112). She pushes her argument further when she insists that the practice of 'getting in' domestic help – Miss Janion's impressive list of her family's help includes a masseur, nursemaid, 'electric shock person', 'hair man', butler and a woman 'to do the flowers for parties' – might be extended to fathers and mothers (ibid.). It is, she insists, an 'eminently rational' scheme:

> How can we wonder that only one person in ten is handsome and well-made, when you reflect that they were most likely haps of hazards, that they were unintended, the offspring of people quite unfitted to have children at all. There are people fitted, for instance, to be mothers, which every woman isn't; there are women fitted to bring up children, who may not be mothers. Think of this: a man may love a woman and marry her; they may be devoted to each other, and long for a child to bring up and to love; but the woman may be too delicate to run the risk. What are they to do? What would be the reasonable thing to do? Sacrifice the poor woman for the sake of a weakly baby? No, of course not, but get in a mother! (ibid.: 113)

Gallia insists that this is the logical extension of having a wet-nurse; it will allow for 'far fewer delicate men and women in the world' (ibid.: 114). The reaction of her friends is rather humorous: the narrator records, '[t]heir brains were a little burdened, and no wonder, by this astounding piece of social reform' (ibid.). Yet despite Margaret's shock – and her insistence that this plan sounds 'like treating the world as a sort of farm, and men and women merely as animals' – she tells Gallia that she should write out her ideas (ibid.). Instead, the remainder of the novel sees her not writing about her ideas but enacting them.

Male Specimens and the New Father

Mark becomes the unwitting (if not unwilling) participant in Gallia's activism. Though I argue that the novel objectifies his body most emphatically, the above passage also makes clear that Gallia evaluates her own body as fitted for motherhood. Essex in fact notes what he sees as a discrepancy between Gallia's New Woman intellectualism and her beauty, bemoaning the fact that she has 'no grain of coquetry to make play with all [her] bodily gifts' (ibid.: 127–8). This makes her, he says, 'the perfectly hapless kind of modern woman. Your whole make-up is an egregious mistake – a complete waste of material' (ibid.: 127). Yet Gallia confesses that she will use the 'material' of her body by becoming a mother. Though her romantic love is 'used up' after Essex's rejection, she will now marry a man of 'healthy stock [. . .] solely with a view to the child I am going to live for' (ibid.: 129). Dowie introduces Mark as that man early in the novel.

He is consistently referred to as a 'specimen' of ideal masculinity. For instance, the narrator claims that Mark is more than just 'an excellent specimen of the average man' and records Mark's assumption that 'most men would call him a very decent specimen' (ibid.: 17; 79). When Gallia first meets him, she studies his attributes, finding that 'there was a firmness and a faint pinkness about his face which did not suggest a London life in any way [. . .] His eyes were bright and clear [. . .] his teeth were perfect; not too small, and very white' (ibid.: 121). This treatment of the male as 'specimen' was present in late-Victorian society due to the cultural developments I have previously mentioned – the repeal of Contagious Diseases Acts and an emphasis on physical fitness – but such terminology can also be related to the burgeoning fields of criminology, sexology and anthropology. As these fields entered the cultural imaginary of late-Victorian England, the evaluation of the male as a physical 'specimen' found its way into literary texts as well. For instance, in George Gissing's *The Odd Women*, the New Woman Mary Barfoot notes that her cousin, Everard Barfoot, 'is a fine specimen of a man, after all, in body and in mind' (Gissing 1977: 87). In Bram Stoker's *Dracula*, John Seward, after reading of Jonathan Harker's adventures with Dracula, notes that he was 'prepared to meet a good specimen of manhood' (Stoker 1997: 199). These specimens of New Manhood are contrasted with men who are somehow contaminated or sickly: the awkward and sexually inept Widdowson in *The Odd Women* and the polluting vampire Dracula. Gallia too compares the robust Mark to the unhealthy Essex in this manner: 'Gallia looked down at [Essex], where he sprawled awkwardly at one side of her, and then over to Mark sprawling gracefully at the other' (Dowie 1895: 160).

By their use of this medicalised term, the novelists seem to position these characters as objects of quasi-scientific study, even without the eugenic terminology so prevalent in Dowie's text. Various New Women novelists represented degenerate men in particular as texts to be deciphered, as displaying their (im)morality on their bodies. In Grand's *The Beth Book*, for instance, the heroine's degenerate husband has a smile that 'was not altogether agreeable, because his teeth were too far apart'; Beth notes too that his 'finely-formed hands would have looked better had they not been so obtrusively white' (Grand 1897: 321). The hands of the degenerate figure were often objects of particular interest: the 'corded and hairy' hands of Mr Hyde in Stevenson's story signal his degenerate masculinity (Stevenson 2003: 58). Gallia, in fact, is unnerved by Essex's small hands and feet, noting:

> with a feeling of dislike, when she handed him a peach with a bit of ice in place of the stone, that his feet were too small. In the Cloisters, just when he took her hands, she had observed that his hands were too small. It was a blemish in so handsome a man; a blemish that gave her a feeling of discomfort. (Dowie 1895: 167)

Just like the reactions to the mysterious Hyde, who elicits from Utterson a 'strong feeling of deformity', Gallia *feels* Essex's imperfections (Stevenson 2003: 11). She does not know of his hereditary illness until the conclusion of the novel, but can somehow intuit his 'inferiority' despite her love for him.

Her evaluation of Mark's hereditary potential, though, is distanced from romantic love, and Gallia's proposal to Mark is remarkable for her lack of feeling. Furthermore, during the proposal, her eugenic impulses are separated not just from her own desire but also from the romantic script of the conventional proposal. The narrator reminds us that while Mark 'was in love with Gallia', she was now 'in love with logic' (Dowie 1895: 183). Both characters – and the narrator – possess a knowing awareness of the proposal scene as just that: as a scene in a book or play. When Mark begins to recite a poem, the narrator records wryly, 'He said it. He had a good voice; he said it very well. There is no need to detail the poem. Everybody has had such a poem in his mind on such an occasion; everybody will remember some of it. It was quite the usual poem' (ibid.: 184). And Gallia announces to him that she won't see him 'suffer the unfairness of the average proposal scene' wherein the man confesses his past sins while the woman 'listens calmly' and passively (ibid.: 185). Instead, she directs the scene – a key example of the novel's playful gendered reversals.

Yet, Gallia battles with convention, as she herself realises. Somehow the environment seems constructed for sentimental feelings. She complains, 'This lane, the scent of those queen-of-the-meadows, the honeysuckle and roses, that sky over there above the fir trees, is too much for me; the whole thing is a stage set, and we are puppets!' (ibid.: 186). Gallia struggles for a sense of individual control and agency, feeling as though 'the press of centuries of tradition is weighing on me' (ibid.). However she does ultimately break with tradition, not allowing Mark his moment of confession and instead shocking him by announcing, 'I believe I was already dreaming of marrying you – possibly, and if you would have me – when the knowledge of the illness of your mistress came to my ears' (ibid.: 192). The narrator notes that if 'a cannon had gone off close to his head, Mark would have been less amazed' (ibid.). Cunningham remarks on the significance of Dowie's choice of words here, stating 'it is not the *existence* of Gurdon's mistress which is at issue, but her *"illness"* – the fact that he has successfully impregnated her' (Cunningham 2001: 100). Indeed, this emphasises not just Mark's sexual past but also specifically his fertility. The story, Cunningham argues, thus ends with Mark's 'capture by a New Woman wanting little from him but healthy sperm' (ibid.: 101). Yet what is perhaps most surprising is that Mark marries Gallia with full knowledge of that fact, telling her, 'you shall take me for whatever you please, no matter in what capacity, for better or worse. I – I am proud that you want me' (Dowie 1895: 194). Mark's stuttering response places him as the doting and emotional lover, while Gallia insists that she does not love him. He furthermore accepts Gallia's assessment of him as an object, urging her to 'take him' for whatever she pleases.

In reversing expected gender roles, Dowie seems to be responding to many anti-feminist narratives that scripted gender reversal as a frightening harbinger of the future. For example, the day after the second Wilde trial in 1895, *Punch*'s 'Angry Old Buffer' wrote a satirical ballad against 'Sexomania' that expressed anxieties about the challenge to gender conventions presented by both the New Woman and dandy:

> But a new fear in my bosom vexes;
> Tomorrow there may be *no* sexes!
> Unless, as end to all the pother,
> Each one in fact becomes the other. (Anon. 1895: 203)

The idea of one sex 'becoming the other' was frequently linked to the relationship between the New Man and New Woman, imagined by conservative commentators as the perverse pairing of an effeminate man with a manly woman. For instance, in a story in *The Speaker*, titled simply 'The New Man' (1894), a sensitive, emotional New Man stays home to write about fashion, while his New Woman partner is an influential politician who presents 'an air of decision as of one who bears the heritage of a ruling sex' (Anon. 1894: 621). In perhaps the most explicit example of the period, Walter Besant's *The Revolt of Man* (1882), we witness a futuristic society in which, after the 'Great Transition', women have taken over public office, have reduced men to house husbands, and have demolished industrialisation and religious institutions. Men are now defined by 'meekness, modesty, submission, and docility' (Besant 1882: 39). Older women force younger men into marriage – perhaps the most pressing issue that leads to the 'revolt' – and art reflects these new social conventions:

> Among the modern pictures a very remarkable change was apparent. The men were painted in early manhood, the women at a more mature age [...] The faces of the men were remarkable for a self-conscious beauty of the lower type: there was little intellectual expression; the hair was always curly, and while some showed a bull-like repose of strength, others wore an expression of meek and gentle submissiveness. As for the women, they were represented with all the emblems of authority — tables, thrones, papers, deeds, and pens. (ibid.: 15–16)

Besant also shows that as men become objects in the marriage market, they fall victim to romantic scripts, a notion that Dowie repeats with Mark and Gallia. In Besant's dystopian novel, for instance, a group of men laugh at the utter ridiculousness of a song featuring a young *woman* who 'pined away and died for love of a man who broke his promise' (ibid.: 90).

These stories present satires of a changing Victorian society while they also warn with great sincerity of dangers that men face in losing political and social ground to the women's movement. Cunningham finds Dowie's feminist story similarly satirical in its treatment of the male body as object, arguing that 'manliness is comically reduced to the functional ability to breed' (Cunningham 2001: 96). While the narrative voice is certainly wry at times, the novel records Gallia's decision to marry Mark purely for his body with uncertainty, as I have noted. Gallia's decision implies the lack of alternative options available to her. And while her rejection of sentimentality – and of a desire to have Mark confess his 'sins' – is rather humorous, her decision to abandon love is depicted as more troubling. When she first announces her plan to throw herself headlong into motherhood, the 'triumph in her voice was somehow pitiful' (Dowie 1895: 131). At the close of the proposal scene between Gallia and Mark, he laughs and grips her tightly, the narrator channelling Gallia's thoughts through free indirect discourse: 'If only Essex had had the grit to go as far – to laugh and go as far' (ibid.: 195). Gallia only learns the fact that Essex has heart disease, which he informs her is 'hereditary', in the final pages of the novel (ibid.: 200). Without knowing of her previous feelings for him, Mrs Leighton predicts ominously that Gallia will 'fall in love with that attractive manifestation of heart-disease yet' (ibid.).

Earlier in the novel, the narrator claims that Essex was the first man that Gallia had ever loved and 'the first man is never a woman's free choice. Like the first fish of the amateur trouter, he is an accident; neither science, skill, nor selection has a hand in landing him' (ibid.: 62). Essex's heart disease – a genetic 'fault' – seems to reinforce the risks inherent in attraction to such 'accidents' and his specific ailment actually gestures to his weak will. In *Victorian Poetry and the Culture of the Heart* (2006), Kirstie Blair describes the way in which, throughout the Victorian period, the heart figured as a symbol of human fallibility. The heart affects the body in a manner that surpasses conscious human control, taking a kind of hidden authority over the mind, or as Blair puts it: 'the rhythm of the heart stands in opposition to the will because it represents an alternative source of control' (Blair 2006: 65). Furthermore, writers, especially poets, were often associated with heart disease because it was popularly thought to stem from susceptibility to feeling. In the novel, Essex is actually less outwardly emotional than Mark, but he does indeed figure as the physical manifestation of feeling, passion and the potentially frightening will of the body for Gallia, his heart disease only further solidifying such associations. And the fact that his heart was, as Essex says, '[b]ust up in my rowing days', further implies his physical frailty (Dowie 1895: 201).

Dark Essex's nickname ascribes to him a racial ambiguity that furthermore puts his eugenic potential into question. After all, Gallia's decision to marry Mark based purely on his physical features means, as Molly Youngkin states, that she is inherently 'choosing him on the basis of racialised characteristics' (Youngkin 2007: 129). Yet Essex's 'darkness' also alludes to a hidden, even Byronic, interiority. When Gallia confesses to Essex her eugenic plans, before knowing that Mark will be her husband, he breaks his façade and is 'sincere, for the first time in his life perhaps' (Dowie 1895: 132). Gallia's honesty and, to Dark's mind, her tragic submission, allows him to find 'another self' that he did not know existed (ibid.). In contrast, the novel does not credit Mark with a similarly complex inner life: his affair with Cara, for instance, paints him as a sexual rather than intellectual being. And he is satisfied with Gallia because his own desire will be met, despite the fact that she does not love him. While the novel might not encourage much sympathy for Mark, it does trouble the role of men like Essex who do not fit neatly into narratives of physical fitness or eugenic ideals.

Near the end of the novel, Essex tells Gallia that he has written her a letter; he shows her the sealed envelope but taunts her with his desire to bury it. Once he learns of her decision to marry Mark, Essex reaffirms his plan to destroy the letter, telling her, '[L]et us burn the letter [. . .] Do you think a sprig of white heather would be so obliging as to spring on the grave of my hopes?' (ibid.: 179). Gallia's response – '*Your hopes?*' – reveals both her surprise and interest in his confession (ibid.). Though she admits that she would have liked to have read it, she announces to Essex, 'I believe I *can* control the woman in me sometimes,' to which he interjects, '[T]hat's your one failing!' (ibid.: 180). Gallia teases him about their decision to reject 'custom' by not kissing one another at their parting, explaining that 'one may over-do one's sacrifices, in order to fly in the face of custom', but Essex doesn't understand her flirtatious request (ibid.). He admits, 'I swear I'm so accustomed to acting as if I've no feelings, that I begin to think I haven't any!' (ibid.). In the context of eugenic feminism, rejecting custom necessarily means rejecting sentiment and even feeling. Gallia's comment regarding the tendency to 'over-do' personal sacrifice in order to challenge social convention is an issue with which the novel wrestles. Upending the custom of treating women as objects in the marriage market only to mimic the same treatment of men does not seem to offer Gallia, or perhaps even late-Victorian feminism, any real solutions to the social problem of sexual inequality. Nor does it seem to present the possibility of her future personal happiness, as her romantic desires are destroyed along with Dark's. While Dark may be her intellectual equal, the novel finally does not provide a New Man that consolidates mental and physical ideals. Instead, the New Man simply becomes the New Father.

Three years after *Gallia* was published, Eugen Sandow went on to edit *Sandow's Magazine of Physical Culture* (1898–1907), a physical fitness guide for the everyman. In the introductory article, Sandow urged his audience to cultivate their bodies as they did their mental faculties. Physical culture's 'ultimate object', he claimed, was to 'raise the average standard of the race as a whole' (Sandow 1898: 7). Once achieved, '[h]ealthier and more perfect men and women will beget children with better constitutions and more free from hereditary taint' (ibid.). That Sandow and various New Women (both fictional and historical) seem to agree on this point is perhaps surprising given their differing placements within late-Victorian popular culture. Although, as Richardson has pointed out, many scholars of the New Woman might wish to obscure her associations with the early eugenics movement, by making this connection we broaden the cultural significance of the New Woman and New Man as well as 'the social significance of the late-nineteenth-century romance plot' (Richardson 1999: 248). It is the very confrontation between the social and the personal that *Gallia* confronts, as the novel implies that the New Woman's victory (however hollow) comes only at the expense of the New Man's conversion into a physical specimen and national symbol.

Notes

1. The competition took place at the Royal Aquarium with the Marquess of Queensberry as a judge.
2. See my *The New Man, Masculinity and Marriage in the Victorian Novel*, 'The Failure of the New Man: Masculinity in *The Odd Women*', and 'Doctors, Dandies and New Men: Ella Hepworth Dixon and Late-Century Masculinities'. While I am attentive to the New Man's body in the above work, in particular distinguishing him from representations of the degenerate dandy, this chapter demonstrates how Dowie's *Gallia* takes the focus on the New Man's 'pure' body to radical extremes.
3. Richardson's later book, *Love and Eugenics in the Late Nineteenth Century: Rational Reproduction and the New Woman*, expands upon this 1999 article.
4. As McHugh relates, they were passed with a degree of secrecy: 'Introduced in a thin house, late at night, a government measure with a title deceptively similar to an Act dealing with veterinary rather than venereal disease, the Bill passed silently through both houses, receiving the royal assent on 29 July without a word being said about it' (McHugh 1980: 37).

Works Cited

Anderson, A. (1993), *Tainted Souls and Painted Faces: The Rhetoric of Fallenness in Victorian Culture*, Ithaca: Cornell University Press.
Anon. (1894), 'The New Man', *The Speaker*, 10 (8 Dec.), pp. 621–2.
Anon. (1895), 'Sexomania', *Punch* (27 April), p. 203.
Besant, W. (1882), *The Revolt of Man*, London and Glasgow: Collins' Clear Type Press.
Blair, K. (2006), *Victorian Poetry and the Culture of the Heart*, Oxford: Oxford University Press.
Cranfield, J. L. (2012), 'Chivalric Machines: The Boer War, the Male Body, and the Grand Narrative', *Strand Magazine. Victorian Literature and Culture*, 40, pp. 549–73.
Crompton, C. (2011), 'Eugen Sandow, 1867–1925', *Victorian Review*, 37: 1, pp. 37–41.
Cunningham, G. (2001), '"He Notes": Reconstructing Masculinity', in A. Richardson and C. Willis (eds), *The New Woman in Fiction and in Fact*, Basingstoke: Palgrave, pp. 94–106.
Dowie, M. M. [1895] (1995), *Gallia*, ed. Helen Small, London: Everyman.
Eldridge Miller, J. (1994), *Rebel Women: Feminism, Modernism and the Edwardian Novel*, London: Virago.
Gissing, G. [1894] (1977), *The Odd Women*, London: W. W. Norton and Co.
Grand, S. (1894), 'The Man of the Moment', *The North American Review*, 158 (May), pp. 620–7.
Grand, S. [1897] (1980), *The Beth Book*, New York: The Dial Press.
Ledger, S. (1997), *The New Woman: Fiction and Feminism at the Fin de Siècle*, Manchester: Manchester University Press.
Leluan-Pinker, A. S. (2007), '"Have everything new and made new again": Gendered Vision and the "great sex question" in M. M. Dowie's *Gallia* (1895)', *Nineteenth-Century Gender Studies*, 3: 3, n.p. Available from: http://www.ncgsjournal.com/issue33/leluan.htm [accessed June 2014].
MacDonald, T. (2012), 'Doctors, Dandies and New Men: Ella Hepworth Dixon and Late-Century Masculinities', *Women's Writing*, 19: 1, pp. 41–57.
MacDonald, T. (2013), 'The Failure of the New Man: Masculinity in *The Odd Women*', in C. Huguet and S. J. James (eds), *George Gissing and the Woman Question: Convention and Dissent*, Aldershot: Ashgate, pp. 41–55.
MacDonald, T. (2015), *The New Man, Masculinity and Marriage in the Victorian Novel*, London: Routledge.
McHugh, P. (1980), *Prostitution and Victorian Social Reform*, London: Croom Helm.
Rappoport, J. (2012), *Giving Women: Alliance and Exchange in Victorian Culture*, Oxford: Oxford University Press.

Richardson, A. (1999), 'The Eugenization of Love: Sarah Grand and the Morality of Genealogy', *Victorian Studies*, 42: 2, pp. 227–55.

Richardson, A. (2003), *Love and Eugenics in the Late Nineteenth Century: Rational Reproduction and the New Woman*, Oxford: Oxford University Press.

Ruddick, N. (2004), 'Introduction', in Grant Allen, *The Woman Who Did*, Peterborough, ON: Broadview Press, pp. 11–43.

Sandow, E. (1898), 'Physical Culture: What is it?', *Sandow's Magazine of Physical Culture* (July), 1: 1, pp. 3–7.

Schreiner, O. (1911), *Woman and Labour*, London: T. Fisher Unwin.

Shannon, B. (2006), *The Cut of his Coat: Men, Dress, and Consumer Culture in Britain, 1860–1901*, Athens: Ohio University Press.

Stevenson, R. L. [1886] (2003), *The Strange Case of Dr Jekyll and Mr Hyde*, ed. K. Linehan, London: W. W. Norton and Co.

Stoker, B. [1897] (1997), *Dracula*, ed. N. Auerbach and D. J. Skal, London: W. W. Norton and Co.

Walkowitz, J. (1980), *Prostitution and Victorian Society: Women, Class and the State*, Cambridge: Cambridge University Press.

Waller, D. (2011), *The Perfect Man: The Muscular Life and Times of Eugen Sandow*, Brighton: Victorian Secrets.

Youngkin, M. (2007), *Feminist Realism at the Fin de Siècle: The Influence of the Late-Victorian Woman's Press on the Development of the Novel*, Columbus: Ohio State University Press.

Part II

Fractured and Fragmented Bodies

Chapter 4

Pirates and Prosthetics: Manly Messages for Managing Limb Loss in Victorian and Edwardian Adventure Narratives

Ryan Sweet

> The generation reared on Captain Pugwash and Tintin will have a very clear idea of what pirates do. They wear striped trousers. They sport eye-patches and cutlasses and wooden legs. (Burrow 2013)

> The staff was cut and handed to the learner, who, planting it firmly on the ground before him, leaned on it, and exclaimed, 'Let it go!' in tones which instantly suggested 'the anchor' to his friends.
> The order was obeyed, and the ex-pirate stood swaying to and fro, and smiling with almost childlike delight. Presently he became solemn, lifted one leg, and set it down again with marvellous rapidity. Then he lifted the other leg with the same result. Then he lifted the staff, but had to replace it smartly to prevent falling forward.
> 'I fear I can only do duty as a motionless tripod,' he said rather anxiously. (Ballantyne 1883: 238)

Many of us associate pirates with prosthetic body parts. From wooden legs to hook hands, prostheses have frequently appeared in imaginative representations of pirates, such as Captain Hook from J. M. Barrie's 1904 play *Peter Pan*, Captain Barbosa and Ragetti from the *Pirates of the Caribbean* (2003–11) film series, the badges of the sports teams the Cornish Pirates and Pittsburgh Pirates, and the products and branding of the Woodenhand Brewery in Truro, Cornwall. Yet this prevalent association has not always existed. Its literary history is, in fact, curious.[1] What we might consider the great age of pirate stories (c. 1858–1904) exhibits relatively few prosthesis-using characters, aside, of course, from one obvious example: Captain Hook. What we do, however, see in the fiction from this period, and what we today unthinkingly assume are wooden leg users, are a number of pirates who persevere with their deplorable duties in spite of disability.

The second quotation above, from Robert Michael Ballantyne's 1883 novel *The Madman and the Pirate*, exposes a rare example of a fictional pirate from this period who does use wooden legs – though it should be noted that this character, Captain Rosco, only loses his legs and begins wearing prosthetic replacements after his piratical career has ended. This quotation in fact gestures towards a rationale that explains why 'prosthetic pirates' were so scant in nineteenth-century adventure fiction: the prostheses that would have been available in the golden age of piracy (c. 1694–1724), the period in which the majority of fictional pirate narratives are set, would have provided their users less physical functionality than other assistive technologies available at this time, such as crutches, deck ropes and bannisters – the latter two are used by Captain Ahab in Herman Melville's *Moby-Dick* (1851) and all three by Long John Silver in Robert Louis Stevenson's *Treasure Island* (1881). Indeed, it is apt that Rosco's career as a buccaneer is already at an end when he receives his prosthetic limbs since his physical mobility is almost entirely compromised by his false legs: to begin with he 'can only do duty as a motionless tripod' (Ballantyne 1883: 238); he is later felled by soft ground and then gets stuck in a hole after again falling over. Ballantyne shows both that prosthetics were often impractical for pirates and that they encompassed far too much comic potential to be given to figures whom an author wished to depict as truly villainous.

The credit for this now long-standing association between pirates and prosthetics is often pinned to Stevenson's characterisation of Long John Silver in *Treasure Island*, which when published as a whole in 1883 was a bestseller and has remained hugely popular ever since. But this attribution of credit is peculiar since Stevenson makes it quite clear that Silver is a crutch rather than false-leg user: 'His left leg was cut off close by the hip, and under the left shoulder he carried a crutch, which he managed with wonderful dexterity, hopping about upon it like a bird' (Stevenson 1915: 62–3). There remains, however, a misconception of Silver as a peg-legged pirate – in spite of evidence to the contrary.[2] Why, then, do we associate Stevenson's pirate with the use of a false leg? We might trace an answer to this question to Silver's status as an amputee and point to his repeated references to his crutch as his 'timber leg' and his infamous catch phrase, 'shiver my timbers' (ibid.: 86; 96; and ibid.: 67; 87; 210; 230; 244; 264).

One might even agree with John Amrhein's claim that Silver was based on the real wooden-leg-using pirate, John Lloyd.[3] And yet it seems strange to assume that such a prevalent cultural association stems from inference or misreading. It is unlikely that readers really know that Silver is based on a wooden leg user when he is not depicted as such in Stevenson's story.

    This chapter reframes these questions as it argues that our association between piracy and prosthetics stems, in part, from the deployment of what David T. Mitchell and Sharon L. Snyder have called 'narrative prosthesis'– the use of disability as a character-defining motif, which in this context equates bodily loss with moral decrepitude (Mitchell and Snyder 2000). The chapter also, however, complicates this disability-studies model by suggesting that the disabled pirates depicted in late Victorian and Edwardian adventure stories display an alluring form of hyper-masculinity that enables them to continue pirating in spite of their physical impairments. While fictional deployments of pirates with prosthetics are less common than one might expect in the adventure narratives from this period, the instances in which they do appear, while revealing the functional, cosmetic and ontological inadequacies of rudimentary prostheses, also draw attention to the ability of impaired figures to earn money in spite of their disabilities. Such a capacity, Martha Stoddard Holmes and Erin O'Connor have shown, was a vital component of manly identity in this period (Stoddard Holmes 2009: 94–132; O'Connor 2000: 102–47). Though clearly not advocating a life of buccaneering to their young, predominantly male, readership, such stories reveal hyper-masculine disabled role models who work to gain a living and, in some cases, even achieve social mobility. The enduring image of the peg-legged pirate thus stems from the ability, in our minds, of prosthetics to enable disabled subjects to perform their various 'duties'.

    In order to understand where the links between pirates and prosthetics, and disability and hyper-masculinity stem from, it is worth exploring the real and fictional precedents of the peg-legged or hook-handed pirate. As the first section of this chapter shows, a complex network of influences inspired Stevenson and Barrie to create their amputee pirates, who are for many the iconic prosthetic pirates. After revealing some overlooked literary forebears and the real-life inspiration for Silver's maimed hyper-masculinity, the chapter then shifts to the question of 'narrative prosthesis' before turning to the complex characterisation of fictional pirates as anti-heroes, figures who are simultaneously villainous and captivating.

Buried Treasure: The Historical and Fictional Roots of Pirates with Prosthetics

While Linda Grant de Pauw has noted that 'It is easy for writers of fiction to romanticize pirates, partly because hard, factual knowledge about them is scarce' (Grant de Pauw 1982: 20), it is probable that the most longstanding fictional depictions of maimed but nonetheless tenacious pirates, such as Long John Silver and Captain Hook, were moulded, at least in part, from real pirates (or at least pirates that their authors thought were real): Silver from a supposedly real pirate and Hook from Silver himself. Neil Rennie argues both that *Treasure Island* was 'a significant prototype and analogue for Neverland' and that Hook's hook was 'Barrie's rejoinder [. . .] to Long John Silver's crutch (Rennie 2013: 197–8). Rennie also suggests that Silver's one-leggedness may have been inspired by a wooden-legged pirate described in Captain Charles Johnson's *A General History of the Pyrates* (1724), a text that London booksellers Nutt and Bain provided for Stevenson after he requested 'the *best* book about the Buccaneers that can be had' (Stevenson 1911a: 60–1).[4] The appearance of the pirate described in *A General History* is certainly familiar to a twenty-first-century reader:

> a Fellow with a terrible pair of Whiskers, and a wooden Leg, being struck round with Pistols, like the Man in the Almanack with Darts, comes swearing and vapouring upon the Quarter-Deck, and asks, in a damning Manner, which was Captain *Mackra*: The Captain expected no less than that this Fellow would be his Executioner; – but when he came near him, he took him by the Hand, swearing, *Damn him he was glad to see him; and shew me the Man, says he, that offers to hurt Captain* Mackra, *for I'll stand by him*; and so with many Oaths told him, *he was an honest Fellow, and that he had formerly sail'd with him.* (Johnson 2012: 123, emphasis in original)

At a glance, the parallels between this supposedly threatening-looking eighteenth-century pirate and Silver seem to suggest that there are legitimate historical roots for the enduring image of the prosthetic (or at least the maimed) pirate; though, as Rennie later explains, the pirate described in *A General History* was 'probably as fictional as Long John Silver' (Rennie 2013: 185). Despite the questionable legitimacy of Silver's possible real-life antecedent, there is a historical figure who we know inspired Silver's maimed hypermasculinity, if not his one-leggedness itself.

Stevenson is widely assumed to have accredited Silver's one-legged characterisation to his friend, the poet, William Ernest Henley, who lost his left leg below the knee after suffering tuberculosis of the bone. While (contrary to popular belief) Stevenson by no means conclusively attributes Silver's one-leggedness to Henley, the author lauds the latter's physical and mental strength as major inspirations:

> I will now make a confession. It was the sight of *your maimed strength and masterfulness* that begot John Silver in *Treasure Island*. Of course, he is not in any other quality or feature the least like you; but the idea of the maimed man, *ruling and dreaded by the sound*, was entirely taken from you. (Stevenson 1911c: 137–8, my emphasis)

Though Stevenson without doubt attributes Silver's '*maimed strength and masterfulness*' to Henley, qualities obtaining to what is labelled in disability studies the phenomenon of the 'supercrip',[5] he at no point states explicitly that Henley inspired him to create Silver as an amputee in the first place (Garland Thomson 2000). Nonetheless, it is clear that Henley, the author of 'Invictus' (written in 1875 but published in 1888) – one of the most-cited Victorian poems about adopting a never-say-die attitude in the face of life's obstacles, which uses the maritime metaphor 'captain of my soul' to conclude its verses – was a major inspiration for Stevenson's characterisation of Silver. In addition to Henley, it is important to consider Silver within a wider network of influences that includes the one-legged pirate from *A General History* and the depictions of wooden-legged pirates that followed – several of which drew directly from Johnson's portrayal. Of these examples, some prelude the maimed hypermasculinity exhibited by pirates like Silver and Hook, whereas others provide a stark contrast to such representations.

Johnson's *A General History* can certainly be considered a forebear for many of the representations of one-legged pirates that we see in nineteenth- and early-twentieth-century fiction and non-fiction narratives. Indeed, Johnson's description of the pirate is plagiarised in Charles Ellms' 1837 book *The Pirates Own Book*. The wooden-legged pirate of *A General History* is again described in John Biddulph's *The Pirates of Malabar, and an Englishwoman in India Two Hundred Years Ago* (1907), though in this text Johnson is cited. Like Rennie over one hundred years later, Biddulph links Stevenson's characterisation of Silver to the 'real' pirate first depicted in *A General History* (Biddulph 1907: 138–9). In addition to Silver, a couple of minor and now largely forgotten fictional pirates bear an uncanny resemblance to the 'non-fiction' representation of the wooden-legged pirate first portrayed by Johnson. For example, the frightful and drunken aspects of the one-legged pirate's portrayal resonate with Harry Gringo's depiction of the barbarous Bill Gibbs in the 1864 novel *Captain Brand, of the Centipede*, a novel that was also loosely based on the life of an infamous eighteenth-century pirate. A pistol-swinging pirate with a wooden leg called 'Timbertoe' is also depicted in George Walter Thornbury's serialised novel *The Little Black Box* (Thornbury 1857: 11). These fictional refigurations of Johnson's one-legged pirate tend to draw from the negative aspects of this buccaneer's representation, in particular his allegedly threatening appearance and alcohol-fuelled conduct. Yet if we look to a wider network of fictional influences that may have contributed towards the characterisation of courageous disabled pirates, such as Silver, we see several characters who bear resemblance to later piratical anti-heroes.

It is, for instance, possible that Stevenson derived the idea of making Silver an amputee from reading Michael Scott's popular novel *Tom Cringle's Log* (1829–33). In this text, a classic of nautical fiction, the narrator describes a pattern by which disabled sailors en masse continue to work in spite of their impairments:

> It seems to be a sort of rule, that no old sailor who has not lost a limb, or an eye at least, shall be eligible to the office; but as the kind of maiming is so far circumscribed that all cooks must have two arms, a laughable proportion of them have but one leg. (Scott 1834: 76)

Stevenson was certainly aware of Scott's work in 1885 – just two years after *Treasure Island* was published in its complete, most famous and most popular form – since he mentions the author in a letter to P. G. Hamerton (Stevenson 1911d: 276).[6] Equally, it is possible that Stevenson may have been inspired by the representation of other famous fictional seafaring leg amputees, such as Old Tom from Frederick Marryat's *Jacob Faithful* (1834) – another figure who maintains an active position on a boat despite physical impairment – or Gruff and Glum from Charles Dickens' *Our Mutual Friend* (1864–5). A clear link between Old Tom and Silver is their shared use of the expression 'shiver my timbers'. Though Silver is today better remembered than Old Tom for the use of this phrase, according to the *Oxford English Dictionary*, the first recorded instance of its usage came in Marryat's 1834 novel. We know for sure that Stevenson read Marryat's work since he gave a scathing review of the latter's 1836 novel *The Pirate* in a letter to

Henley dated September 1881. At this time Stevenson was nineteen chapters through writing *Treasure Island*, up to then entitled 'The Sea Cook' (1911b: 63–4).[7] It may be a curious coincidence that the two fictional antecedents of the phrase 'shiver my timbers' are both amputees, yet the expression appears to perform a dual function, drawing attention to the speaker's prosthetic device and thus his physical impairment, while focalising his ability to work by directly referring to the 'timbers' of a ship – his place of work. This stock nautical phrase inherited by Stevenson is therefore implicitly tied to not just wooden-leggedness but also to a capacity to work regardless of physical disability.

Along similar lines, a major literary figure whose work may have inspired Silver's one-leggedness and indeed Hook's hook-handedness, but whose influence is often neglected, is Robert Michael Ballantyne, an author whose importance to Stevenson is revealed in the prefatory poem to *Treasure Island*, 'To the hesitating purchaser':

> If studious youth no longer crave,
> His ancient appetites forgot,
> Kingston, or Ballantyne the brave,
> Or Cooper of the wood and wave:
> So be it, also! And may I
> And all my pirates share the grave
> Where these and their creations lie! (Stevenson 1915: ix)

Like Stevenson, Barrie also acknowledged his indebtedness to Ballantyne in a preface he wrote for a 1913 edition of the latter's most famous novel, *The Coral Island* (1857): 'Ballantyne was for long my man' (Barrie 1913: vi). Barrie's comment, which establishes a decidedly masculine appreciation of Ballantyne's work, is telling of the widespread appeal of the earlier writer's stories: they were for a male readership and concerned decidedly masculine issues. As I will show, a particular aspect of Ballantyne's portrayal of an amputee sailor makes manifest an aspect of disabled pirate characterisation that has remained an enduring trope: the association between physical impairment and violent villainy.

While best known for his enduringly popular Robinsonade, Ballantyne was seemingly obsessed with limb injuries, amputation and prosthesis use. Indeed, in *The Young Fur-Traders* (1856), a doctor is suddenly called to set a broken leg for a trapper; in *Hudson's Bay; or Every-Day Life in the Wilds of North America* (1859), a Native American has the whole calf of his left leg bitten off and walks with a limp as a result; in *The Pirate City: An Algerine Tale* (1874), the narrator notes how under Turkish rule theft is punishable by amputation; in *Wrecked But Not Ruined* (1881), a clerk pledges to make an injured sailor 'a splendid wooden leg', providing that his chief performs an amputation (Ballantyne 1881: 89); and, as earlier noted, in *The Madman and the Pirate,* Rosco is eventually fitted with a pair of wooden legs after his feet are so badly burnt that they are amputated following a near-death experience at the hands of 'savages'. Most notably, though, amputation, prosthesis use and subsequent madness are depicted in Ballantyne's fabular 1864 novella *Why I Did Not Become a Sailor* (1864), a text that I argue displays parallels with Stevenson's novel and Barrie's play in terms of its depiction of the effect of seafaring injury. As I will suggest in the following section, this story, like the popular pirate narratives that followed it, sets up physical injury as a visual signifier for, and cause of, a violent disposition.

Peg-Legged Pirates: Narrative Prosthesis?

Why I Did Not Become a Sailor features a dream in which a teenager is transformed from an adventurous but nonetheless fairly domesticated, kind-hearted, able-bodied young man, into a wild, bloodthirsty amputee. A clear link is therefore established between disablement and moral aberrance. Jack, the best friend of the narrator and protagonist, is injured and his leg is amputated after the boys are unwittingly inducted as pirates and their ship embarks on a bloody battle with a Russian merchant vessel. Soon after Jack's leg is amputated, he fits himself with a wooden leg that 'is three inches too short [. . .] caus[ing him] to hobble in a most undignified manner' (Ballantyne 1864: 315). The narrator, Bob, grows increasingly concerned by his companion's rash conduct. Following their escape from the pirates and landing on an unknown island, Jack first insults a slave keeper, who with his allies assaults and captures the two young boys. Jack continues to berate his captors, resulting in Bob's assessment of his friend as 'probably under the influence of madness' (ibid.: 342). Jack's behaviour grows increasingly reckless and irrational as his captivity draws on. To Bob's horror, Jack eventually throws all caution to the wind and attempts to take the lives of his captors. He convinces them to lock the door of the building in which he and Bob are chained and then starts a fire. The scene that follows is bewildering:

The men uttered a yell, and rushing forward, threw themselves on the smoking heap in the hope of smothering it at once. But Jack applied the torch quickly to various parts. The flames leaped up! The men rolled off in agony. Jack, who somehow had managed to break his chain, hopped after them, showering the blazing straw on their heads, and yelling as never mortal yelled before. In two seconds the whole place was in a blaze, and I beheld Jack actually throwing somersaults with his one leg over the fire and through the smoke; punching the heads of the four men most unmercifully; catching up blazing handfuls of straw, and thrusting them into their eyes and mouths in a way that quite overpowered me. I could restrain myself no longer. I began to roar in abject terror! (ibid.: 352–3)

Here Jack's wild and barbarous behaviour is shown to come as a direct result of his injuries: after his assault and capture, he brashly exclaims, 'A man with only one leg, no head, and an exposed brain, isn't worth caring about. *I* don't care for him – not a button' (ibid.: 339). He is thus shown to have lost all hope and all self-respect as a result of his damaged physical state. His violence is depicted as a consequence of his despondent mentality.

While Jack is not a pirate, his eventual ferocious conduct matches him in terms of brutality with the buccaneers displayed earlier in this novella, and even the vicious kidnappers who arrest him and Bob. By aligning physical disability with moral decrepitude this story fits Mitchell and Snyder's model of 'narrative prosthesis'. Now an important theory in disability studies, 'narrative prosthesis' describes 'the myriad relations between the literary and the historical' focusing specifically on the way that physical and mental difference is used as a form of supplement by authors and filmmakers to perform a number of narrative functions: 'as a character-making trope', 'as a social category of deviance', 'as a symbolic vehicle for meaning-making and cultural critique', and 'as an option in the narrative negotiation of disabled subjectivity' (Mitchell and Snyder 2000: 9; 1). A particular aspect of narrative prosthesis is evident in Ballantyne's novella: that is, 'the pervasiveness of disability as a device of characterization in narrative art' (ibid.: 9). Indeed, the association that Ballantyne draws in this tale between loss of body and loss of mind is almost identical to the way that '[d]isability conjures up a ubiquitous series of associations between corrupted exterior and contaminated interior' in Melville's *Moby-Dick* (ibid.: 139).

The bond between disability, villainy and violence is indeed a strong one in the pirate adventure fiction from this period. In many instances, the loss of a body part is reflective of injuries sustained while performing piratical duties, as in the case of Silver and Hook. In these instances, the prosthetics and/or assistive technologies that are used stand as unwanted yet alluring trophies of their violent escapades. Often, such characters are shown to be vengeful to those who inflicted injuries upon them. Hook, of course, is the best example of this kind of portrayal. Revealing that Peter Pan was responsible for the amputation of his arm, he threatens, "Twas he cut off my arm. I have waited long to shake his hand with this. (Luxuriating) Oh, I'll tear him!' (Barrie 1977: 28–9). In other cases, the loss of a body part is seen as either secular or divine punishment for previous piratical deeds: see Bill Gibbs from *Captain Brand*, whose leg is crushed and piratical career all but ended by an enraged slave protecting his mistress (Gringo 1864), and Rosco from *The Madman and the Pirate*, whose double-foot amputation coincides with his redemption as a character: 'the ruin of his body had been the saving of his soul' (Ballantyne 1883: 216).

While narrative prosthesis is certainly a useful theoretical apparatus for considering why physical aberrancies and the primitive prosthetics that were used to mask them have so often been associated with pirates, the characterisation of popular pirate figures, such as Silver and Hook, as anti-heroes complicates this framework somewhat. Despite being out for revenge against Peter Pan, Hook nonetheless has a number of amicable and admirable attributes, which make him comical and likeable as well as compellingly criminal. He is, for instance, charming, polite and well-spoken. Perhaps even more so than Hook, Silver, though a cold-blooded murderer, is likeable in many ways. He is physically strong, brave and commanding. He is also, according to Squire Trelawney, a man of considerable integrity: 'Silver is a man of substance; I know of my own knowledge that he has a banker's account, which has never been overdrawn' (Stevenson 1915: 57). Silver is, in fact, so likeable that he is all but forgiven by Jim Hawkins and his comrades in spite of him leading the mutiny that put their lives in danger in the first place. Jim goes so far as to pledge to save Silver from the gallows should he go to court for his evil deeds. Silver also avoids dramatic justice. He escapes the reclaimed *Hispaniola* in a shore boat rather than facing the consequences for his piratical endeavours back in England, thus revealing his place in the author's heart. Our most famous fictional pirates are, therefore, more than just villains whose evil is made manifest by their injuries. Silver and Hook are complex figures who are not quite evil through and through. They actually possess some qualities that are compelling to a young male readership. Above all, these fictional pirates adapt remarkably well to their physical impairments, displaying to their readership how a manly man 'should' respond to physical loss.

Message in a Bottle: Manly Markers for Managing Limb Loss

In a time when dangers to physical integrity came in many forms and the importance of bodily wholeness could not be underestimated,[8] a contingency plan was needed for those aspiring to go places in life but whose bodies did not meet the establishing standards for the bodily 'norm', which came to the fore in the nineteenth century.[9] For many, prosthetics provided a solution to this problem. A burgeoning profession of prosthesis makers promulgated the mimetic capacities of their devices, which they claimed could 'substitute for the handiwork of nature' (Bigg 1855: 2). Such claims were supported by some journalists, who were awestruck by the 'ingenuity shown by [. . .] wooden-leg makers' and other prosthetists, such as glass-eye makers, a profession pioneered by Auguste Boissonneau, who coined the term 'ocularist' to describe those working in the trade (Anon. 1875: 463). Others, however, were less sure about prosthetics, and lambasted what they saw as a means of deception: devices that could disguise bodily difference thereby obscuring popular physiognomic prejudices. William Blanchard Jerrold, for instance, famously debated the virtues and vices of prosthetics, identifying that some saw artificial body parts as 'emblem[s] of deceit', 'device[s] of ingenious vanity', or items that 'cover[ed] the wearer with gross and unpardonable deceit' (Blanchard Jerrold 1851: 64). A concern for those who had lost limbs was that certain prosthetics came to be associated with beggary. David Copperfield's sweetheart, Dora, for instance, associates beggary with 'a yellow face and a nightcap, or a pair of crutches, or a wooden leg, or a dog with a decanter-stand in his mouth, or something of that kind' (Dickens 2004: 545–6). Thus while prosthetics provided a practical material solution for those who could afford top-end products, such as those created by British prosthetists Henry Heather Bigg or Frederick Grey, such devices were not available to everyone and the efficacy of them was debatable. In his 1855 treatise on artificial limbs, for instance, Grey lamented that 'from the expense entailed by their elaborate construction, they are not within the reach of the poorer class of sufferers' (Grey 1855: 107). If prostheses did not provide a complete solution to the perceived problems caused by bodily loss – loss of function, respect and job prospects – what was needed was a specific attitude to deal with physical loss. As I suggest, a piratical approach to dealing with physical loss – that encompassed adaptability, defiance, determination, courage and resilience – was promulgated by late-Victorian and Edwardian adventure narratives.

The developmental role of late-Victorian adventure fiction has received increased critical attention in recent years. David Head has suggested that late-nineteenth-century educators, librarians and psychologists thought pirate stories good for boys' physical masculine development. He argues that 'Pirate stories could [...] encourage boys to be vigorous, fighting the perceived tendency of modern middle-class life to create soft boys and softer men' (Head 2012: 112). Discussing a very different Victorian genre, Karen Bourrier has outlined the capacity of disabled male figures in fiction to 'train the reader emotionally' (Bourrier 2009: 117). As she contends, in mid-century sentimental fiction, disability opens up a more capacious emotional range for male characters, while the physical limitations of disability mirror the emotional restraint expected of both able-bodied male characters and readers (ibid.: 118). Tom Shakespeare, meanwhile, suggests that 'non-disabled men have things to learn from disabled men' (Shakespeare 1999: 63). While studies on disability and masculinity have tended to dwell on the incompatibilities between the realities of male disablement and traditionally held ideals of masculinity, which usually hold physical strength in high regard,[10] pirate stories tend to exhibit quite the contrary: disabled male figures who persevere by exhibiting a kind of hyper-masculinity. The disabled pirates depicted in Stevenson and Barrie's adventure stories serve as disabled male role models, whose ability to battle through life's obstacles – in their cases limb loss – provide a masculine model of resilience to both able-bodied and disabled readers. It is, however, noteworthy that the messages promulgated by disabled pirates are buttressed by an ablest philosophy that encouraged men with disabilities simply to 'get on with it' rather than hope for social changes to lessen their disablement – disability being a condition now considered at least in part, if not largely, socially constructed.[11]

Silver and Hook, however, are not the only disabled characters in pirate adventure fiction that display the hyper-masculinity described above. Though not a pirate per se, but a character unwillingly and unwittingly formerly employed on a pirate vessel, who adopts the blood-thirsty traits of his former comrades because of injury, Jack from Ballantyne's *Why I Did Not Become a Sailor* is another character who exhibits extreme adaptability and surprising physical capacities in spite of his limb loss. Jack not only manages to engulf his eventual captors with flames while performing somersaults, but earlier bludgeons an alligator, kills a dog, and injures a slave keeper all by using his wooden leg as a club. With some significant adaptation to his prosthesis (Bob and Jack fashion an artificial foot out of a 'square piece of bark off a tree') Jack is also able to traverse a swamp (Ballantyne 1864: 327). Jack's bravery is probably the most impressive aspect of his characterisation. The narrator notes:

> Poor Jack was very gentle and uncomplaining. He even made light of his misfortune, and laughed a good deal at himself; but I could see, nevertheless, that his spirits were at times deeply affected, in spite of his brave efforts to bear up and appear gay and cheerful. (ibid.: 329)

Why I Did Not Become a Sailor thus presents a complex portrayal of disability that, on the one hand, shows some alluring, hyper-masculine ways of dealing with limb loss while, on the other hand, supports prejudices that associate disability with villainy and violence.

Ballantyne's other prosthetically adorned pirate, Rosco, from *The Madman and the Pirate*, also shows a relatively stoical attitude to disability while revealing the functional inadequacies of primitive lower-limb prosthetics. Notwithstanding the humorous trials of his double-prosthesis use – he is first unable to walk with his prosthetics, then breaks one of his false legs, realises that his prostheses are poorly suited to the terrain of the island, wears defective limbs with lifted toes, and finally falls over repeatedly, requiring the assistance of others to return him to his feet – Rosco perseveres and eventually achieves a degree of physical mobility and, more importantly, happiness: he reacquires the art of walking 'to such perfection' that he is seen 'almost at all times and in all weathers, stumping about the village' (Ballantyne 1883: 240). His contentedness is revealed by the image presented at the close of the novel, where he is described to be sitting 'slightly bent, with eyes gazing sometimes at the children, and sometimes at his wooden toes' (ibid.: 246). Acceptance is, above all, the quality encouraged here.

If acceptance is the favoured response to disability espoused by Ballantyne, then defiance is the preferred attitude propagated by *Treasure Island*. Silver's physical capacities are no doubt aided by his otherwise impressive physique ('He was very tall and strong, with a face as big as a ham' [Stevenson 1915: 62–3]) and yet his mobility and physical prowess in the text are, at times, remarkable – if not, to an able-bodied Victorian reader, somewhat disconcerting. As Alan Sandison has commented, 'perhaps the two most striking things about Silver are his remarkable physical agility, given his missing limb, and a parallel and equally notable mental agility' (Sandison 2005: 238). Silver is at one point described as moving 'with the speed and security of a trained gymnast' and in the same scene, the one where he murders the seaman Tom, he is also said to be as 'agile as a monkey, even without leg or crutch' (Stevenson 1915: 117). Possibly a nod to the also 'monkey-like' double-amputee Miserrimus Dexter from Wilkie Collins' *The Law and the Lady*, who is said to move 'as lightly as a monkey, on his hands', Silver's portrayal is similarly sensational and transgressive in this scene (Collins 1876: 212). The reader is simultaneously shocked, impressed and terrified by the acrobatics of Stevenson's disabled anti-hero. Though Silver's physicality is impressive, it is, more than anything else, his ability to work and at times climb the social ladder that is truly admirable. If, like Jim, the doctor, or Stevenson himself, we forgive Silver for his misdeeds, one can do little more than marvel at the pirate's unwavering commitment to self-betterment throughout *Treasure Island*. He progresses from respected sea-cook to pirate captain, and is only reduced to a valued crew member and eventually an unpursued exile after his mutiny attempt is compromised and he forms an alliance with his former enemies. Silver begins *Treasure Island* a landlord with a bank account and ends it with a sack of coins 'worth, perhaps, three or four hundred guineas', an amount roughly equal to the annual income of a middle-class household at this time (Stevenson 1915: 288). Though by no means a rich man at the close of the novel, Silver ends it with more than he began with. He also earns decidedly more than he would have had he remained an honest sea-cook. Although his means of securing an income are dubious, he certainly works for it, and this elevates him above the status of the stereotypical wooden-leg user from this period – the street beggar.

A considerable amount of stigma surrounded disabled men who were reduced to begging in the nineteenth century. Wooden legs were commonly associated with mendicants. They were also routinely seen as fraudulent props used to dupe alms givers into giving more. A number of reasons why wooden legs were seen as beneficial to street vendors, a class barely above beggars in the Victorian class hierarchy, was propagated in an anonymous 1877 *All the Year Round* article titled 'Mr Wegg and his Class'. In this piece, the author describes the various duplicitous strategies of a one-legged crossing sweeper for increasing his income: he uses his wooden leg to inspire the idea that he is a war veteran; he draws upon the sympathy of others, claiming to be in constant pain; after his wooden leg breaks, he uses this as an excuse to demand extra money from passers-by; and finally, he claims to have found Salvation and so uses Christian verses to encourage charitable donations (Anon. 1877). Other fraudulent wooden-legged street dwellers are depicted in Mark Twain's *Roughing It* (1872) and Arthur Melbourne Cooper's 1903 short film *Blind Man's Bluff*. Though Silver is certainly deceptive, his cunning, unlike other calculating amputee characters, such as Silas Wegg from Dickens' *Our Mutual Friend*, is less deplorable because of his activeness and robustness. Unlike Wegg's scheme for success, Silver's designs rely on his actions rather than the mistakes of others. Silver's activeness, work ethic and ability to accrue capital in contemporary eyes elevate him above the status of street 'cripples', as does his decision to not use a peg leg, which was seen as a signifier for paupers. Certainly a slippery character, Silver nonetheless commands respect and is an anti-hero not only in the novel's context but also for both able-bodied and disabled men in general. Young male readers are not intended to aspire to Silver's piratical ways, but are encouraged to admire his unrelenting attitude to physical injury and perhaps life's obstacles more generally. Stevenson was, after all, impressed by his friend Henley's 'maimed strength and masterfulness' (Stevenson 1911c: 137).

Hook is another impaired fictional pirate who transcends the association of prosthetics with beggars. Indeed, Hook's aristocratic attire – based on the apparel of Charles II – and stately diction elevate him from the lower echelons of society in spite of his piratical career. Like Silver, Hook is also separated from street beggars by his apparent work ethic and ability to continue his duties in spite of his loss of a hand. Unlike Silver, however, Hook is not driven by financial reward but is motivated by vengeance. Though physically compromised and once defeated by Peter Pan, Hook continues his buccaneering career in order to avenge his bodily loss. Despite his neglect of looting, Hook remains apparently wealthy. His ability to continue working as a pirate stems primarily from his adaptability. He adjusts profoundly well to his hand loss, claiming to prefer his hook to his remaining organic hand: conversing with Hook, Smee comments, 'I have oft heard you say your hook was worth a score of hands, for combing the hair and other homely uses,' to which Hook responds, 'If I was a mother I would pray to have my children born with this instead of that' (Barrie 1977: 29). Hook's success as a pirate therefore relies on the efficacy of his hook prosthesis and also on the unflinching way in which he has adapted to using it. Like Silver, Hook adopts a never-say-die attitude to his loss of a body part.

To return finally to the question of where the enduring image of the prosthesis-using pirate comes from, a piece of biographical conjecture sheds light on another possible inspiration for Stevenson's depiction of Silver – and thus Barrie's portrayal of Hook – and also explains why the image of the disabled pirate remains so pertinent. While the stimulus of Stevenson's friend Henley has been well documented and we cannot dismiss the complex network of influences discussed earlier in this chapter, few have considered how Stevenson's own experience of disabling illness shaped his depiction of a resilient physically impaired character. Stevenson was a long-term sufferer of nervous exhaustion and various lung problems, rendering him, by Victorian standards, 'a cripple'. Oliver S. Buckton has observed the impact of Stevenson's body on his literary work: 'Disease was an apt metaphor by which Stevenson could represent subjection to power, being a state of oppression under which he had long suffered' (Buckton 2007: 28). Reading the mobility of Silver in light of Stevenson's often bed-ridden lack of it may encourage us to consider whether Silver represents a disabled fantasy of physical and social mobility. Alternatively, we may wish to view Silver as imbued with some of Stevenson's own mechanisms for coping with impairment. In 1901, former Free Church of Scotland minister William Robertson Nicoll, who himself was forced to retire from pastoral ministry after contracting pleurisy, praised Stevenson's resilience to illness and gestures towards his enduring success:

> He was simply the bravest of men. Now and then, as in his letter to George Meredith, he lets us see under what disabling conditions he fought his battle. Human beings in a world like this are naturally drawn to one who suffers, and will not let himself be mastered or corrupted by suffering. They do not care for the prosperous, dominant, athletic, rich, and long-lived man. They may conjecture, indeed, that behind all the bravery there is much hidden pain, but if it is not revealed to them they cannot be sure. (qtd in Hammerton 1907: 148)

Though Stevenson's own struggles with his body are little-known to popular audiences in the twenty-first century, the image of Long John Silver, a physically impaired character so durable and resilient that he manages without a prosthetic and who inspired our most famous prosthesis-using pirate, Captain Hook, endures as a Stevensonian role model for coping with life's obstacles. While Silver is not the archetype for our association between pirates and prosthetics, the fantasy of disabled durability that he embodies gestures towards an explanation for this enduring stereotype: the image of wooden-legged and hook-handed pirates stems from a complex web of real and fictional influences, an admiration for the piratical attitude towards disability displayed by maimed buccaneers, and an ablest assumption that sees prostheses as a logical, practical and materially effacing solution to the difficulties occasioned by limb loss. Our understanding of fictional pirates' resistance to disability is thus propped up by a peg leg.

Notes

Special thanks to Jason David Hall, Richard Noakes, Matt Hayler, Karen Bourrier and the editors of this collection for their helpful comments on earlier drafts of this piece.

1. Hans Turley and Mel Campbell suggest that the association between pirates and prosthetics, in addition to various other 'fashion plates' – such as 'dashing rogues waving Jolly Rogers and sporting puffy shirts, parrots, rakish bandannas, gold earrings [. . .] eye-patches and velvet coats' – 'would seem at odds with the economic, political and legal realities of piracy in eighteenth-century Europe' (Campbell 2011: 11; see Turley 1999: 37–42).
2. For recent examples of where Silver has been referred to as a wooden leg user, see Kemp 2009: 8–9, Narain 2011, BBC News 2011 and Burrow 2013.
3. See Amrhein 2012: Chap. 13.
4. See Rennie 2013: 179–87.
5. Garland Thomson argues that 'Modernity secularized wonder into the stereotype of the supercrip, who amazes and inspires the viewer by performing feats that the nondisabled viewer cannot imagine doing. Contemporary wonder rhetoric emphasizes admiration rather than amazement, in part because bourgeois respectability now deems it inappropriate to delight in staring at disabled people' (Garland Thomson 2002: 60–1).
6. David Cordingly, a leading expert on pirate history, notes some other possible cultural influences, including a one-legged sea cook depicted by Thomas Rowlandson (Cordingly 2006: 8).
7. Stevenson describes Marryat's novel as an 'arid, feeble, vain, tottering production' (1911b: 64).
8. For work on the perceived importance of physical wholeness, see Haley 1978 and O'Connor 2000. For work on possible dangers to this integrity, see Kirkup 2007.
9. As Lennard J. Davis has argued, the idea of the bodily norm came to prominence in the nineteenth century when statistics emerged as a powerful model for modern life (Davis 1995: 23–49). It is also worth considering the effect of legislative reforms, such as the Poor Law Amendment Act of 1834, which tightened poor relief eligibility requirements, thereby placing the physical capacities of those with impairments under the spotlight (Stoddard Holmes 2009: 108–22).
10. See Shakespeare 1999, Serlin 2003, Shuttleworth 2004, Wilson 2004 and Bionaz 2005.
11. See Shakespeare 2006 for a thorough yet concise survey of literature, discussion and interrogation of the social construction of disability.

Works Cited

Amrhein, J., Jr (2012), *Treasure Island: The Untold Story*, Kitty Hawk, NC: New Maritima Press.

Anon. (1875), 'Legs: Wooden and Otherwise', *All the Year Round*, 14: 350, pp. 463–7.

Anon. (1877), 'Mr Wegg and his Class', *All the Year Round*, 18: 441, pp. 250–3.

Ballantyne, R. M., (1856), *The Young Fur-Traders*, London: Thomas Nelson and Sons.

Ballantyne, R. M. (1859), *Hudson's Bay; or Every-Day Life in the Wilds of North America*, Boston, MA: Phillips, Sampson, and Company.

Ballantyne, R. M. (1864), *Why I Did Not Become a Sailor*, in R. M. Ballantyne, *Freak on the Fells; or Three Months' Rustication and Why I Did Not Become a Sailor*, Philadelphia: The John Winston Co., pp. 263–379.

Ballantyne, R. M. (1874), *The Pirate City: An Algerine Tale*, London: James Nisbet and Co.

Ballantyne, R. M. (1881), *Wrecked But Not Ruined*, London: James Nisbet and Co.

Ballantyne, R. M. (1883), *The Madman and the Pirate*, London: Nisbet and Co.

Barrie, J. M. (1913), 'Preface', in R. M. Ballantyne, *The Coral Island*, London: Nisbet, pp. v–viii.

Barrie, J. M. [1904] (1977), *Peter Pan: A Fantasy in Five Acts*, London: Samuel French.

BBC News (2011), 'Long John Silver "based on two Welsh brothers"', *BBC News*, 2 August, available at http://www.bbc.co.uk/news/uk-wales-north-east-wales-14380085 [accessed 26 February 2014].

Biddulph, J. (1907), *The Pirates of Malabar, and an Englishwoman in India Two Hundred Years Ago*, London: Smith, Elder and Co.

Bigg, H. H. (1855), *On Artificial Limbs, their Construction and Application*, London: Churchill.

Bionaz, R. E. (2005), 'Unmanly Professional Athletes: Disability and Masculinity in the United States, 1888–1908', *Disability Studies Quarterly*, 25: 2, available at http://dsq-sds.org/article/view/546/723 [accessed 18 February 2014].

Blanchard Jerrold, W. (1851), 'Eyes Made to Order', *Household Words*, 4: 81, pp. 64–6.

Blind Man's Bluff (1903), film, dir. A. M. Cooper, USA: Alpha Trading Company.

Bourrier, K. (2009), '"The spirit of a man and the limbs of a cripple": Sentimentality, Disability and Masculinity in Charlotte Yonge's *The Heir of Redclyffe*', *Victorian Review*, 35: 2, pp. 117–31.

Buckton, O. S. (2007), *Cruising with Robert Louis Stevenson: Travel, Narrative, and the Colonial Body*, Athens: Ohio University Press.

Burrow, C. (2013), Review of *Treasure Neverland: Real and Imaginary Pirates* by Neil Rennie, *Guardian*, 27 November (amended 3 December), available at <https://www.theguardian.com/books/2013/nov/27/treasure-neverland-neil-rennie-review> [accessed 25 February 2014].

Campbell, M. (2011), 'Pirate Chic: Tracing the Aesthetics of Literary Piracy', in G. Moore (ed.), *Pirates and Mutineers of the Nineteenth Century: Swashbucklers and Swindlers*, Farnham: Ashgate, pp. 11–22.

Collins, W. [1875] (1876), *The Law and the Lady*, London: Chatto and Windus.

Cordingly, D. (2006), *Under the Black Flag: The Romance and the Reality of Life among the Pirates*, New York: Random House.

Davis, L. J. (1995), *Enforcing Normalcy: Disability, Deafness, and the Body*, London: Verso.

Dickens, C. [1864–5] (2000), *Our Mutual Friend*, London: Everyman.

Dickens, C. [1849–50] (2004), *David Copperfield*, London: Penguin.

Ellms, C. [1837] (2004), *The Pirates Own Book; or, Authentic Narratives of the Lives, Exploits, and Executions of the Most Celebrated Sea Robbers*, available at <https://www.gutenberg.org/ebooks/12216> [accessed 14 March 2014].

Garland Thomson, R. (2002), 'The Politics of Staring: Visual Rhetorics of Disability in Popular Photography', in S. L. Snyder, B. J. Brueggemann and R. Garland Thomson (eds), *Disability Studies: Enabling the Humanities*, New York: MLA, pp. 56–75.

Grant de Pauw, L. (1982), *Seafaring Women*, Boston, MA: Houghton-Mifflin.

Grey, F. (1855), *Automatic Mechanism, as Applied in the Construction of Artificial Limbs, in Cases of Amputation*, London: H. Renshaw.

Gringo, H. (1864), *Captain Brand, of the* Centipede, New York: Harper and Brothers.

Haley, B. (1978), *The Healthy Body and Victorian Culture*, Cambridge, MA: Harvard University Press.

Hammerton, J. A (ed.) (1907), *Stevensoniana: An Anecdotal Life and Appreciation of Robert Louis Stevenson*, Edinburgh: John Grant.

Head, D. (2012), 'Howard Pyle's Pirates: Late Victorian Children's Literature and the Best Reading for Over-Refined Boys', *Topic: The Washington & Jefferson College Review*, 58, pp. 93–112.

Henley, W. E. (1888), 'Invictus', available at < https://www.poetryfoundation.org/poems-and-poets/poems/detail/51642> [accessed 21 March 2014].

Johnson, C. [Daniel Defoe?] [1724] (2012), *A General History of the Pyrates*, available at http://www.gutenberg.org/ebooks/40580 [accessed 14 March 2014].

Kemp, R. (2009), *Pirates*, London: Penguin.

Kirkup, J. (2007), *A History of Amputations*, London: Springer-Verlag.

Marryat, F. (1834), *Jacob Faithful*, London: Richard Edward King.

Marryat, F. [1836] (2007), *The Pirate*, available at <http://www.gutenberg.org/ebooks/21580> [accessed 14 March 2014].

Melville, H. [1851] (2012), *Moby-Dick*, London: Penguin.

Mitchell, D. T. and S. L Snyder (2000), *Narrative Prosthesis: Disability and the Dependencies of Discourse*, Ann Arbor: University of Michigan Press.

Narain, J. (2011), 'Was Long John Silver a Peg-Legged Welshman? The Real Pirate could have been Born near Rhyl', *Daily Mail*, 2 August, available at <http://www.dailymail.co.uk/news/article-2021178/Treasure-Islands-Long-John-Silver-based-real-man-WELSH.html> [accessed 26 February 2014].

O'Connor, E. (2000), *Raw Material: Producing Pathology in Victorian Culture*, Durham, NC: Duke University Press.

Rennie, N. (2013), *Treasure Neverland: Real and Imaginary Pirates*, Oxford: Oxford University Press.

Sandison, A. (2005), '*Treasure Island*: The Parrot's Tale', in H. Bloom (ed.), *Robert Louis Stevenson*, Philadelphia: Chelsea House, pp. 211–44.

Scott, M. [1829–33] (1834), *Tom Cringle's Log*, Paris: Baudry's European Library.

Serlin, D. H. (2003), 'Crippling Masculinity: Queerness and Disability in US Military Culture, 1800–1945', *GLQ: A Journal of Lesbian and Gay Studies*, 9: 1, pp. 149–79.

Shakespeare, T. (1999), 'The Sexual Politics of Disabled Masculinity', *Sexuality and Disability*, 17: 1, pp. 53–64.

Shakespeare, T. (2006), 'The Social Model of Disability', in L. J. Davis (ed.), *The Disability Studies Reader*, 4th edn, London: Routledge, n.p. [Kindle version].

Shuttleworth, R. P. (2004), 'Disabled Masculinity: Expanding the Masculine Repertoire', in B. G. Smith and B. Hutchison (eds), *Gendering Disability*, New Brunswick, NJ: Rutgers University Press, pp. 166–78.

Stevenson, R. L. [1881] (1911a), Letter to W. E. Henley, in S. Colvin (ed.), *The Letters of Robert Louis Stevenson*, vol. 2 of 4, New York: Charles Scribner's Sons, pp. 59–61.

Stevenson, R. L. [1881] (1911b), Letter to W. E. Henley, in S. Colvin (ed.), *The Letters of Robert Louis Stevenson*, vol. 2 of 4, New York: Charles Scribner's Sons, pp. 63–4.

Stevenson, R. L. [1883] (1911c), Letter to W. E. Henley, in S. Colvin (ed.), *The Letters of Robert Louis Stevenson*, vol. 2 of 4, New York: Charles Scribner's Sons, pp. 137–8.

Stevenson, R. L. [1885] (1911d), Letter to P. G. Hamerton, in S. Colvin (ed.), *The Letters of Robert Louis Stevenson*, vol. 2 of 4, New York: Charles Scribner's Sons, pp. 274–76.

Stevenson, R. L. [1881] (1915), *Treasure Island*, New York: Harper and Brothers.

Stoddard Holmes, M. [2004] (2009), *Fictions of Affliction: Physical Disability in Victorian Culture*, Ann Arbor: University of Michigan Press.

Thornbury, G. W. (1857), 'The Little Black Box: A Story of a Shaftesbury Plot, Chapter VIII', *National Magazine*, 3: 13, pp. 8–12.

Turley, H. (1999), *Rum, Sodomy and the Lash: Piracy, Sexuality and Masculine Identity*, London: New York University Press.

Twain, M. [1872] (1988), *Roughing It*, London: Penguin.

Wilson, D. J. (2004), 'Fighting Polio like a Man: Intersections of Masculinity, Disability and Aging', in B. G. Smith and B. Hutchison (eds), *Gendering Disability*, New Brunswick, NJ: Rutgers University Press, pp. 119–33.

Chapter 5

Tuberculosis and Visionary Sensibility: The Consumptive Body as Masculine Dissent in George Eliot and Henry James

Meredith Miller

> He would fain be always tripping and waltzing, and is sorry that he cannot be allowed to walk about in the morning with yellow breeches and flesh-coloured silk-stockings. He sticks an artificial rosebud in his button hole in the midst of winter. He wears no neckcloth, and cuts his hair in imitation of the Prints of Petrarch. In his verses, he is always desirous of being airy, graceful, easy, courtly and ITALIAN. (Lockhart 1817: 39)

Thus John Gibson Lockhart's famous vitriol directed at Leigh Hunt, in the review which coined the epithet 'Cockney School'. The passage reveals this critique as formed not only around class, but also through constructions of proper and improper British masculinity. Leigh Hunt is presented here in terms of the foppish masculinity which, in the decades after the French Revolution, was associated with popular Romanticism, and the threat of national social disintegration through class contamination. Here, I want to examine the manner in which, through the literary afterlife of John Keats, the Victorian imaginary retains this picture of the socially/nationally disruptive, improperly gendered, male body, and its associations with both illness and visionary sensibility. In the 1870s and 1880s, George Eliot and Henry James draw on six decades of popular associations linking aesthetic sensibility, masculine dissent and the wasting, youthful, tubercular male body to trouble the fixed boundaries of national identity and robust Anglo masculinity.

It is a critical commonplace that Victorians saw consumption as a female illness, a pathological, but also purifying expression of feminine virtue and gentleness. This feminising of consumption extends even to the reading of male characters in Victorian fiction. Katherine Byrne, in her thorough study *Tuberculosis and the Victorian Literary Imagination*, reads Ralph Touchett, hero of James' *The Portrait of a Lady*, as 'feminised' by tuberculosis. Byrne concludes her chapter on *Portrait* by reiterating a common biographical reading which sees James' tubercular characters (in *The Wings of the Dove* and *Portrait*) as transpositions of his real life friend Minnie Temple. Reading by substitution, she concludes that, 'the portrayal of a male consumptive in *The Portrait of a Lady* emerges as a portrayal of a female consumptive after all' (Byrne 2011: 169), thus maintaining the unity of her argument that 'with some significant and usually emasculated exceptions [. . .] the classic literary consumptive is inevitably a woman in the Victorian era' (ibid.: 6).

The ubiquity of female consumptives in later nineteenth century literature is undeniable. This essay, however, will trace another, often overlooked, thread in the cultural imagining of the tubercular body, that of the wasting male youth of visionary sensibility. It will first note several key moments during the nineteenth century at which both the story of Keats' death and *Blackwood's* critique of the 'Cockney School' reappear, and then examine the manner in which Eliot and James take advantage of and reposition the structure of feeling which associates the tubercular male body, visionary aestheticism and masculine dissent.

Lockhart's critique of Hunt and Cockney School poetry employs the language of diseased vision, as well as foppish masculinity. It rails against 'the unhealthy and jaundiced medium through which the Founder of the Cockney School views everything' (Lockhart 1817: 40). Through Keats and Shelley, this conflation of diseased vision and dissenting masculinity became specifically associated with pulmonary tuberculosis. In his *Romanticism and Colonial Disease*, Alan Bewell (2003) examines Keats' own letters alongside contemporary criticism of the 1817 *Poems* and of *Endymion*, for their structuring of the experience of consumption across the geography of empire. Bewell traces associations in the reviews between orientalist aesthetic excess and the construction of the tubercular body. Keats' poetry, like Hunt's, is seen as aesthetically unhealthy in its imperfect, in his case tubercular, masculinity. As Bewell puts it, Lockhart's criticism of Hunt and the Cockney School portrays 'a new mode of British urban vulgarity, a tawdry tropicalized urbanism, the product of an effeminizing commerce with the East' (Bewell 2003:174).

A further look at contemporary responses to the 1817 *Poems* reveals, in both positive and negative reviews, tropes of luxuriance, fevered vision and dissident masculinity. An enraptured reviewer in the *Monthly Magazine* (April 1817) sees in Keats 'the fertile fancy and beautiful diction of our old poets [. . .] There is in his poems a rapturous glow and intoxication of the fancy – an air of careless and profuse magnificence in his diction – a revelry of the imagination and tenderness of feeling' ('New Publications in March' 1817: 248). On the other hand, the offended reviewer of *The Eclectic Review* ('Poems, by John Keats' 1817) figures Keats, and other 'imitators' of Wordsworth and Scott, as dangerous in their lack of active masculine vigour.

The story of Keats' visionary promise and tragic death took shape and developed through Shelley's *Adonaïs* and, from 1848, through Richard Monckton Milnes' *Life, Letters and Literary Remains of John Keats*. Monckton Milnes' two-volume production, based largely on Charles Armitage Brown's material, was widely reviewed in the later part of 1848, and these reviews dwelt at length on Keats' 'orientalist' excesses and his tubercular body, both associated with his visionary sensibility. The August *Athenaeum* review contains a very erotic description of the poet's masculine beauty, then quotes almost in full his frank description of his sexual desire for an 'Eastern' beauty with whom he became acquainted. The same review then spends more than 50 per cent of its space on detailed descriptions of Keats' wasting body and fading consciousness, reproduced in lengthy quotations from letters between Keats, Hunt, Severn and Brown. These letters also reveal the passionate homosocial love expressed among this circle of men, which achieves physicality through detailed descriptions of the solicitous, quasi-maternal care of Keats' sick body ('Life, Letters and Literary Remains of John Keats' 1848: 825–7). The particular narrative choices that begin to form the canonical story of Keats' life and his death marry a luxuriant, sexualised, orientalist excess of spiritual vision with a wasting masculine body and a strong sense of homosocial bonding. This combination of elements continues, as we shall see, to form a significant counterpoint to the robust and self-willed, positivist masculinity that underpinned evolving ideas of British imperial nationhood as the century moved on. A troubling counter-narrative of Romantic masculinity lived on in the later decades of the nineteenth century in pre-Raphaelitism, popular Gothic fictions, and the increasing concern with subjective consciousness in imaginative writing.

In an editorial published in *Macmillan's* in November 1860, David Masson seeks to reinvent Keats as the embodiment of healthy masculine vigour through a repositioning of both the poetry and the poet's masculine body. Masson repeatedly uses words such as 'vigour', 'pugnacity' and 'courage' to describe the young, pre-tubercular Keats. The poet's emotional sensibility is written as an aberration caused by illness, both in his family history and in himself. Writing to his conception of a restrained and physically robust normative masculinity, Masson is at pains to recuperate the image of Keats from these emotional excesses. Significantly, Masson contrasts Keats to the dangerous Shelley in terms of the contemporary discourse of subjective and objective writing. Shelley is, of course, the over-subjective poet. In conclusion, Masson interestingly reverses the narrative of a progressively feminising illness to reposition Keats' life as a narrative of progress from the 'sensuous', wild, excessive sensibilities of youth to a mature attainment of 'sublimity and action' (Masson 1860: 15–16). The implication is that, had Keats lived longer, his healthy masculinity would have triumphed. The use of 'action' is important here, in its evocation of a particular masculine type, the robust and positivist man of action, the imperial self, posed against Romantic lassitude and decadence. Masson is working one side of a particular current here, a nineteenth-century structure of feeling which associates Romantic radicalism, dissident masculinity, visionary sensibility and aesthetic excess. He obviates these associations in seeking to position Keats outside of them. In doing so, he is at pains to unpick his 'true', or latent, poet from the imaginary associations which accrue to Keats' tubercular body.

In dismissing the male consumptive, Katherine Byrne asserts that, though his

> body too is reduced and wasted by the disease, the consequences are different. The results are not fashionably or aesthetically pleasing, and the passive role of self-sacrifice and suffering he as invalid is obliged to take up is the antithesis of all his gender is meant to represent. Health and strength are vital to the Victorian concept of the virile male. (Byrne 2001: 34–5)

Like Byrne, Susan Sontag moves quickly on from the masculine consumptive to the increasing feminisation of pulmonary tuberculosis and concludes that the tubercular body 'became more and more the ideal look for women, while great men of the mid- and late nineteenth century grew fat, founded industrial empires, wrote hundreds of novels, made wars and plundered continents' (Sontag 1990: 30). The association of robust masculinity with novel-writing is significant, as Sontag argues specifically for *poetic* creativity written as tubercular. We might stop momentarily to point to Gissing's sickly Edwin Reardon, who undoes this critical narrative on several counts, being male, occurring late in the century, and being a novelist who dies of 'an inflammation' of the lungs (Gissing 2016: 397). Reardon's rarefied 'literary' sensibilities, famously posed against the capitalist marketplace of modern fiction, are expressed in the form of the newly conceived art novel of the *fin de siècle*.

For a generation which grew up on reproductions of idealised drawings and paintings of the wasting Keats produced by Brown, Severn and others, the consumptive male body certainly could be fashionably, aesthetically (and erotically) pleasing. There is no singular masculinity in the Victorian (or any) era, though there may be a hegemonic one. What we might call the Keatsian body is significant because it locates a collection of dissident masculine expressions in this period. This is the unremarked role of the masculine consumptive in later nineteenth-century novels. His wasting body and fevered, visionary spirit locate a dissent from the robust masculinity of the bourgeois epoch. Its deviance from national masculine norms also provides a standpoint for dissent from the imperial self. The tubercular male body in late nineteenth-century fiction is just that, a standpoint; it locates a nexus where masculine dissidence meets tragically, transcendentally elevated sensibilities.

Typology and Transmission: *Daniel Deronda* and Realism

The uses of this fictional male body illuminate a particular function of realism in terms of character types and the relation between the realist imaginary and its material referents. It is here that we find the consumptive male characters of *Daniel Deronda* and *The Portrait of a Lady*. Mordecai Cohen and Ralph Touchett exemplify the function of the tubercular male character in the latter nineteenth century as the location of dissent from both nation and reason. Both George Eliot's and Henry James' use of the tubercular masculine character lie within their broader interventions in the realist project. *Daniel Deronda* and *The Portrait of a Lady* both dissent from the formal structure and narrative conventions expected of novelistic realism. This fact was clearly remarked upon in contemporary reviews of both novels, broadly as regards *Deronda*'s plot structure and *Portrait*'s narrative style.

As Mikhail Bakhtin, Georg Lukàcs, Ian Watt and others have written, the notion of novelistic realism rests on the relationship between the idea of individual character and the elucidation of the material, social, and political life within which the modern novel might be usefully embedded. The dominant idea of the realist project is one in which characters are 'types' of people produced by social conditions in the world outside the novel, and therefore stand in for these conditions and their effects. Contemporary reviews of *Daniel Deronda* during its serial release (eight volumes in as many months in 1876) critique its generic position in terms of the realist project, and after the release of its fifth volume in June, the construction of Mordecai's character as a 'type'.

R. E. Francillon's very positive October 1876 review of *Deronda* argues that the novel is not realist, is in fact Eliot's first 'romance', because here Eliot is 'not dealing with types' (Francillon 1876: 412). Critics also noted Eliot's studied use of sensational effects in *Deronda*, again taking Eliot out of the stylistic territory of *Middlemarch* and *Adam Bede*, to which *Deronda* was pointedly contrasted. These generic interventions were at times related to expressions of critical confusion and debate about how the character of Mordecai Cohen should be received. The *Examiner* of August 1876 asks whether we are meant to receive Mordecai as comic or ideal, and concludes that this will depend on whether we accept 'the inherent reasonableness of the idea with which she over-informs his frail body [. . .] that every race has its special mission in the world' ('Mordecai' 1876: 885). Earlier, in June of 1876, the *Examiner*'s review of Book V describes Mordecai in terms which show us that Eliot's audience will receive his tubercular body as the expression of visionary sensibility without her having to spell out the connection. The critic reproduces the mystic inversion of wasting body and enlarged soul which Eliot has never quite stated outright: 'But his soul, the intense workings of which have worn his fragile body to a skeleton, and given a consumptive brilliance to his eye, is filled with sublime enthusiasm and mystic aspiration' ('Daniel Deronda, Book V' *Examiner* 1876: 632). Eliot never explicates the meaning of Mordecai's consumption in the novel because, as this critic demonstrates, it is there already in the cultural imaginary.

Joseph Jacobs, writing in *Macmillan's* in June 1877, continues to situate the terms of the debate on the novel's Jewish content in the relation between characterisation and genre. Jacobs' discussion brings together the ideological effects that underpin Mordecai's characterisation and its reception with the larger, troubled project of the novel, a questioning of national identity, cultural transmission and scientific notions of heredity. Well aware of the problem of types, inheritance and the individual in this sophisticated and complex discussion of the operations of race, Jacobs frames his intervention in typology by subversively heading his article with the author-name 'A. Jew' and then signing his own individual name at the close (Jacobs 1877: 633).

For Eliot, the relation between Mordecai and Daniel functions as a working out of the slippage between nation and race, and of the problem of heredity and aesthetic apprehension, through the medium of cultural transmission. Mordecai's tubercular body, the wasting house which fosters his mystic vision, is the tool Eliot uses to stage the drama of these relations. She picks it up because its long-established cultural effects enable her critique of the relations among nation, race and masculine identity. In *Deronda*, Mordecai Cohen's consumption conveys both refinement and tragic status on his character. The disease also services those interventions in characterisation and genre which were remarked on both positively and negatively by critics during and immediately after the serial run.

Our first view of Mordecai himself, presented through Daniel's gaze, introduces the mingled themes of cultural inheritance and spiritual transmission which will form both Mordecai's tubercular body and the novel's central critique. On entering an East End bookshop at random, Daniel is arrested by the sight of a man Eliot explicitly marks as both ordinary type and extraordinary tragic figure.

> A man in threadbare clothing whose age was difficult to guess – from the dead yellowish flatness of the flesh, something like an old ivory carving [. . .] the thought glanced through Deronda that precisely such a physiognomy as that might possibly have been seen in a prophet of the Exile, or in some New Hebrew poet of the mediæval time. It was a finely typical Jewish face, wrought into intensity of expression apparently by a strenuous eager experience in which all the satisfaction had been indirect and far off, and perhaps by some bodily suffering also [. . .] with its dark, far-off gaze, and yellow pallor in relief on the gloom of the backward shop, one might have imagined one's self coming upon it in some past prison of the Inquisition [. . .] while the look fixed on a customer seemed eager and questioning enough to have been turned on one who might have been a messenger either of delivery or of death. The figure was probably familiar and unexciting enough to the inhabitants of this street; but to Deronda's mind it brought so strange a blending of the unwonted with the common. (Eliot 1892: 288–9)

However contemporary critics perceived Eliot's generic positioning of *Deronda* and its characters, it is clear that she herself invoked the language of both realism and high tragedy, and that she makes a particular point of blending them. From Dickens to Gissing, the blending of the naturalistic everyday and tragic sentiment is of course a common strategy for the nineteenth-century realist novel with a particular social agenda. Mordecai is both ideal and possible, and Eliot takes pains to establish both qualities.

He is the character of cultural spirit within the everyday flesh of the citizen of the world. At this first introduction Daniel feels suddenly, 'a thin hand pressing his arms tightly, while a hoarse, excited voice' asks him a startling question about his origin (ibid.: 288). From the outset, Mordecai is presented in terms which separate the spirit within him from his physical body: 'The grasp was relaxed, the hand withdrawn, the eagerness of the face collapsed into uninterested melancholy, as if some possessing spirit which had leaped into the eyes and gestures had sunk back again' (ibid.: 288).

This scene, and others throughout the novel, employ the language of the nervous body developed in popular sensation fiction throughout the 1860s. In her *Somatic Fictions*, Athena Vrettos (1995) demonstrates that Gwendolyn's bodily agitations and nervous terrors are also drawn from the generic language of the sensation novel, and in turn from the longer tradition of bodily sensibility. Mordecai is in many ways the classic patient whose disposition is rendered nervous by 'hectic fever'. He suffers from 'the consciousness of misapplied agitation; sane as well as excitable' and, as he anticipates meeting with Daniel, feels 'an increasing agitation of that subdued hidden quality which hinders nervous people from any steady occupation on the eve of an anticipated change' (Eliot 1892: 360; 361). In several ways, Eliot locates this nervous disposition specifically within the tradition of the Keatsian body. Given Mordecai's scholarly history and the content of his historical, philosophical intervention, we might expect him to write essays. Yet he is a poet, and his identity as such is repeatedly conflated with his consumption, which, like Keats, he believes he developed during an unfortunate exposure while travelling. With 'his emaciated figure, and dark eyes deep in their sockets' (ibid.: 355), Mordecai recites, 'in a strong high baritone, with its variously mingling hoarseness, like a haze amidst illuminations' (ibid.: 359), 'a verse on which he had spent some of his too scanty heart's blood' (ibid.: 358). Keats' own expression of the spirit imprisoned in the wasting body, from 'Sonnet on Seeing the Elgin Marbles', forms the epigraph to *Deronda*'s Chapter XLIII. The most pronounced use of the nervous body in the novel regards this construction of Mordecai's tubercular body as the house of the visionary spirit. The 'hopefulness which is often the beneficent illusion of consumptive patients', is 'in Mordecai wholly diverted from the prospect of bodily recovery and carried into the current of this yearning for transmission' (ibid.: 355).

The 'transmission' for which Mordecai yearns, and which he believes he can enact with Daniel, brings together ideas of heredity and racial typing with the novel's critique of English masculinity and its vision of national transcendence. At their second meeting, affect overcomes reason as something passes between them which both evokes and transcends the nervous body:

> the two men, with as intense a consciousness as if they had been two undeclared lovers, felt themselves alone in the small gas-lit book-shop and turned face to face, each baring his head from an instinctive feeling that they wished to see the other fully. (ibid.: 372)

From our standpoint, the scene feels distinctly homoerotic, though for Eliot's contemporary readers it would have expressed something else, or also – an excess of sensibility and a sense of some communication possible at the limit of the nervous body. It is the same something that was felt perhaps in that much-related moment when Coleridge met the 'loose, slack, not well-dressed' Keats in the street and shook his hand, feeling the poet inside him (see for example Masson 1860: 4). Whether and what Coleridge in fact felt, it is the ubiquity of the myth which is significant, a story of masculine communion in poetic vision through proximate bodies which informs the relationship between Daniel and Mordecai. Nor is its homosocial physicality incidental. From the 1790s forward, such expressions of sensibility in dissident masculine bodies locate a subversive position in relation to the increasingly hearty, self-contained and robust heterosexual masculinity which expressed the ideal of the imperial self.

This contrast between two masculinities joins the novel's two plots, focused on a pair of very different 'English gentlemen'. The perfect English gentleman, Daniel, is not English by heredity, while Henleigh Grandcourt is English to the core and not at all a true gentleman. Many conversations on national spirit and cultural inheritance embed this pointed critique of the masculine national ideal. The novel ultimately calls for a blending of 'Eastern' and 'Western' culture, embodied in Daniel.

Questions of the individual, types and national identity, of the relation between the mass and historical change, form the substance of the wonderful philosopher's club scene which takes up Chapter XLII. Here Eliot presents alternative philosophical positions and alternative

Jewish types to those she has chosen as her central vehicles. We catch a glimpse of the Jewish secular socialism which enlivened the East End in this period, as well as various degrees of assimilation. Eliot also troubles the unified idea of English identity with a small array of Celtic types and with working-class Anglo radicalism. These associations are an important aspect of the novel's project, which is to disrupt England's unified national identity, and its basis in racialised masculinity.

Mordecai, initially marked as radically Jewish, makes a point of his Englishness in terms of both culture and bodily inheritance; 'English is my mother-tongue,' he says, 'England is the native land of this body, which is but as a breaking pot of earth around the fruit-bearing tree' (Eliot 1892: 374). In spite of language and body, heredity endures and transcends. Eliot writes as both bodily heredity *and* spiritual transmission what is increasingly written as biological race in this period. The boundaries of the nation are permeable, and Jewishness is the sign of this permeability here, as it is throughout the nineteenth-century novel. It exists at the limit of national/racial identity as contemporary slippages in the signification of the words race and nation reveal. Yet while writers such as Anthony Trollope pose this as a threat, Eliot poses it as heroic transcendence. Throughout *Deronda*, nation is used to signify both the boundaries of England and the transcendent inheritance of the Jewish people.

The vehicle for this inheritance, in *Deronda*, is the tubercular breath. Mordecai's first hope for a receptacle to hold his Zionist poetic vision is in little Jacob Cohen. He recites his 'unintelligible' words into Jacob's ear, seeking to imprint ideas beneath language. Jacob plays along at imitation, 'as long as the teacher's breath would last out' (ibid.: 358). Presented in physical contrast to Daniel's body, Mordecai's bears:

> the pathetic stamp of consumption, with its brilliancy of glance to which the sharply-defined structure of features, reminding one of a sacred temple, give already a far-off look as of one getting unwillingly out of reach [. . .] a Jewish face naturally accentuated for the expression of an eager mind—the face of a man little above thirty, but with that age upon it which belongs to time lengthened by suffering, the hair and beard still black throwing out the yellow pallor of the skin, the difficult breathing giving more decided marking to the mobile nostril. (ibid.: 372–3)

Haunting historical vision, heightened sensibility revealed in physiognomy, and the acquired spiritual effects of consumption are all blended here. Throughout the novel, Mordecai's consumption is one with his spiritual grandeur and his mystical poetic vision. His body is Gothic, a house haunted by a spirit that doesn't quite belong to it, and sometimes itself a haunting. Yet it is acted upon, shaped by the fire of this spirit, expressed through consumption. If we could view these associations out of context, they would seem strangely incongruous. In the 1870s, though, they are part of a decades-long tradition which knows the consumptive male body as the house of poetic vision and the site of resistance to the hegemonic narrative of unified English masculinity.

Eliot uses Mordecai to stage transcendence from the hereditary, racialised body to cultural inheritance as spirit. For that, the tubercular male body, as imagined in Victorian culture, is perfectly constructed as a wasting, ethereal prison for an inflamed spirit. It is, in effect, a secular version of the mystical body. He is 'a frail incorporation of the national consciousness, breathing with difficult breath' (ibid.: 433).

Narrative Disembodiment: *The Portrait of a Lady*

A strong thread in the critical tradition on *Deronda* reads the novel through Henry James' satirical 'Daniel Deronda: A Conversation', published in the *Atlantic* of December 1876, two months after the completion of *Deronda*'s serial run (in *Harper's* in the US). Though it is clearly a send-up of the various positions taken up by contemporary critics and readers, this piece is often read unproblematically as representing James' stance on *Deronda*. The two-plot reading is there, with compliments on the 'Englishness' of the first two books and complaints that the whole is too 'German', that is, too Romantic and philosophical. James also satirises the common complaint that Daniel's character is unrealistic, too perfect, *not embodied*. He 'has no blood in his body' and 'is not a man at all' (James 1876: 684–94). Together with other contemporary reviewers, James makes fun of Daniel's constant tugging at his shirt collar, as a pathetic attempt of Eliot's to give him an embodied human character. The notion is that Daniel stands in for an idea, and that it is a failure of Eliot's realist craft that he is more type than individual.

Daniel is, in fact, quite pointedly embodied, characterised with the kind of exotic, over-sexualised masculine magnetism with which Trollope imbues that other male character at the limit of Englishness, Phineas Finn. Like Phineas', Daniel's masculine beauty is racialised. He has 'a face not more distinctively oriental than many a type seen among the Latin races: rich in youthful health and with a forceful masculine gravity in repose' (Eliot 1892: 373). Daniel lives up to Mordecai's very physical requirements in having, 'an embodiment unlike his own [. . .] his face and frame must be beautiful and strong [. . .] his voice must flow with a full and easy current' (ibid.: 355). Daniel's physical body appears explicitly during interactions with Mordecai, as a foil for the consumptive house of Mordecai's spirit. He puts 'out his ungloved hand' (ibid.: 381) to shake Mordecai's, and often touches him with sensitive care. Significantly, their relationship is repeatedly characterised as that of mother and child, with Mordecai written as maternal. He holds little Jacob 'with a maternal action' (ibid.: 360) and he looks at Daniel with 'something of the dying mother's look when her loved one visits her bedside [. . .] for the sense of spiritual perpetuation in another resembles that maternal transference of self' (ibid.: 373).

Henry James' Ralph Touchett, the consumptive 'reflector' of his *The Portrait of a Lady*, also enacts 'a maternal transference of self' on several levels. Ralph's actions are specifically marked as maternal in the opening chapter, where three male characters take tea on the lawn of the Touchett house and Ralph pays solicitous attention to his sickly father. Many critics read this, and Ralph's characterisation in general, as a biographically determined queerness or 'failed masculinity' belonging to James himself and presented through the screen of his fiction. In such readings, critics such as Lyndall Gordon and Katherine Byrne construe Ralph's consumption both as failed masculinity and as a transposition of the illness and death of James' friend Minnie Temple (Gordon 2012; Byrne 2011). Yet, there is more complexity here than a mere reading by substitution – female for male, real-life friend for fictional character – can account for. Ralph is made out of available cultural material, and deployed in service to a critique of modern nationhood as masculinity which goes beyond the limits of fixed biographical projection.

Like the successive books of *Deronda*, early chapters of *Portrait* pose a clear, self-reflexive intervention in the formal structure and characterisations of the realist novel. James plays with the idea of types, while characters discuss the romance plot and the infidelity of gendered characterisations in the popular novel. There are a set of 'reversed' gender characterisations as well as several contrasting types of masculine embodiment, which illustrate a pointed critique of national character. In all, this adds up to an intervention in the techniques of realism and the formal structure of the romance plot. In the opening chapters, Isabel Archer is established reflectively as the young woman at an interesting time of life. As our view of her suitors is focalised through her matrimonial choices, we are invited to critically examine national character as masculinity.

Masculine bodies, including Ralph's, are associated with national critique from the novel's opening scene. Daniel Touchett, still at this point simply the unnamed 'old gentleman', has come from America with 'at the top of his baggage, his American physiognomy; and he had [. . .] kept it in the best order, so that, if necessary, he might have taken it back to his own country with perfect confidence' (James 1997: 7). Lord Warburton possesses 'a face as English as that of the old gentleman I have just sketched was something else' (ibid.: 7). The novel's complex net of gender inversions includes the characterisations of Ralph's 'maternal' father and his 'gubernatorial' mother and the 'lady journalist' Henrietta Stackpole, whom we ought to count among the masculine types on display. Isabel's 'native land' produces not 'personages', but rugged, individual men of action like her suitor Caspar Goodwood. Goodwood is 'intrinsic enough', individual rather than type' (ibid.: 425). Qualities of individual purpose and action in Henrietta Stackpole and Caspar Goodwood are contrasted with the sterility and decadence of a kind of *ancien régime* represented by Gilbert Osmond and his erstwhile mistress, Madame Merle.

The notion of characters as types is invoked again and again in jokes about 'specimens'. Isabel, who is 'theoretical', is in the habit of talking about specimens, 'a word that played a considerable part in her vocabulary; she had given him [Ralph] to understand that she wished to see English society illustrated by figures' (ibid.: 61). She likes Lord Warburton 'as a specimen very much' (ibid.: 66), though she rejects him as a husband. The journalist Henrietta Stackpole tells Isabel she would like to write a story on Ralph, because there is 'a great demand just now for the alienated American, and your cousin is a beautiful specimen' (ibid.: 80).

James underlines this play with characters as types by refusing to name the characters for almost the whole of Chapter 1. Daniel Touchett is simply 'the old man', and Ralph 'the ugly young man', or they are 'the father' and 'the son'. Lord Warburton is named as such, but of course his name merely marks an outdated and transferable social function, not a fully incentivised individual. Like all male aristocrats, Warburton's title might equally refer to any man in his line in any generation before or after him. He is a cypher. As the lens homes in on this group and the action moves forward, Ralph and his father Daniel finally acquire the name Touchett only at the close of the first chapter.

This play with characters as specimens harks back to Daniel Deronda's supposed lack of embodied characterisation, as Ralph's conspicuous habit of putting his hands in his pockets echoes Daniel's constant play with his collar (ibid.: 275; 316; 322). This continual self-conscious marking of Ralph's body counterpoises his Gothic disembodiment at the novel's climactic moments. It also renders Ralph's baffled lack of action within an array of characters whose degree of masculinity marks the successful or unsuccessful embodiment of national character. Isabel Archer and Daniel Touchett throw the question specifically back on gender, realism and the romance plot in Chapter 6. Isabel reflects that she doesn't think the English are very nice to girls, since they are never very nice to them 'in the novels'. Daniel Touchett replies:

> I don't know about the novels [. . .] I believe the novels have a great deal of ability, but I don't suppose they are very accurate. We once had a lady who wrote novels staying here; she was a friend of Ralph's and he asked her down. She was very positive, very positive; but she was not the sort of person that you could depend on her testimony. (ibid.: 53)

It is not only femininity here that renders people cyphers, it is gendered social form in total. Tuberculosis sets Ralph outside of this, outside of masculinity, allowing him to realise psychological personhood. He is marked early on as materially sterile, in terms of the reproduction of both children and capital. While Ralph is 'cheerful' and 'interested' in spite of his illness, his tubercular character is formed more by lassitude than by the sense of enervation Eliot uses to portray Mordecai Cohen. He tells his father early on, that 'it is impossible for a man in my state of health to spend much money' and that 'people in an advanced state of pulmonary weakness had better not marry at all' (ibid.: 168; 169). With this argument he diverts half of his inherited wealth and all of his active agency to Isabel, thus upsetting both the order of gender within the plot and the formal structure of the novel within which it makes meaning.

While passivity is a product of illness for Ralph, in Warburton it is a sense of aristocratic anomie in the face of a changing social political landscape, and in Osmond a suspicious cosmopolitan decadence which some critics have read as a specific reference to Wilde (for example, Eastham 2008). Ralph's reflections on lassitude and positive action are a frame for the work's self-reflexive performance of masculine narration and characterisation in the realist novel. Stepping outside of its own space to comment on the rules of its construction, this generic portrait of 'a lady' both undoes its representation of the real and promises a more real representation than other novels. As the novel moves to Italy and to Isabel's marriage to Osmond, the techniques of realism are temporarily set aside. James moves back and forth between the established free indirect style of the realist novel and a more radically subjective imprisonment in consciousness. In the July *Macmillan's* instalment, the latter reaches its fullest expression in Chapter 41 (42 in volume editions), where the reader is enclosed entirely in Isabel's consciousness and almost no action occurs.

In Chapter 5, the reader is carried into Ralph's consciousness and he emerges as the novel's focaliser, what James called a 'reflector' character. Absent for much of the action of the novel, he nevertheless forms our sympathies and our narrative desires. As Katherine V. Snyder puts it, James' reflector characters 'provide an off-center perspective on the novel's main characters and action. They also vicariously center themselves in another character or characters. They are, one might say, "off-centers of consciousness"' (Snyder 1999: 85). Chapter 5 delivers the original story of Ralph's consumption in a remarkable passage which splits his subjectivity into two distinct orders of third-person narration. At first a unified narrator focalises Ralph's thoughts, then these thoughts themselves split from Ralph, who sees himself in the third person. Ralph must take care of 'his unattractive *protégé*', himself (James 1997: 37). He winters abroad and generally takes up the life of an invalid, which is presented to us in terms of passive and active modes of existence:

> A certain fund of indolence that he possessed came to his aid to help reconcile him to doing nothing; for at the best he was too ill for anything but a passive life. As he said to himself, there was really nothing he had wanted very much to do, so that he had given up nothing. At present, however, the perfume of forbidden fruit seemed occasionally to float past him, to remind him that the finest pleasures in life are to be found in the world of action. (ibid.: 37)

Ralph's illness, conflated with the novel's narrative perspective, is first the condition of his passive role as spectator. As Madame Merle reflects, Ralph's illness is 'a kind of intellectual advantage; it absolved him from all professional and official emotions and left him the luxury of being simply personal' (ibid.: 312). This quality of being an individual, rather than a 'specimen' or cypher, forms a pointed contrast to Isabel's position. Ralph's radically subjective quality is specifically related to Romanticism when Ralph arrives at Rome to lie at the brink of Keatsian death.

A decadent dilettantism troubles the English characters from the outset. In the opening chapter, Ralph and Warburton joke about Warburton's *ennui*, and Isabel's several suitors are characterised chiefly by their attitudes to the productive life of action. The novel sets up its masculine characterisations in terms of positivist action and Romantic lassitude, and these are written along the axis of masculine national identity, from the energy of the new republic to the disintegrating power of European monarchy. Warburton only finds redemption once he devotes his radical principles to parliamentary reform. Isabel reflects that 'British politics have cured him' of his purposeless lassitude (ibid.: 355). The tubercular Ralph Touchett with his national hybridity, permeable body and dissolute character, stands at the limit of these relations. Both an idealistic Tory and a young aesthete in a brown velvet jacket, he is an American 'infected' by the disease of European over-refinement. Almost the whole of Chapter 10 contrasts Ralph's alienated over-sophistication with Henrietta's forthright and ethical engagement. Later appealed to with regard to the danger in which Isabel stands, he cannot construe the open simplicity of Henrietta's request because he lacks the 'purity of mind'. His 'fault was that he was not quite sure that anything in the world could really be as candid as this request of Miss Stackpole's appeared' (ibid.: 112). Europe has rendered Ralph incapable of simple, open constructions. While Ralph's consumption is clearly used to strip him of sexual agency, it is also the vehicle through which James renders the excessive finitude which focuses his critique of national character. Trapped between national sympathies, Ralph recognises the power of action, but can only achieve it vicariously through Isabel.

I have noted elsewhere the disavowed relation between James' experiments in this period and generic techniques developed in more popular forms of the novel (Miller 2013). As the novel draws to a close, its occasional Gothic eruptions (Pansy's imprisonment, Isabel's architectural interiority, the empty London house, the Gardencourt ghost) come to the fore and dominate a plot in which Ralph's consumption becomes both instrumental, allowing Isabel to leave Rome, and generic, moving the novel into pronounced sentimentality at its close. Within this shift, Ralph's consumptive body emerges as a Gothic vehicle. The novel's sympathetic characters all conspire to get Ralph back to Gardencourt for an English, rather than a Roman death, and Isabel follows him to a house now funereal and haunted.

Early in the novel, he is a superfluous, sad spectator who takes 'his entertainment wherever he could find it' (James 1997: 233).

In the end this spectatorship, as a kind of displaced subjectivity, is all that animates his body. 'What kept Ralph alive was simply the fact that he had not yet seen enough of his cousin; he was not yet satisfied' (ibid.: 365). Increasingly, as the novel draws to a close, the watching becomes a spiritual, and eventually a ghostly one. For Isabel, his visits are 'a lamp in the darkness; for the hour that she sat with him her spirit rose' (ibid.: 400). He is her 'apostle of freedom' (ibid.: 425). As Ralph fades, his realised disembodiment enables a spiritual transference something like that between Daniel and Mordecai. It is impossible to keep his spirit from Isabel's, however hard Osmond may try.

In Chapter 5, during one of Ralph's first conversations with Isabel, he tells her that no-one can see Gardencourt's ghost until they have suffered greatly. In the final chapter Ralph is revealed as that very ghost, appearing to her in another room at the instant of his death, 'a dim, hovering figure in the dimness of the room. She stared a moment; she saw his white face—his kind eyes; then she saw that there was nothing' (ibid.: 533). In an inversion of the usual pattern, Isabel goes from Ralph's ghost to the solid fact of his dead body in the sick room. This death scene draws on the long tradition of tubercular deaths in Victorian fiction, and James deploys the well-recognised markers, developed in popular fictions both sentimental and Gothic.

In their final conversation, Ralph tells Isabel that he is no longer of any use but to give the 'sensation of life' to others (ibid.: 529). We might read this specular sterility as the sign of the death of the narrator in the face of radically psychological fiction. Characters are now conscious interiorities rather than types; in Chapter 41 Ralph is no longer necessary and James can stage his rejection of the realist focaliser. In doing so he picks up other generic conventions, chiefly those orders of fragmented, multiple, intersubjective consciousness developed in the popular Gothic.

In terms of the novel's many gender subversions, Ralph's tubercular body is the standpoint for a critique of masculine action, acquisition and purely social, exterior being. These subversions are more multiple and complex than a mere reading by substitution of the desires of the author can account for. In her *Bachelors, Manhood and the Novel*, Katherine V. Snyder (1999) reads Ralph Touchett as one of a group of bachelor narrators in whom we can trace the stylistic move into Modernism. Her significant intervention acknowledges queer desires and their repression but argues for a polymorphous, rather than equivalent, reading of masculinity and masculine sexuality. She argues that, as well as what we think of as an emerging gay male subjectivity, 'the intrasubjective and intersubjective relations by which these figures define themselves and each other also signal [...] the presence of the perverse within what has conventionally been demarcated as normative masculinity' (Snyder 1999: 5). We might also place Mordecai Cohen, a bachelor, and even the marrying but racialised Daniel Deronda, in Snyder's group of 'threshold figures who marked the permeable boundaries that separate domesticity, normative manhood, and high cultural status, from what was defined as extrinsic to these realms' (ibid.: 7). The tubercular body, and its associations with both aesthetic vision and national leakage, locate this threshold in a dissenting physicality with a history stretching back to the second generation of Romantic poets.

We know that these anxious associations are alive and well into the 1880s, because we can read them, remarkably unchanged, in the periodical literature. Harry Quilter's 'The New Renaissance; or, the Gospel of Intensity', appearing in *Macmillan's* one month before the first chapters of *Portrait*, rails against the detriment to the national health caused by the contagious influence of pre-Raphaelitism. Quilter's critique, like Lockhart's sixty-three years earlier, associates radically subjective vision, homosociality, sickly bodies and democratised aesthetics. Together, these form, 'a source of corruption which cannot be too soon fully understood' (Quilter 1880: 392).

Both *Daniel Deronda* and *The Portrait of a Lady* contain pointed critiques of British masculinity as imperialist and rigidly positivist. Tubercular male characters locate this critique in their aesthetic sensibility and negative capability and in the association of these capacities with the dissident masculine body. They are the inheritors of a tradition of Romantic dissent from modernity, tying subversive masculine embodiment to subversion of realist orthodoxy.

These characters exist at the Gothic limit of the body, troubling the muscular and active masculinity of the age through a constant suggestion of disembodiment and escaping spirit. The nervous, over-refined sensibility associated with pulmonary tuberculosis, and the special relations of the sick-room allow for a continuation of the homosocial physicality already evident in descriptions of Keats' final days in Rome. Together these associations work against the idea of restrained will, positivist relation and radical exteriority which uphold the imperial self. Tubercular male bodies, permeable, Gothic and liminal, figure a diffuse counter-current to the robust masculinity of late-Victorian era. The structure of feeling which surrounds them allows both Eliot and James to stage their particular interventions in orders of gender, nation and realism.

Works Cited

Bakhtin, M. M. (1986), 'The *Bildungsroman* and its Significance in the History of Realism (Towards a Historical Typology of the Novel)', trans. V. W. McGee, in C. Emerson and M. Holquist (eds), *Speech Genres and Other Late Essays*, Austin: University of Texas Press, pp. 10–59.

Bewell, A. (2003), *Romanticism and Colonial Disease*, Baltimore: Johns Hopkins University Press.

Byrne, K. (2011), *Tuberculosis and the Victorian Literary Imagination*, Cambridge: Cambridge University Press.

'Daniel Deronda' (1876), *Edinburgh Review* (October), pp. 442–70.

'Daniel Deronda, Book V' (1876), *Examiner* (June), pp. 632–3.

Eastman, A. (2008), '"Master of Irony": Henry James, Transatlantic *Bildung* and the Critique of Aestheticism', *Symbiosis*, 12: 2 (October), pp. 167–90.

Eliot, G. [1876] (1892), *Daniel Deronda*, Edinburgh: Blackwood.

Francillon, R. E. (1876), 'George Eliot's First Romance', *The Gentleman's Magazine* (October), pp. 411–27.

Gilman, S. (1995), *Health and Illness: Images of Difference*, London: Reaktion.

Gissing, G. [1891] (2016), *New Grub Street*, Oxford: Oxford World's Classics, Oxford University Press.

Gordon, L. (2012), *Henry James: His Women and His Art*, London: Virago.

Jacobs, J. (1877), 'Mordecai: A Protest against the Critics', *Macmillan's* (June), pp. 101–11.

James, H. (1876), 'Daniel Deronda: A Conversation', *Atlantic Monthly* (December), pp. 684–94.

James, H. [1881] (1997), *The Portrait of a Lady*, London: Penguin.

Leavis, F. R. (1948), *The Great Tradition*, London: Chatto and Windus.

'Life, Letters and Literary Remains of John Keats' (1848), *Athenaeum* (August), pp. 824–7.

'Life, Letters and Literary Remains of John Keats' (1848), *Critic of Books, Society, Pictures, Music and Decorative Arts* (November), pp. 425–7.

Lockhart, J. G. (1817), 'On the Cockney School of Poetry', *Blackwood's Edinburgh Magazine* (October), pp. 38–41.

Martin, C. A. (1994), *George Eliot's Serial Fiction*, Columbus: Ohio State University Press.

Masson, D. (1860), 'The Life and Poetry of John Keats', *Macmillan's* (November), pp. 1–16.

Miller, M. (2013), *Feminine Subjects in Masculine Fiction: Modernity, Will and Desire, 1870–1910*, New York: Palgrave Macmillan.

'Mordecai' (1876), *Examiner* (5 August), pp. 885–6.

'New Publications in March, with an Historical and Critical Proemium' (1817), *Monthly Magazine, or, British Register* (April), pp. 245–8.

Novak, D. (2004), '"Literary Photographs" and the Jewish Body in *Daniel Deronda*', *Representations*, 85: 1 (Autumn), pp. 58–97.
'Novels of the Week' (1876), *Athenaeum* (July), pp. 14–15.
'*Poems*, by John Keats' (1817), *Eclectic Review* (September), pp. 267–75.
Quilter, H. (1880), 'The New Renaissance; or, The Gospel of Intensity', *Macmillan's* (September), pp. 391–400.
Sontag, S. (1990), *Illness as a Metaphor; and AIDS and its Metaphors*, New York: Picador.
Snyder, K. V. (1999), *Bachelors, Manhood and the Novel, 1850–1925*, Cambridge: Cambridge University Press.
Vrettos, A. (1995), *Somatic Fictions: Imagining Illness in Victorian Culture*, Redwood City, CA: Stanford University Press.
Watt, I. (1957), *The Rise of the Novel: Studies in Defoe, Richardson and Fielding*, London: Chatto and Windus.
Young, T. (1815), *Historical Treatise on Consumptive Diseases*, London: Underwood and Callow.

Chapter 6

Monstrous Masculinities from the Macaroni to Mr Hyde: Reading the Gothic 'Gentleman'

Alison Younger

> Come trollops and slatterns
> Cock't hats and white aprons
> This best our modesty suits
> For why should not we
> In dress be as free
> As Hogs' Norton squires in boots?
>
> (Jerrold 1911: 92)

Citing Kelly Hurley in her 2004 text, *Fashioning Gothic Bodies*, Catherine Spooner suggests:

> The province of nineteenth-century human sciences was after all very like that of the earlier Gothic novel: the pre-Victorian Gothic provided a space wherein to explore phenomena at the borders of human identity and culture – insanity, criminality, barbarity, sexual perversion – precisely those phenomena which came under the purview of social medicine in later decades. (Spooner 2004: 87)

While Hurley draws a timeline between Romantic Gothic and late Victorian Gothic via scientific and pseudo-scientific means, Spooner augments this by focusing on 'another equally discriminating gaze: that of fashion' (ibid.: 87). Fashion, as she argues, finds its apogee in the discourse of the dandy, a 'monstrous spectacle' who 'seems to reproduce a Jekyll-and-Hyde dualism whereby public self and monstrous self are inextricably linked' (ibid.: 87). Such a comment deserves to be unpicked as it points to what might be defined as a crisis of masculinity, spanning the nineteenth century, wherein deviant masculinities (such as the dandy), are coded as effeminate, feminine or freakish in heteronormative discourses. In opposition and stark contrast to these lesser masculinities, the discourse of the gentleman was both a social ethos and a badge of honour based on a Greco-Roman ideal which brooked no blemish, parody or imitation. The gentleman embodied civic humanism, independence and martial attributes as masculine virtues. As Lawrence E. Klein observes:

> Civic humanism was preoccupied with the threat of decay and dissolution of the body politic as well as with the conditions for its survival and health. Its view of history was cyclic: states moved from savage to more advanced stages, but following loss of virtue or corruption they would become effeminate, degenerate and decline. Morality was seen as the way to achieve political stability, while moral failures (corruption, effeminacy and selfishness) were seen as threats to the welfare of the state. Civic virtues such as courage, frugality, and military prowess were pitted against such vices as luxury, corruption, cowardice and 'feminine' characteristics (such as softness and sensuousness). (Klein 1989: 593)

The ideal (labelled the Corinthian), based on representations of masculinity in classical art and literature was determined, particularly in the early nineteenth century, by status, wealth and breeding. 'Manliness' was the prerogative of men of standing, 'biologically predisposed to superiority, hardiness, self-discipline' (Gilmour 1990: 220) while behaviours that were coded as feminine and effeminate were considered as moral failures and a form of self-degradation and abasement which was incommensurable with English national character. This is summarised in an 1867 tract by Samuel Roberts Wells, who uses a combination of culturally accepted pseudo-sciences including physiognomy, phrenology and anatomy to classify the English gentleman, thus:

> The English cranium is large [. . .] brain is power; and the more you have of it the better, provided it be in the right place and you have the physical system to sustain it (as the Englishman has).
> Physically the Englishman is broadly built, stout, and amply developed throughout. He has a full chest, a good stomach, an active liver, a large heart. His digestion, circulation and nutrition are perfect; and the supply of vitality is always equal to the demand. He is hale, rosy and rotund.
> Mentally he is proud, self-sufficient, combative, ambitious, energetic, aggressive, persevering, practical, acquisitive, economical, cautious, secretive, firm, affectionate, benevolent and religious. He is often rough in his manners and bluff in his speech but is at heart kind and tender. (Wells 1867: 399)

This dashing band of brothers was further distinguished by their clothing, which, according to the pamphleteer Charles Tilt, was the outward expression of a gentleman's character. As he writes:

> When we speak of excellence in dress we do not mean richness of clothing, nor manifested elaborations. Profusion of ornaments, rings, charms, etc [. . .] are in bad taste. Faultless propriety, perfect harmony, and a refined simplicity, – these are the charms which always fascinate [. . .] A gentleman will always be tastefully dressed [. . .] avoiding foppery on the one hand and carelessness on the other. (Tilt 1837: 13)

Notably the focus is on an unadorned elegance and refined simplicity that shuns the gaudy, the outré and the ostentatious. Here, clothing and conduct combine to indicate social power, privilege and elite status. In what later became known as 'the great masculine renunciation' nineteenth-century men of the upper ranks sought, as Susan Kingsley Kent observes: 'to demonstrate their public virtue by deploying a modest and sober style [. . .] By adopting a style of "noble simplicity" and denouncing the world of fashion and luxury, gentlemen trumpeted their virtue, asserting their claims to social, moral, and political leadership' (Kent 1999: 62). Luxury, as David Kuchta observes was seen 'as the vice of middle-class upstarts who ambitiously lived above their social station' (Kuchta 1996: 63). The ideal was an 'inconspicuous consumption' and sartorial sobriety. In light of this, the haute couture, torturous toilettes, ornamentation and ostentation of 'dandies' and 'macaronis' (also known as 'swells' and 'gents') caused an affront to the English gentlemanly classes.

In what follows I examine the ways in which the 'gentleman's' body was viewed as emblematic and constitutive of heterosexual, national masculine values, and how any transgression from these values rendered the transgressor as deviant, perverse, monstrous or less than a man. As Barbara Creed suggests: 'The male body [. . .] is represented as monstrous only when it assumes characteristics that are associated with the female body; his monstrosity is defined by the characteristics that make him not male' (Creed 1993: 118). In common with scholars such as Creed, Elaine Showalter, John Tosh and Michael Roper I argue that encounters with fear shaped the way 'degenerate' or deviant masculinity was constructed in the nineteenth century, looking at how writers during the period capitalised on fear and paradigmatic notions of monstrosity to represent masculinity and masculine anxieties in Gothic texts.

Beginning with a brief examination of heteronormativity and degenerate masculinities at the start of the century, I move on to non-literary texts, such as dictionaries of slang, to examine dialogues of the male body from the excessively masculine sporting Corinthian of the late eighteenth and early nineteenth century (latterly the Muscular Christian), to the Decadent dandy of the fin de siècle, as grotesque and derivative parodies of the English gentleman. Referring to two iconic *fin de siècle* novels: Robert Louis Stevenson's *The Strange Case of Dr Jekyll and Hyde* (1886) and Oscar Wilde's *The Picture of Dorian Gray* (1890), I discuss the redefinition and degeneration of the gentlemanly ideal during the nineteenth century and suggest that, irrespective of the relative levels of masculinity or machismo displayed by the central characters in these novels, the monstrous protagonists are incapable of living up to an ideal model of virility (with its cultural associations of bravery, courage and morality) which constituted gentlemanly conduct.

Queering the Pitch

One year before Robert Louis Stevenson published *Dr Jekyll and Mr Hyde* in 1886, the Criminal Law Amendment Act included a clause introduced by Henry Labouchère which legislated against gross indecency between men, whether in 'public or private'. Prior to this, sodomy laws (although capital) were difficult to enforce as penetrative sex had to be proven. The Labouchère Amendment, as it came to be known, signalled 'a marked shift in the codes of manliness' during the latter half of the nineteenth century' (Roper and Tosh 1991: 3), and in what was permissible within codified definitions of masculinity. As the century drew to a close, masculinities became multiple, sexual preferences became pathologised and male homosexuality, along with being criminalised, was labelled deviant by sexologists such as Richard von Krafft-Ebing and Havelock Ellis. This resulted in what Eve Kosofsky Sedgwick describes as 'Homosexual Panic' in *The Coherence of Gothic Conventions* (1986). Unsurprisingly, the Gothic literature of the period, focused as it was on the deviant, the uncanny and the perverse, made connections between monstrous and threatening homoerotic desires. As Harry Benshoff suggests, these *fin de siècle* works were 'even more explicit than their [Gothic] predecessors regarding the conflation of the monstrous with some form of queer sexuality' (Benshoff 1997: 19). Simultaneously the effete and death-obsessed

Decadents with their pallor, delicacy and dandified dress were seen as a threatening affront to English manliness.

The illicit and illegal practices associated with male homosexuality combined with the social anxieties it provoked in the late Victorian period rendered the subject 'Gothic' and 'queer', in the sense that: 'to be queer, when taken outside of the sexual connotations of that term, is to be different' (Hughes and Smith 2009: 3). Continuing with this thread Hughes and Smith argue: 'to be queer is to be different, yet it is also unavoidably associated with the non-queer, the normative which, though it implicitly represses through the mechanisms of conformist culture, may yet serve as a catalyst for liberation' (ibid.: 3). The two states exist in 'reciprocal tension' (ibid.: 3), much like the reciprocal tension between the philanthropic idealist, Dr Henry Jekyll, and his troglodytic, monstrous alter-ego, Edward Hyde.

The Grotesque Gent

Edward Hyde is an enigma. He cannot be identified by his corporeality or appearance. As Stevenson has Gabriel Utterson recall:

> He is not easy to describe. There is something wrong with his appearance, something displeasing; something downright detestable. I never saw a man I so disliked and yet I scarcely know why. He must be deformed somewhere; he gives a strong feeling of deformity, although I couldn't specify the point. He is an extraordinary looking man and yet I can really name nothing out of the way [. . .] And it's not for want of memory, for I declare I can see him this moment. (Stevenson 2004: 7)

As Richard Dury points out 'of the socially condemned activities that Hyde is associated with, veiled allusions to homosexuality are particularly frequent. They are also appropriate since this hidden vice was often referred to indirectly as "unspeakable" (so resembling the indescribable Hyde)' (Dury 2004: xxx). These hidden vices and the all-male cast of gentlemanly flâneurs, along with Hyde's unspecified nocturnal routines, lead critics such as Dury and Elaine Showalter to suggest that Hyde is a metaphor for sexual and homosexual repression and that the novella 'can most persuasively be read as a fable of fin-de-siècle homosexual panic, the discovery and resistance of the homosexual self' (Showalter 1990: 107).

> The Victorian homosexual world had evolved into a secret but active subculture, with its own language, styles, practices, and meeting places. For most middle-class inhabitants of this world, homosexuality represented a double life, in which a respectable daytime world often involving marriage and family, existed alongside a night world of homoeroticism. (ibid.: 106)

Thus, Hyde can be viewed as a physical manifestation of Jekyll's double life – his homosexuality. It is a plausible argument, prefaced on the notion that Hyde does not exist as a separate entity to Jekyll, but rather as a hidden self; a necessity during a time when 'deviance from sexual norms was identified as both a symptom and a cause of social degeneration, so that by posing a challenge to traditional gender roles, liminal subjects like the homosexual [...] were seen as causes of social unrest and potential threats to national health' (Hurley 2002: 199).

If, as some scholars have suggested, Hyde represents unrepressed homosexual desire, Jekyll can be seen as a hypocrite, hiding behind respectable, gentlemanly façade, but concealing desires that are largely unacknowledged, unidentified and unacceptable. This is evident in the full statement wherein he writes 'it came about that I concealed my pleasures; and that when I reached years of reflection, and began to look round me and take stock of my progress and position in the world, I stood already committed to a profound duplicity of life' (Stevenson 2004: 58). Such duplicity is particularly interesting in relation to Jekyll's admission that:

> when I wore the semblance of Edward Hyde, none could come near to me at first without a visible misgiving of the flesh. This, as I take it, was because all human beings, as we meet them, are commingled out of good and evil: and Edward Hyde, alone in the ranks of mankind, was pure evil. (ibid.: 51)

It is evident then, that Jekyll has an awareness and a consciousness of his other self that is quite deliberate: he puts on a semblance. Elsewhere it is noted that Jekyll and Hyde's handwriting is 'almost identical' and bears a 'singular resemblance' (ibid.: 28). Despite this, the figure of Hyde is degenerate: physically inelegant, ugly (though indescribable) and degraded in his habits. A gentleman, to paraphrase Elizabeth Foyster, was measured by the prized attributes of controlled emotions and taciturnity (traits that can, for the most part, be associated with Henry Jekyll). As Foyster suggests: 'for those who aspired to be regarded as gentlemen, angry behaviour was to be avoided at all costs' (Foyster 1999: 62). If we follow this argument, Hyde's homicidal rage debars him from the gentlemanly fraternity. Doubtless, he is conventionally masculine. He has the machismo of the pugilistic bruiser, but his roaring defiance, and lack of restraint and decorum are the opposite of what was defined as gentlemanly fortitude. In the language of the Fancy (the boxing fraternity), he is a 'mug-miller' – a churlish, bare-knuckle brawler – who is free of self-restraint in all things, and consorts for the most part with low company in scandalous settings. He is unequivocally not a gentleman. He is a post-Darwinian, barbaric and atavistic nightmare compared to the polite, decent and distinguished gentleman that Jekyll presents himself to be.

Yet, some scholars argue that Jekyll and Hyde have more that unites them than that which divides them. For example, while Jekyll resides in an affluent West End residence, furnished with costly cabinets of oak, Hyde lives in Soho, in what Stephen Arata describes as 'surprisingly well-appointed rooms', 'furnished with luxury and good taste' (Arata 1995: 35). Arata also notes, 'Hyde's palate for wine is discriminating, his plate is of silver, his napery elegant, Art adorns his walls', while 'carpets of many plies and agreeable in colour' cover his floor. This is not a savage's den, but 'the retreat of a cultivated gentleman' (ibid.: 35). While there is no doubt that Hyde is far from destitute, he is equally far from being a cultivated gentleman according to nineteenth-century definitions. He is violent, irresponsible and decayed in morals. His world revolves around uncontrolled hedonism, more in keeping with the received image of the Decadent than the demonstrably brave and neo-chivalric Victorian gentleman as espoused in self-help manuals such as Samuel Smiles' *Self Help: With Illustrations of Conduct and Perseverance* (1859). Undoubtedly, he has strength and physical prowess, but it appears he is devoid of the conventional qualities of reason, logic and rationality, and his implied masturbatory tendencies suggest what the sexologists described as a degenerate psychopathology. Notably also, he is without that basic requisite of honour pretended by the English gentleman, in that he uses weapons to belabour and kill his opponents. Not only was this dishonourable, this behaviour was also considered 'terribly un-British', as the English gentleman was expected to fight fist to fist (without weapons), a point of honour which the *Annals of Sporting and Fancy* (1823) colourfully describe thus: 'John Bull manfully enters the lists and uses those weapons only which nature has given him, and with which indeed he seems gifted in a manner superior to all the world' (*The Annals of Sporting and Fancy Gazette*, vol. 3 (1823): 11–12). The use of weapons was considered caddish behaviour usually associated with foreigners. For example, in a popular song much chanted during the Peninsular War (1807–14), the propensity of the French to use pistols was roundly mocked. As for Mediterranean peoples:

> Italians stab their friends behind,
> In darkest shades of night;
> But Britons they are bold and kind,
> And box their friends by light. ('A Boxing We Will Go', *Sporting Magazine*, vol. 38 (1811): 294)

Britons are therefore associated with courtesy, fair-mindedness and magnanimity, compared to the undignified slyness and savagery of non-Britons. Fisticuffs was a serious business in the discourse of the gentleman and was governed by the Broughton Rules, which included: 'that no person is to hit his adversary when he is down, or seize him by the ham, the breeches, or any part below the waist; a man on his knees to be reckoned down' (Gee 1998: 14). Trampling on elderly men and children was such low, caddish and ungentlemanly behaviour that it simply didn't appear in the pamphlets relating to the Fancy.

Hyde, then, despite his Herculean strength, is not a gentleman (at least by British standards). Indeed, in his appearance, his dress and his behaviours, he could be described as a 'gent' or sham 'swell': a counterfeit gentleman in his appropriation and emulation of gentility. The term, as Peter Bailey points out 'carried an early suggestion of the bogus [. . .] denoting a class of pickpockets who dressed in style to escape detection as they mingled with their fashionable victims' (Bailey 2003: 109). The gent (as opposed to the gentleman) was viewed as a disreputable, vulgar fraud who frequented less salubrious establishments and aped the manners and mien of the gentleman. Theirs was a 'spurious gentility' (ibid.: 109) according to Bailey, and because of this inauthenticity they were mercilessly mocked as upstarts and phonies. For example, Albert Smith's *The Natural History of the Gent* (1847) lampoons them as an offensive body of blackguards. His suggestion is to establish a 'Court of Propriety' at which gents can be convicted of misdemeanours against '*comme il faut*' (Smith 1847: 103). After their extinction (which is devoutly to be wished), their effigies would be displayed along with ibises, *scarabaei* and taxidermy specimens at the Egyptian room of the British Museum' (ibid.: 104).

While the purpose is no doubt satirical, *The Natural History of the Gent* and similar publications highlight how Victorian cultural elites represented the lower middle class as risible, dangerous (as in the case of Edward Hyde), vulgar and pitiable. These were the people who flocked to buy shilling shockers, penny dreadfuls and Gothic tomes, such as Stevenson's novella. Devoid of authenticity, the gent was considered a dangerous and disruptive influence by cultural and economic elites. An exemplar of the masses, the gent ignited class-based concerns about infecting his cultural betters (authentic, aristocratic gentlemen) with his passion for frivolous and debauched pursuits such as music hall, consorting with prostitutes, smoking, clandestine drinking and frequenting gaming houses and haunts of ill repute. The real danger was in his ability to ape the aristocracy without the character, breeding or intelligence with which they prided themselves. A crucible of anxieties, the gent, with the assistance of skilful tailoring, could look the part, but beneath his surface lustre he was a dangerous moral contaminant, much like Edward Hyde.

The *Homme com il faut*

As stated earlier, the idea of what constituted a gentleman had long predated the publication of Stevenson's novella, and definitions of the same appeared in popular dictionaries and conduct manuals. For example, in 1823, John Badcock (pseudonymously known as John Bee) defined 'the Gentleman' in his *Slang: A Dictionary of the Turf, the Ring, the Chase, the Pit, of Bon-ton*:

> <u>Gentleman</u>: gamblers denominate themselves gent. if not Esq. even when detected and had up; but the bills of indictment dub them labourers, every man, yea, labourers at the treadmill. Tailors are the most blameable of all tradesfolk; 'tis they who transform blackguards into gentlemen. Gentleman – he only is one, and 'a real gentleman' who spends his money upon those who bestow the distinction upon him; otherwise he must be so undeniably such a one, that none think of questioning the issue; none can be understood a true English gentleman by us who has not stored his mind with English lore, spells every word rightly, and is capable of forming a sane off-hand judgement upon every subject that may come upon the carpet. (See swell, Tulip, Corinthian) (Badcock 1823: 87)

Badcock's definition is illuminating not only because of the scorn it pours on those (such as Hyde) who ape 'the gentleman' (who are described as blackguards) but for the fact that tailors, 'the most blameable of all tradesfolk', are culpable of disguising the lowly classes as gentlemen by dressing them in gentlemanly attire. What it makes clear is what a gentleman is not: a gambler or one of the lower orders or working classes, despite the near alchemical skills of the tradesman tailor. Paradoxically, as we shall see, a gambler cannot be a gentleman, though a gentleman can be a gambler, providing it is done in the correct establishments and undertaken in a 'manly' way. What a gentleman is, according to Badcock, is one who is suitably educated in 'Englishness', and has genteel accomplishments such as grammatical skills and rhetorical *sprezzatura*, which allow him to converse on any subject, in any circumstance and in any setting.

It appears that in the first instance clothes make the man, as the visible marker of the gentleman is his luxurious, though not ostentatious garb. Clothes do not make the gentleman, though, as the 'well-dressed prig' or the 'seedy sordid knave' (both apt descriptions of Edward Hyde) are excluded from the gentlemanly mode (ibid.: 181). These egregious, tailor-aided charlatans lack the noble bearing and gentrified education and also the requisite grammatical and oratorical skills which mark the gentlemanly orders. Equally they have 'no souls', which hinders them from appreciating the sports of the turf and the ring – manly pursuits which the pro-boxing lobby argued were synonymous with patriotism and a sense of essential Englishness.

In terms of physical appearance, according to Badcock, the *Homme com il faut*, or 'man as he ought to be': 'must have 32 teeth, thick curly hair, and calves six inches diameter each. Around both ankles, placed across should measure the same' (ibid.: 111). Supposing that the gentleman was as 'a man ought to be', he should be strong, aesthetically pleasing, and symmetrical in form, virile, vigorous and agile. Moreover, as Revathi Krishnaswamy points out, the 'manly' form of the superlative English gentleman marked him as one of an elite fraternity which was based in part on the exclusion of those less physically endowed, and, therefore, less gentlemanly and indubitably less 'English': 'the ideal appearance of the English male (the tall, strong, clean-cut English man) specifically excluded those who were stunted, narrow-chested, excitable, easily wearied, or inefficient – qualities associated with women, the lower classes, Jews, Papists, Spaniards, the French, and colored peoples' (Krishnaswamy 2002: 292). If this list demarcates what an English gentleman was not, we can say by opposition what he was supposed to be: an upper-class, barrel-chested, well-nourished, mentally and physically robust, white male with boundless stamina, and, if Badcock is to be believed, all of his teeth and thick curly hair. Notably, all of these attributes are lacking in the characters of Edward Hyde, Dracula and Dorian Gray, for reasons of class, race and gender. Hyde is too churlish, Dracula too foreign and Dorian too Hellenistically effeminate to aspire to the lofty ideal of the English gentlemanly classes.

In the late eighteenth and early nineteenth centuries the English gentleman was a Teutonic ideal composed of latter-day chivalry, neo-Spartan virility and active physicality; attributes which can be sharply distinguished from the uninterested languor and fastidious sartorial elegance of the dandies and their eighteenth-century counterparts: the flamboyantly attired and elaborately bewigged 'Macaroni Club', thus named because of their taste for foreign foods and fashions. With the concomitant move towards inconspicuous consumption, the 'macaroni', attired in unpatriotic, continental garb, came to symbolise the luxurious profligacy of the *ancien régime* aristocrat. According to James Laver in his *Costume and Fashion: A Concise History*: 'They wore very thin shoes with enormous buckles made of gold, silver, pinchbeck or steel and set with real or imitation stones. They affected very large buttons on their coats. Their hats were extremely small, but their wigs were designed high on the head, prodigiously curled' (Laver 2002: 139). Defined thus in the 1911 text, *The Beaux and the Dandies*, the macaronis represented a deviant and grotesque form of masculinity that could be defined as Gothic in its excess:

> The macaronis, in fact went to the extreme in femininity, giving most of their attention to ribbons, laces and fashions – sitting amongst the ladies simpering, mincing, sniffing at scent bottles. They made a cult of inane frivolity and regarded a curl awry as of more importance than a life in jeopardy. They carried muffs or fans [...] Long canes hung with silver or gold tassels were essential to their equipment, as also gilt scent bottles, dainty gloves and jewelled spying glasses, sometimes set at the top of a cane, through which to ogle women – the ogling being of a distinctly bold and forward character. Their conversation was of embroidered waistcoats, worked stockings, patterns from abroad, described with an accompaniment of French phrases and mincing oaths; and their love making was as unhealthy as the rest of their actions and habits. (Jerrold 1911: 178–9)

As Michele Cohen argues, these flamboyant and extravagant clothes and coiffures came to represent a 'dilemma of masculinity' (Cohen 2005: 567) in the late eighteenth century indicating, as Rauser suggests, an 'embrace of artifice, decadence, and the pursuit of pleasure'

(Rauser 2004:103). This made them the subject of repeated lampoons and satires, and resulted in them becoming the recipients of soubriquets such as 'rump riders', 'rubsters' and 'dancing girls'.

One such squib from George Alexander Stevens in his 1765 'Celebrated Lecture on Heads' suggested: 'grammarians are at a loss whether to rank them with the masculine or feminine, and therefore put them down as the Doubtful Gender' (Stevens 1765: 4). Later, a 1772 song entitled 'The macaroni: A New Song' characterised the ambiguous sexuality of the figure thus: 'His taper waist, so strait and long, / His spindle shanks, like pitchfork prong, / To what sex does the thing belong? / Tis call'd a macaroni' (cited in Eisenberg 1996: 9). Thus, the macaroni is mocked, not only as the antithesis of manliness, but also as being beyond codification, barely male and, as a result of his foreign-induced, modish effeminacy, an unnatural, monstrous and degenerate sodomite. Shape shifters and supposed sexual deviants, macaronis, like vampires, embody an ambiguity and unknowability which makes them a threatening conduit for social anxieties surrounding normative notions of masculinity. It is precisely the fact that they are unclassifiable that makes them troubling, paradoxical, and fundamentally grotesque and monstrous figures. As Jeffrey Jerome Cohen points out, monsters evoke anxiety precisely because they refuse to 'participate in the classificatory "order of things" [. . .] they are disturbing hybrids whose externally incoherent bodies resist attempts to include them in any systematic structuration' (Cohen 1996: 6). In short, their transformative and performative bodies mark them as boundary crossing, ontologically liminal beings who resist definition in a society which depends on absolutes and binarisms. Peter K. Garrett writes,

> This nightmare of a world where all transcendental support or guarantees of the intrinsic have disappeared may be the deepest terror of the nineteenth century Gothic, but it is also confronted by persistent reminders of dialogical possibilities that resist such reduction. (Garrett 2003: 27)

Besides their grotesquely outré fashions macaronis were beset with accusations that they engaged in 'feminine vices' such as slander, gossip and frivolity. Added to this, as a sub-culture they were known to frequent molly houses and to cross-dress as women during dancing and sexual intercourse (Edwards 2012: 45–6; Mackie 2009: 116–17; Senelick 1990: 50–1). In a period such as the *fin de siècle* which, at least on the surface, lauded 'Muscular Christianity' – 'an aggressive, robust, and activist masculinity [designed] – to create brave, true, and Christian men' (Mosse 1996: 49), it is unsurprising that these practices were pathologised and comprehended in terms of disease and degeneracy, and these feminised men with dubious libertine morals and embrangled gender identities were seen as both a national and a moral threat to British masculinity. As Valerie Steele points out, in the post-revolutionary period: 'modish male attire in England came to be associated with tyranny, political and moral corruption, and a "degenerate exotic effeminacy" of the aristocracy, while plainer and soberer dress became increasingly associated with bourgeois notions of "liberty, patriotism, virtue, enterprise, and manliness"' (Steele 1985: 52–3).

As the Tory-cum-radical William Cobbett counselled in 1829: 'Let your dress be as cheap as may be without shabbiness, for no-one with sense in skull will love or respect you on account of your fine or costly clothes' (Cobbett 1906: n.p.). In those more sober and stoical times, the macaroni came to be seen as the epitome of luxury and effeminacy in a country where an elegant uninterest in fashion was being lauded in aristocrats and the emergent middle classes alike. An arriviste, inauthentic social parvenu who haunted elegant assembly rooms and masquerade balls, the jigging, ambling and lisping macaroni in his modish continental fashions and powdered toupée, was considered a potential contaminant to British manliness and thus was satirised, caricatured and generally derided as effeminate or perverse. By the end of the nineteenth century, during a time when there was what Elaine Showalter describes as 'the crisis in masculinity' of the British *fin de siècle* (Showalter 1990: 17) the macaroni, and latterly the dandy, were viewed in one of two ways: risible, or more often, grotesque, threatening and irredeemably Gothic, as is evident in Oscar Wilde's *The Picture of Dorian Gray*.

Diabolical Dandies

As Catherine Spooner notes, 'For the Victorian public, artificiality was the dandies' greatest crime' (Spooner 2004: 94), because it blurred the distinction between the middle classes and the upper classes and thereby upset the moral order. Dandies were all about the surface, projecting an exterior that was lazy, aloof and self-indulgent, and these were qualities not associated with manly virtue.

The manly gentleman displayed his virility and virtue through membership of exclusive gentlemen's clubs, gaming houses and coteries wherein young sporting minded bucks ate, drank, debauched and often wagered considerable amounts of money on the outcome of a bout, the turn of a card or the tumble of a dice. Such men epitomised a new masculine ideal, based on the medieval concept of chivalry which had been revived in the late eighteenth century to replace the refinement and politeness of the early eighteenth-century notion of manliness which was defined in Charles Richardson's *Dictionary of the English Language* in 1837 as: strong, robust, courageous, with the courage, dignity, fortitude of, or belonging to a man. This was a manliness based on the knightly virtues of service and duty, on a sense of 'espirit de corps' and on the conventionally male attributes of competitiveness, combativeness, bravery, sporting accomplishment and honour. The manly man subdued his passions, or projected them into sporting activities. If he yielded to what was known as the acceptable vices of gambling, drinking and debauchery (activities which, paradoxically, carried connotations of manliness), the manly man would not indulge to excess, as this, it was thought, enfeebled the character. The manly man would be a model of strength, courage and firmness while eschewing the conventionally feminine attributes of vanity and shallowness associated with an interest in fashionable attire and beauty products. As the Earl of Chesterfield remarked in 1807, some men: 'poise themselves in such a dainty way, and paint and powder themselves to such an extent, that it induces us to believe that they are but Women in Men's clothing' (Chesterfield 1807: 30). To engage in such activities resulted in imprecations of effeminacy being levied at the perpetrator via biting satires and grotesque caricatures. An 1818 cartoon by George Cruikshank entitled 'Dandies Dressing', for example, shows a dandy undertaking his extravagant toilette, including the application of shoulder pads and stays along with false calves to feign a well-turned leg. 'D–n it,' says one lisping young blade, contorted by the size of his cravat, 'I really believe I must take off my cravat or I shall never get my trowsers on' (Jerrold 1911: 2).

The dandies emerged around 1815, flaunting their superficiality and supercilious sang froid in their promenades and daily fashion parades in Hyde Park (after which, it is worth noting, Edward Hyde is named), wherein they consorted with the nobility with whom they had ingratiated themselves. Emulating the aristocracy in matters of taste and lifestyle, the dandies elevated luxury, taste and connoisseurship to a fine art. First and foremost, as Thomas Carlyle argues in *Sartor Resartus*: 'the dandy is a clothes wearing Man; a Man whose trade, office and existence consists in the wearing of Clothes [. . .] where others dress to live, he lives to dress' (Jerrold 1911: 10). Like Dorian Gray, the dandy is a walking work of art and, as Felski points out, '[H]e can be perceived in aestheticist doctrine as quite useless, exalting appearance over essence, decoration over function, he voices a protest against prevailing bourgeois values that associate masculinity with rationality, industry, utility and thrift' (Felski 1991: 1096). This posturing reflects the philosophy and personal style of Walter Pater, which consisted of flamboyant, attention-seeking behaviour designed to create an aura of fascination and mystery. Wilde, also, was a mannered aesthete who had flowing locks, frock coats and stockings, in keeping with Victorian depictions of dandies and homosexuals. This 'New Hedonism', as Pater described it, is evident in Wilde's characterisation of the eponymous protagonist in *The Picture of Dorian Gray*. Indeed, under the influence of Lord Henry, Dorian becomes a symbol of the aesthetic propagated by Pater and Wilde:

> New Hedonism was to recreate life and to save it from that harsh uncomely puritanism that is having, in our own day, its curious revival. It was to have its service of the intellect, certainly, yet it was never to accept any theory or system that would involve the sacrifice of any mode of passionate experience. Its aim, indeed, was to be experience itself, and not the fruits of experience, sweet or bitter as they might be. Of the asceticism that deadens the senses, as of the vulgar profligacy that dulls them, it was to know nothing. But it was to teach man to concentrate himself upon the moments of a life that is itself but a moment. (Wilde 2011: 104–5)

By defying the moral, and embracing the sensual and hedonistic in all aspects of his life, Dorian 'assumes the office of art' (ibid.: 48) before he is ready for it, and with fatal effect.

The Picture of Dorian Gray is a complex, multivalent and multilayered text which has been read as a manifesto for aestheticism and decadence that champions the precedence of art; a social satire which attacks Victorian social hypocrisy; a reinterpretation of classical myth; and a psychobiography of Oscar Wilde as a transgressive, Dionysian rebel. Without doubt the Paterian myth of heedless hedonism features in the text along with questions regarding the moral and/or social function of art, liberally interspersed with the unforgettable witty aphorisms of the effete Lord Henry who lives to and for desire. Undoubtedly, as Sedgwick has argued (1985), the novel is suffused with over-determined homosexual codes (such as opium smoking, same-sex relationships and erotic art), which challenge and supplant Victorian patriarchal values such as heteronormativity, propriety and order. Perhaps, then, it is an allusive meditation on the love that dare not speak its name, or perhaps an ironic rendering of a moral message on the transience of beauty and/or pleasure. All of these themes make for plausible readings, which are easily supported by the text. The

Gothic multiplication of contrary narratives and meanings is echoed by the trope of the poisoned book that poisons Dorian. The narrative I want to pursue to conclude this chapter, though, is Dorian as dandy.

In his *New Physiognomy* published in 1867, Samuel Roberts Wells described the dandy thus:

> Gentlemen express their characters in displaying their equipage. The best minds – those which are free from eccentricity – display the best taste in dressing in such a way as not to attract particular attention. Vulgar minds – or those not cultivated – pile on the gew-gaws; cheap jew-ellery, frills, flounces and wriggle themselves through the dirty streets. (Wells 1867: 33)

The vulgar wriggling gait, here described, sees its apex, according to Wells, in the effete flouncing of the 'exquisite', who apes the 'attitudes of the ballroom and the stage': 'his brain is small; his mind narrow; his features pinched up and the whole miserably mean and contracted' (ibid.: 315). Furthermore, Wells suggests: 'his walk is simply Miss Nancyish', and he himself 'a bundle of egotism, vanity, deceit and pride; vulgar, pompous and bad' (ibid.). Gentlemanliness, by stark comparison, is described thus: 'in the walk of a tall, healthy, well-built perpendicular man both dignity and firmness may be seen' (ibid.: 317). Yet, as Ellen Moers points out, 'To the question – What is a gentleman? the dandy made the most frivolous answer conceivable. He was a gentleman – it was a visible fact – by virtue of a "certain something", a "je-ne-sais-quoi" which could not be defined – or denied' (Moers 1959: 17).

To the question, is Dorian Gray a dandy, the answer is a resounding yes – quintessentially so. Androgynous, elusive, sartorially flamboyant, with an exacting toilette and hedonistic disposition, Dorian, though dissipated and deviant, exudes savoir vivre. Like his creator, Dorian's raison d'être is art for art's sake and the pursuit of beauty in every aspect of life. There is a crucial moment of aesthetic self-knowledge which the main character experiences in front of his artistic likeness, which the painter has just finished. For the first time, Dorian sees himself as a dandy: a living work of art.

> Dorian made no answer, but passed listlessly in front of his picture, and turned towards it. When he saw it he drew back, and his cheeks flushed for a moment with pleasure. A look of joy came into his eyes, as if he had recognised himself for the first time. He stood there motionless and in wonder, dimly conscious that Hallward was speaking to him, but not catching the meaning of his words. The sense of his own beauty came on him like a revelation. He had never felt it before. (Wilde 2011: 20)

Here there is a lingering narcissistic joy, and a Paterian passion for beauty that is a precondition for art. But the story moves on from this to paint a disturbing picture of descent into dissolute living, while the lifeless picture absorbs all the ugliness that should adhere to the living man. The storyline panders to the Victorian equation of physical beauty with goodness, and it seems that the story is an extended refutation of this underlying moral assumption. Dorian is a self-fashioning peacock of startlingly beautiful and decorative appearance. This is made evident when Lord Henry Wotton first sets eyes on him:

> Lord Henry looked at him. Yes, he was certainly wonderfully handsome, with his finely-curved scarlet lips, his frank blue eyes, his crisp gold hair. There was something in his face that made one trust him at once. All the candour of youth was there, as well as all youth's passionate purity. One felt that he had kept himself unspotted from the world. No wonder Basil Hallward worshipped him. He was made to be worshipped. (ibid.: 90)

Dorian is a picture of pastoral innocence in his rosy-cheeked, youthful beauty, but underneath this exterior lies a terrible, supernatural and dangerous secret. He is as corrupt as he is seductive; a lethal and, as it transpires, fatal combination for those who fall prey to his charms. Having lived the credo of dandyism in his superficial sensation-seeking, façade and masquerade, Dorian is forced into the troubling terrain of his moral ugliness, and the macabre realisation that he is all form and no content. Indeed, like Hyde and Dracula, he is a pretence; a grotesque parody of a noble idea, sans mobility or standards: a monster.

To conclude, in the words of Hughes and Smith: 'Gothic has, in a sense, always been queer' (Hughes and Smith 2009: 1). As a genre it is elusive, self-conscious and camp, dangerous, morally pernicious and haunted by the spectres of bad taste and popular culture. In much the same way as the dandy and the macaroni, it is a conduit for anxieties about death, decay, degeneration, sexuality, status and nation. Within its pages, boundaries break and moribund notions of manliness become porous, resulting in monstrous masculinities fraught with anxiety. In showing masculinity to be mutable, these 'deviant', inassimilable fictional men in flux imperil classificatory certainties, bludgeoning the concept of the English gentleman to death in an East End Street, sucking its lifeblood each time the notion is reprised, and vampire-like, corrupting it with monstrous otherness. In this way, the concept of heteronormativity falters and the dandy, the unclassifiable symbol of Decadent manhood, turns a well-shod heel, and with impeccable timing, insouciance and *je-ne-sais-quoi*, bows out nonchalantly, dressed to the nines.

Works Cited

Arata, Stephen D. (1995), 'The Sedulous Ape: Atavism, Professionalism, and Stevenson's "Jekyll and Hyde"', *Criticism*, 37. 2 (Spring), pp. 233–59.
Badcock, J. (1823), *Slang: A Dictionary of the Turf, the Ring, the Chase, the Pit, of Bon-ton, and the Varieties of Life, Forming the Completest and Most Authentic Lexicon Balatronicum hitherto Offered to the Notice of the Sporting World . . . Interspersed with Anecdotes and Whimsies . . .* London: printed for T. Hughes.
Bailey, Peter (2003), *Popular Culture and Performance in the Victorian City*, Cambridge: Cambridge University Press.
Benshoff, H. M. (1997), *Monsters in the Closet: Homosexuality and the Horror Film*, Manchester: Manchester University Press.
Botting, F. (1996), *Gothic*, London and New York: Routledge.
Chesterfield, Earl of (1807), *The Art of Pleasing: or Requisite Qualities in a Youth to be Loved and Held in High Esteem in the World*.
Cobbett, W. [1829] (1906), *Advice to Young Men*, available at: <https://archive.org/stream/cobbettsadvicet00cobbgoog/cobbettsadvicet00cobbgoog_djvu.txt > [accessed 30 May 2017].
Cohen, J. J. (1996), 'Monster Culture: Seven Theses' in Jeffrey Jerome Cohen (ed.), *Monster Theory: Reading Culture*, Minneapolis: University of Minnesota Press, pp. 3–25.
Cohen, M. (2005), '"Manners" Make the Man: Politeness, Chivalry and the Construction of Masculinity 1750–1830', *Journal of British Studies*, 44: 2, pp. 321–9.
Creed. B. (1993), *The Monstrous-Feminine: Film, Feminism, Psychoanalysis* (Popular Fictions Series), London: Routledge.
Dury, R. (2004), 'Introduction', in R. L. Stevenson, *Strange Case of Dr Jekyll and Mr Hyde*, Edinburgh: Edinburgh University Press, pp. xix–lxii.
Edwards, T. (2012), *Erotics and Politics: Gay Male Sexuality, Masculinity and Feminism*, London: Routledge.
Eisenberg, Davina L., *The Figure of the dandy in Barbey d'Aurevilly's 'Le Bonheur dans le crime'* (New York: Peter Lang, 1996).
Felski, R. (1991), 'The Counterdiscourse of the Feminine in Three Texts by Wilde, Huysmans, and Sacher Masoch', *PMLA*, 106. 5 (October), pp. 1094–105.
Flugel, J. C. (1930), *The Psychology of Clothes*, London: Hogarth.
Foyster, E. (1999), 'Boys will be Boys? Manhood and Aggression, 1660–1800', in T. Hitchcock and M. Cohen (eds), *English Masculinities*, London: Longman, pp. 151–66.
Garrett, P. K. (2003), *Gothic Reflections: Narrative Force in Nineteenth-Century Fiction*, London: Cornell University Press.
Gee, T. (1998), *Up to Scratch: Bareknuckle Fighting and Heroes of the Prize Ring*, Harpenden: Queen Anne.
Gilmore, D. D. (1990), *Manhood in the Making: Cultural Concepts of Masculinity*, New Haven, CT: Yale University Press.

Gorn, E. J. (1986), *The Manly Art: Bare-Knuckle Prize Fighting in America*, Ithaca: Cornell University Press.

Hughes, W. and A. Smith (eds) (2009), *Queering the Gothic*, Manchester: Manchester University Press.

Hurley, K. (2002), 'British Gothic Fiction, 1885–1930', in Jerrold E. Hogle (ed.), *The Cambridge Companion to Gothic Fiction*, New York: Cambridge University Press, pp. 189–207.

Jerrold, C. (1911), *The Beaux and the Dandies*, New York, John Lane.

Kent, S. K. (1999), *Gender and Power in Britain, 1640–1990*, New York: Routledge.

Klein, L. E. (1989), 'Liberty, Manners, and Politeness in Early Eighteenth-Century England', *The Historical Journal*, 32: 3, pp. 583–605.

Krishnaswamy, Revathi (2002), 'The Economy of Colonial Desire', in Rachel Adams and David Savran (eds), *The Masculinity Studies Reader*, Malden, MA and Oxford: Blackwell, pp. 292–317.

Kuchta, D. (1996), 'The Making of the Self-Made Man: Class, Clothing, and English Masculinity, 1699–1832', in V. De Grazia and E. Furlough (eds), *The Sex of Things: Gender and Consumption in Historical Perspective*, Berkeley: University of California Press, pp. 54–78.

Laver, J. (2002), *Costume and Fashion: A Concise History*, 4th edn, London: Thames and Hudson.

Mackie, E. R. (2009), *Highwaymen and Pirates: The Making of the Modern Gentleman in the Eighteenth Century*, Baltimore: Johns Hopkins University Press.

Moers, E. (1959), *The dandy: Brummell to Beerbohm*, London: Secker and Warburg.

Morgan, T. (1993), 'Reimagining Masculinity in Victorian Criticism: Swinburne and Pater', *Victorian Studies*, 36: 3 (Spring), pp. 315–32.

Mosse, G. L. (1996), *The Image of Man: The Creation of Modern Masculinity*, New York: Oxford University Press.

Rauser, A. (2004), 'Hair, Authenticity and the Self-Made macaroni', *Eighteenth-Century Studies*, 38: 1, pp. 101–17.

Revathi K. (2002), 'The Economy of Colonial Desire', in Rachel Adams and David Savran (eds), *The Masculinity Studies Reader*, Malden, MA and Oxford: Blackwell, pp. 292–317.

Roper, M. and J. Tosh (eds) (1991), *Manful Assertions: Masculinities in Britain since 1800*, Oxford: Taylor and Francis.

Sedgwick, E. K. (1985), *Between Men: English Literature and Male Homosocial Desire*, New York: Columbia University Press.

Senelick, L. (1990), 'Mollies or Men of Mode? Sodomy and the Eighteenth-Century London Stage', *Journal of the History of Sexuality*, 1: 1, pp. 33–67.

Showalter, E. (1990), *Sexual Anarchy: Gender and Culture at the Fin de Siècle*, New York: Penguin.

Smith, Albert (1847), *The Natural History of the Gent*, London: David Bogue

Spooner, C. (2004), *Fashioning Gothic Bodies*, Manchester: Manchester University Press.

Steele, V. (1985), *Fashion and Eroticism: Ideals of Feminine Beauty from the Victorian Era to the Jazz Age*, New York: Oxford University Press.

Stevens, George Alexander, 'A Lecture on Heads', https://archive.org/details/alectureonheads00stevgoog p. 4 [accessed 17 March, 2017].

Stevenson, R. L. [1886] (2004), *Strange Case of Dr Jekyll and Mr Hyde*, ed. Richard Dury. Edinburgh: Edinburgh University Press.

Tilt, C. (1837), *Etiquette for Gentlemen*, London: 86 Fleet Street.

Trumbach, R. (1990), 'Birth of the Queen: Sodomy and the Emergence of Gender Equality in Modern Culture, 1660–1750', in Martin Duberman, Martha Vincinus and George Chauncey, Jr (eds), *Hidden from History: Reclaiming the Gay and Lesbian Past*, New York: Meridian, pp. 129–40.

Wells, S. R. (1867), *New Physiognomy*, New York: Fowler and Wells.

Wilde, O. [1890] (2011), *The Picture of Dorian Gray: An Annotated, Uncensored Edition*, ed. Nicholas Frankel, Cambridge, MA: The Belknap Press of Harvard University Press.

Chapter 7

Visible yet Immaterial: The Phantom and the Male Body in Ghost Stories by Three Victorian Women Writers

Ruth Heholt

In the ghost story 'Thurnley Abbey', Alastair Colvin, an old colonial hand, points out that 'there are few ghosts outside Europe – few, that is, that a white man can see' (Landon 1984: 228). Although he is of course proved wrong, white men's vision, it is suggested, is impaired or impeded when it comes to apprehending the supernatural. There is much they cannot (or will not?) see. Women (white or otherwise) are not mentioned here, yet in 'Thurnley Abbey', the two men and one woman who apprehend the terrifying ghost figure (or fragments of it), are equally petrified and appalled. They spend the night huddled together to save their reason and provide comfort for each other, still terrified of what they have seen. In this story and in many others, the echoing question of the ghosts that 'a white man can see' resonates through English ghost stories of the long nineteenth century.

This chapter considers the ghosts that become visible to white men, but it also examines the phenomenon of the appearance of white men *as* ghosts. It references the work of three women writers of ghost stories from across the Victorian period: Catherine Crowe, writing in the early Victorian era, Rhoda Broughton from the middle of the age, and Edith Nesbit's late Victorian tales. Exploring the question of men and ghosts through the work of these three popular women writers, we can trace the way that ghosts and ghost sightings reflect on Victorian ideas of masculinity. Victorian ghost stories have long been discussed by scholars in relation to gender, and the writing and reception of these tales enabled women to have a voice and allowed a sort of veiled criticism of patriarchal society. Ghost stories were written by both sexes, but some of the most successful, radical and progressive were written by women. For many women the act of writing ghost stories was liberating. Diana Wallace states that

> [t]he ghost story as a form has allowed women writers special kinds of freedom, not merely to include the fantastic and supernatural, but also to offer critiques of male power and sexuality which are often more radical than those in more realistic genres. (Wallace 2004: 57)

Indeed, critical attention has, to date, focused on the female ghost in Victorian ghost stories as echoing the social and domestic position of the Victorian woman who was 'above all the ghost in the noontide, an anomalous spirit on display at the center of Victorian materialism and progress' (Dickerson 1996: 11). However there has been virtually no critical consideration of the male ghost figure. Whilst the ghost-body of a woman who is ephemeral and transparent may be less troubling to contemporary Western conceptualisations of gender, in the Victorian period the ghostly body of the white male phantom presented an anomaly that is yet to be explored.[1]

Victorian moral doctrine advocated the principle of 'a healthy mind and a healthy body', and presented an idealised form of masculinity that emphasised physical power and mental control (Hall 1994: 116). The male phantasmal bodies in many ghost stories, however, visibly display the direct antithesis to this ideal. Cyndy Hendershott in *The Animal Within: Masculinity and the Gothic* contends that '[s]table gender identity is predicated on the stability of the body itself' and the ghost-body must be the most unstable of all (Hendershott 1998: 9). Phantom bodies take up no space, they have no corporeality or materiality and yet they are present and visible, open to scrutiny and often literally transparent. These immaterial bodies are left being *only* body: barely there, most often reactive and compelled to act, they radiate need. Yet while these ephemeral figures emphasise the weakness of the male body, there is another aspect to the male ghost, where it may be that it is the iron will of the dead man which is expressed in the manifestation of his phantom body. Thus, conversely, the male ghost body could be seen as the epitome of the 'mind/body' dichotomy, whereby the spirit (mind) revives and reanimates the memory of the fleshly body in order to intervene in the material world.

This chapter traces three positions in relation to female authored Victorian ghost stories: men seeing ghosts and their affective reaction to these experiences; the male phantom as an emasculated figure, immaterial and needy; and finally the male ghost as exuding a more manly version of active, determined masculinity. I will argue that the male ghost body signifies very differently from that of female ghosts, and while on the one hand it can present a disempowered, disembodied state for men, particularly in later texts it can also point to the possibility of the survival of the masculine will from beyond the grave, proving that the mind can truly transcend the body. Throughout the discussion of men and ghosts there are paradoxes, complications and questions that sometimes require more than one answer, yet it is a discussion that I believe bears fruit. At a time of flux and ambiguity for the signification of the white male body, of all Victorian male bodies, the upper-class white male ghost body is arguably the most paradoxical. Within the literature of the time these bodies are always and inevitably disturbing and contentious, bringing uncertainty to hegemonic, naturalised notions of Victorian masculinity.

Women's Ghost Stories and the Ghosts of the Marginal

The Victorian period was the 'golden age' of the ghost story and Cox and Gilbert contend that '[g]host stories were something at which the Victorians excelled' (Cox and Gilbert 1991: x). The mid-to-late nineteenth century saw the rise of the literary ghost story and these tales became 'as typically part of the cultural and literary fabric of the age as imperial confidence or the novel of social realism' (ibid.: x). Over the years critics have discussed and argued about the changes in the representations of ghosts over the Victorian period. However, all agree that ghosts bring into question gender expectations, and the literary ghost story was a space where gender conventions were disturbed.

In the early Victorian period one of the most famous authors of ghost tales was Catherine Crowe. Published just before the advent of spiritualism, Crowe's influential text, *The Night Side of Nature: Or Ghosts and Ghost Seers* (1848), is a collection of 'real' ghost tales: reports garnered from people's first-hand experience of the supernatural. These encounters with the unexplained were imparted to her through conversations, letters and anecdotes, and have a strong connection with earlier oral traditions associated with tales of the supernatural. *The Night Side of Nature* was intended as testimony to people's true experiences of ghosts and was to be presented as evidence to the scientific community. Crowe believed in ghosts and she felt strongly that science and scientific men were arrogant about this matter, perpetuating ignorance through their persistent refusal to investigate the supernatural. Indeed Crowe says that it is often 'the "weak and foolish" [. . .] women and unscientific persons' who apprehend and investigate paranormal phenomena as they are more intuitive and open minded (Crowe 2000: 138). Crowe was not quite a feminist as we might understand it today, but she had a keen eye for injustice and was certainly not to be silenced when it came to women's educational rights, generally advocating a more respectful appreciation of the 'feminine' virtues of intuition and insight.[2] Crowe was a pioneering figure in many ways and Nicholas Freeman contends that *The Night Side of Nature* 'was to prove inspirational for many writers of ghost stories as the nineteenth century progressed' (Freeman 2014: 188).

The second author this chapter will consider, Rhoda Broughton, wrote ghost stories as well as very popular sensation fiction. She too was an advocate for women's education, and perhaps unsurprisingly, as she is writing in the mid- rather than the early Victorian period (*Twilight Stories* was published in the 1870s), she is more radical in her outlook on gender than Crowe. Indeed, Tamar Heller argues that her work 'anticipates the more explicitly feminist fiction of the 1890s' and cites her 'association with rebellious femininity' (Heller 2011: 283; 290). Heller is speaking particularly about Broughton's sensation fiction, but Emma Liggins suggests that her tales of the supernatural allowed other freedoms, contending that, 'Broughton's ghost stories [. . .] allowed her to comment on taboo subjects such as female sexuality and women's attitudes to money' (Liggins 2009: vi). As a popular ghost story writer her tales are ostensibly fictional, but as Joellen Masters contends, 'Broughton wrote her "nasty" little stories within a cultural *milieu* driven to chronicle, to record, and to prove the existence of an afterlife' (Masters 2015: 224). Additionally, Masters quotes a letter from Broughton written on 9 October 9 1872 claiming that the ghost story considered in this chapter, 'Poor Pretty Bobby', is 'founded on fact' (ibid.: 229), echoing the folkloric, oral tale telling evident in Crowe's work.

Liggins says that Broughton's work 'set a trend for other women writers like [Edith] Nesbit' and Nesbit is the third author of supernatural tales considered here (Liggins 2009: iii). Nesbit's feminist credentials are not quite fully formed, for example she was against women's suffrage (Briggs 1987: 335). However, she was acutely aware of the gender politics of her day and Nicholas Freeman calls her 'a politically radical "new woman"' (Freeman 2012: 101). In her own life Nesbit had, as Julia Briggs asserts, 'enjoyed the benefits of independence, both financial and sexual' (Briggs 1987: 335). Victoria Margree argues that although Nesbit was ambivalent towards feminism, 'a feminist orientation is in evidence more widely in her works of supernatural short fiction. A preoccupation with gender is discernible in several stories that offer distinct gender critiques' (Margree 2014: 246). Writing in the late nineteenth century, she was a member of the occult group, the Hermetic Order of the Golden Dawn, and was known to attend meetings of the Society for Psychic Research (Briggs 1987: 63). Nesbit was very superstitious and believed in ghosts (ibid.: 173; 336). Although Victorian ghost stories were usually fictional stories, throughout the genre there is a strain of 'real' ghost tales present in the period that saw the foundation of spiritualism (c.1848) and the establishment of the Society for Psychical Research in 1882. Andrew Smith asserts that 'it is important to distinguish [. . .] between stories about ghosts and the literary ghost story' (Smith 2010: 3), and we have both sorts in Crowe's, Broughton's and Nesbit's tales. However, it is the suggestion of the 'truth' of the ghost stories that echoes the widespread belief in the supernatural apparent in the Victorian period. This belief resonates through all these women's ghost stories, adding a frisson of the real to the gender politics they present.

It was not just ghost stories that offered women a space in which to critique and question the society they lived in, interestingly the ghost figure itself is argued as being the site of radical critique. Those of us familiar with Victorian ghost stories recognise that very many ghost figures signify the 'other' and most scholarly work about Victorian ghosts examines the phenomenon of female ghosts. Yet far from viewing the female ghost as a mere extension of the repressive expectations placed on Victorian women, this phantom body is seen as liberated from the material expectations and conventions of the age. Indeed, Vanessa Dickerson contends that the appearance of the female ghost as a central feature in Victorian tales allowed for some visibility, agency and physical presence for women. She says 'the ghost corresponded [. . .] particularly to the Victorian woman's visibility and invisibility, her power and powerlessness, the contradictions, and extremes that shaped female culture (Dickerson 1996: 5). Ghosts, she argues, are like Victorian women whose position was 'ambiguous, marginal, ghostly' (ibid.: 5). Figurations of ghosts and hauntings can bring to light that which has been obscured, forgotten or hidden. More than this, the ghost as a marginalised figure itself can bring to the fore the *presence* of the disavowed. The ghosts of those who are marginalised force notice onto themselves and will not be ignored.

However, while the ghost figure may be liberating for those who have historically been marginalised, for the men that witness them, ghost-seeing is not such a positive thing. That many male ghost-seers are affected in a way that is detrimental to certain notions of masculinity has long been documented. In the introduction to *The Virago Book of Victorian Ghost Stories* Jennifer Uglow notes 'how the experience of seeing a ghost pushes men into conventional female roles: timid, nervous and helpless' (Uglow 1992: xvii). The experience of seeing a ghost can unman even the most masculine of men, introducing elements of doubt into the world-view of those who are vigorous, rational and materialistically inclined. Catherine Crowe details the case of two soldiers in a military hospital. Corporal Q is being treated for an ulcerated leg and, in the neighbouring bed, Private W has consumption. In his testimony Private W recounts:

> 'I was lying awake,' said he, 'last Tuesday night, when I saw someone sitting on Corporal Q's bed. There was so little light in the ward that I could not make out who it was, and the figure looked so strange that I got alarmed, and felt quite sick. I called out to Corporal Q that there was somebody sitting upon his bed, and then the figure got up; and as I did not know but it might be coming to me, I got so much alarmed, that being but weakly' (this was the consumptive man), 'I fell back, and I believe I fainted away.' (Crowe 2000: 215)

Private W has a bodily reaction to the apparition. The ghost is of the deceased wife of a colleague of theirs who desires Corporal Q to write something to her husband. Corporal Q has a similar reaction to the visitation from the ghost. He tells his superior officer who then questions him: '[a]fter a while, she came towards me again; and while my eyes were upon her, she somehow disappeared from my sight altogether, and I was left alone. It was then that I felt faint-like, and a cold sweat broke out over me' (ibid.: 214). The reaction of both military men is physical: weakness, sickness, cold sweats and faintness. Both men feel the encounter strongly and it disturbs them deeply. They are in hospital, already in a position of dependency and vulnerability; these men themselves are not physically healthy but Crowe emphasises that they were 'both men of good character, and neither of them suffering from any disorder affecting the brain' (ibid.: 213). Yet they are undeniably in a powerless, physically fragile state and the ghost-sighting weakens them further. Frank Barrett contends that historically, '[m]ilitaries around the world have defined the soldier as an embodiment of traditional male sex role behaviours'; for these men, however, there is not the possibility of a 'manly' soldier's reaction (Barrett 2008: 77). Ghost seeing has affected their bodies and turned them into fainting, sweating wrecks. Both men are questioned by their superior officer, they attest to the truth of the experience, and he notes that 'six months afterward, on being interrogated, their evidence and their conviction were as clear as at first' (Crowe 2000: 215).

In the more conventional ghost story, Rhoda Broughton's 1872 tale, 'The Truth, the Whole Truth and Nothing But the Truth' the narrative is completed, but a note comes after: 'The is a true story' (Broughton 1995: 16). In this 'true' story, on taking the inevitable 'small compartment of heaven' (ibid.: 9) at a ridiculously low rental price our narrator, Elizabeth de Wynt begins to comprehend something is wrong with the house. It is narrated through letters to her dear friend Cecilia, and we eventually find out that the house is haunted. The two people who see whatever shape/form the apparition takes (we are never told) both can only state: 'Oh! My God, I have seen it!' (ibid.: 13; 16). A maid goes mad and is carted off to a lunatic asylum whilst the handsome young man Ralph Gordon has a different fate. After hearing what has happened he asks permission to sleep in the affected room, saying, 'I should like nothing better' (ibid.: 15). The daughter of the house, Adela, pleads with him not to stay there as he too might be sent mad:

> He laughed heartily, and coloured a little with pleasure at seeing the interest she took in his safety. 'Never fear,' he said, 'it would take more than a whole squadron of departed ones, with the old gentleman at their head, to send me crazy.' (ibid.: 15)

Reluctantly Mrs de Wynt agrees and Ralph happily goes upstairs. They wait 'for exactly an hour; but it seemed like two years' (ibid.: 16), then the bell from upstairs rings urgently and they rush up. Mrs de Wynt writes to her friend:

> There he was, standing in the middle of the floor, rigid, petrified, with that same look – that look that is burnt into my heart in letters of fire – of awful, unspeakable, stony fear on his brave young face. For one instant he stood thus; then stretching out his arms stiffly before him, he groaned in a terrible, husky voice, 'Oh, my God! I have seen it!' and fell down *dead*. Yes, *dead*. Not in a swoon or a fit, but *dead*. (ibid.: 16, emphasis in original)

Ralph is affected even more deeply than the maid: his body is so affected that it cannot support his life any longer. He dies from fright – he does not sweat or faint or even just lose his wits; Ralph Gordon expires. Seeing ghosts for all these men is a visceral, bodily experience. The horror is not just in the imagination – the mind – it manifests through the flesh and the physicality of their bodies. This relates to our contemporary notions of 'affect' whereby there is a re-turn to the body and the emotions, away from any attempt at objectivity. Patricia Clough states that affectivity is 'a substrate of potential bodily responses, often automatic responses, in excess of consciousness' (Clough and Halley 2007: 2). These responses are instinctive, automatic and beyond the comprehension of the mind. The immateriality of the ghost form, perhaps paradoxically, is comprehended and apprehended through the bodies of those who witness it.

In one of the most striking stories about a man seeing a ghost, E. Nesbit's 'From the Dead', the narrator's experience brings a chilling new dimension to the tradition of men who see ghosts being frightened out of their wits. After abandoning her for years, a repentant husband has a change of heart and rushes to the deathbed of his wronged and neglected wife. Alas, he is too late for forgiveness; she has died before he arrives. That night he lies in the room next to her corpse full of guilt, grief and remorse. He begins to be spooked by perceived tiny sounds from next door but rebukes himself:

> 'You fool!' I said to myself; 'dead or alive, is she not your darling, your heart's heart? Would you not go near to die of joy if she came to you. Pray God to let her spirit come back and tell you she forgives you!'
> 'I wish she would come,' myself answered in words, while every fibre of my body and mind shrank and quivered in denial. (Nesbit 2015: 75)

The narrator's rational self calls out loud for his dead wife to come to him, while he shrinks and quivers at the idea both in body and mind. Interestingly here his mind also revolts and is equated with his physical self as his disembodied words ring out. Unfortunately for him, his wish is granted:

> The door opened slowly, slowly, slowly, and the figure of my dead wife came in. It came straight towards the bed, and stood at the bed-foot with its white grave-clothes, with the white bandage under its chin. There was a scent of lavender. Its eyes were wide open and looked at me with love unspeakable. I could have shrieked aloud. (ibid.: 75)

This is an active ghost who moves and speaks. It is most certainly a purposeful ghost and it/she has come to express her undying love to her husband in this memorable encounter:

> 'You'll love me again now, won't you now I'm dead? One always forgives dead people.'
> The poor ghost's voice was hollow and faint. Abject terror paralyzed me. I could answer nothing.
> 'Say you forgive me,' the thin, monotonous voice went on; 'say you'll love me again' [. . .]
> 'I suppose,' she said wearily, 'you would be afraid, now I am dead, if I came round to you and kissed you?'
> She made a movement as though she would have come to me.
> Then I did shriek aloud, again and again, and covered my face with the sheet, and wound it round my head and body, and held it with all my force. (ibid.: 76)

Our narrator is immobilised by fear. Passive and petrified, he can only lie in his bed and shriek. M. Grant Kellermeyer, who annotates my copy of Nesbit's horror stories, says that the wife is making an offer to her erring husband: 'Accept me as a [sic] corruptible flesh rather than an idealistic spirit, and you shall have absolution' (Kellermeyer 2015: 77). He continues:

> While we may forgive her rueful spouse for not wanting to partake in necrophilia (the subtext is very clear – she is offering him the absolving baptism of sexual intercourse), symbolically his failure to accept his wife as a flawed mortal – decay and all – is a condemnable miscarriage of love and action. (ibid.: 77)

The husband fails twice – first, when out of pride he rejects his living wife, but more importantly in his position as husband and man when he rejects her ghost, succumbing to 'abject terror' which paralyses him, shrieking, 'again and again', while he hides his head in the bed-clothes like a child.

All these ghostly encounters have the effect of unmanning the ghost seers, which serves to feminise them, leading to physical affect that in a paradoxical manner returns them to their bodies: sweating, shaking, paralysed, shrieking and even dying. None of these reactions could be classed as a 'manly' response to a supernatural encounter. This form of account was particularly apparent in the ghost stories of the mid- to late nineteenth century, a period which saw the hardening of gender divisions and the rise of the cult of manliness. John Tosh argues that the concept of manliness 'implied that there was a single standard of manhood, which was expressed in certain physical attributes and moral dispositions' (Tosh 2005: 2). These are (white) colonial values and, John Beynon argues, rest on an ideal of 'hard masculinity' that involved discipline and self-sacrifice, and the 'manly' virtues of 'grit, self-reliance, determination, leadership and initiative' (Beynon 2002: 28). Self-sacrifice, a stiff upper lip, leadership and a strong sense of Britishness (or more likely Englishness) were 'manly'. Manliness was an expression of a certain type of idealised masculinity – muscular, fearless, bold, daring and forthright. It was a cult which celebrated spaces of homosociality, encompassing the public school system, the British Empire, Christianity, and, of course, the military. 'Real' men could boast of a 'manly character' and a 'manly figure' (Tosh 2005: 3). At the same time the rise of the movement of Muscular Christianity combined the physical with the spiritual: espousing a robust, healthy, moral masculinity which served the nation. A ghost, however, has no place; it has moved beyond any question of national boundaries.

In relation to the accepted 'supernatural' (the Holy Ghost is still a ghost), although Christian belief was expected, it was not to be taken too far. David Newsome says that Charles Kingsley, one of the greatest proponents of the 'godly' version of manliness, believed that:

> manliness was the antidote to the poison of effeminacy [. . .] which was sapping the vitality of the Anglican church. Young men came to the church for spiritual nourishment: they went away perverted. Their enthusiasm was diverted into unnatural, un-English pursuits. They were encouraged to think of themselves as beings set apart from other men, their minds bent on other-worldliness. (Newsome 1961: 207)

When Christianity remained straightforward and non-reflexive it was acceptable: men needed a rationalistic, materialistic grasp of the world and their place within it. Forthright, down-to-earth and undoubting, a manly man was to have 'nothing odd about him' (ibid.: 98).[3] Solitude and contemplation of the 'other-worldly' were not seen as conducive to proper expressions of manliness, and ghosts inevitably smack of the 'other world'.

Always contradictory, though, Victorian society was never a unified entity and it created its own anxieties. While such straightforward manliness was encouraged from some quarters, elsewhere it was suggested that other reactions to the spiritual (and supernatural) were both possible and desirable. Brett Carroll adds a different dimension to the idea of men and ghosts in his study of Victorian men and spiritualism. The purpose of spiritualist practice was to court communication with spirits, and Carroll contends that this opened up a new dimension of masculinity for Victorian men. He argues that far from being a negative thing, the feminised position of the male ghost seer allowed new insights and the possibility of new expressions of masculinity. Carroll says, 'Spiritualist ideology and ritual provided ideal theoretical and physical settings for [the] rethinking of masculinity' (Carroll 2000: 5). His point is that in opposition to the ideal of manliness as strength, competition and aggression, there was another type of masculinity being espoused, one that manifested itself into a kind of Victorian New Man:

> Countless Victorian advice manuals warned against excessive absorption in public pursuits [. . .] offering an alternate ideal of 'sentimental' or 'domestic' manliness that identified masculine fulfilment with the moral responsibilities and emotional and spiritual ties of marriage and domestic life [. . .] Men conforming to this ideal would emulate their wives and mothers – that is, integrate into their identities traits they defined as feminine – by softening competitive aggressiveness, seeking close domestic involvement, replacing expression of patriarchal anger with an openly affectionate style of governance. (ibid.: 5)

Carroll claims that from this model some men turned to spiritualism 'for relief' from more aggressive models of manliness and suggests that the acceptance of a concept of a higher spiritual plane, an engagement with emotions, especially grief, led to a 'reorientation of manhood' (ibid.: 7). Here, communication with spirits can be a liberating experience for men. Carroll cites what he calls the 'Spiritualist's androgynous spiritual aspirations' (ibid.: 6), which disrupt conventional notions of manly masculinity in very many ways, and indeed ghosts themselves are often degendered and referred to as 'it'. Apart from poor dead Ralph Gordon, the men who encounter ghosts in the stories we have examined must have learned some kind of lesson. Crowe argues that women are more likely to see ghosts than men because women are more sensitive and receptive; she claims that this sort of insight is 'more frequently developed in women than in men' (Crowe 2000: 176). Ghost seeing, it appears, can create an empowered female gaze, and she states quite clearly that 'experience, observation, and intuition must be our principle if not our only guides' (ibid.: 16). If allowed, ghost seeing and an openness to the supernatural can enable a fruitful melding of masculinity with a more feminine, intuitive outlook.

The Male Ghost Body

We have argued that seeing ghosts in these female-authored tales usually forces men into a feminised position and this can be seen as either demasculinising or as presenting an opportunity for enhanced intuition and feeling. We will now turn to the presence of the male phantom as it is seen, witnessed and apprehended by others. Issues of seeing and believing inevitably follow any report of ghost sighting, and scholars from the margins have long questioned the concepts of seeing, vision and visibility. Richard Dyer contends that 'the ultimate position of power in a society that controls people in part through their visibility is that of invisibility, the *watcher* (Dyer 1997: 44–5, emphasis in original). This is a different type of invisibility from that which overlooks and denies the humanity and agency of women or those who are seen as 'other' in whatever way. This is the invisibility of the centre as it surveys, categorises and marks 'difference'. Judith Butler explains this phenomenon in relation to the idea of the (neutral/objective) white gaze that looks outwards, describing: 'the masculine privilege of the disembodied gaze, the gaze that has the power to produce bodies, but which is itself no body' (Butler 1990: 136). However, it is possible to argue that the surveillance of the male ghost-body entirely reverses this power dynamic. The type of 'no-body' manifested by the male ghost does not produce a disembodied, empowered gaze; rather, in its immateriality and transparency, it is a body that is *looked at*. In her discussion of postcolonial masculinities Stephanie Newell states that '[i]f postcolonial women's writing is generally regarded as re-visionary, then (post)colonial masculinity [. . .] tends to be dys-visionary, acting out the failure of the visual economy during bodily encounters' (Newell 2009: 246). A similar interchange may be happening in relation to the visibility of the ghostly white male body. The apparition of the dead white man reverses the power of the gaze. The body of this ghost figure is surveyed: it is seen and it needs to be seen. An invisible, unseen ghost is no ghost at all: a ghost needs someone else to witness it and testify to its existence.

In the section 'Apparitions', Crowe recounts the tale of a ghost that is desperate to communicate; one that has a pressing need to speak:

> [s]ome years ago, during the war, when Sir Robert H E was in the Netherlands, he happened to be quartered with two other officers, one of whom was despatched into Holland on an expedition. One night, during his absence, Sir R H E awoke, and, to his great surprise, saw this absent friend sitting on the bed which he used to occupy, with a wound in his breast.

> Sir Robert immediately awoke his companion, who saw the spectre also. The latter then addressed them saying that he had been that day killed in a skirmish, and that he had died in great anxiety about his family, wherefore he had come to communicate that there was a deed of much consequence to them deposited in the hands of a certain lawyer in London [. . .] He therefore requested that, on their return to England, they would go to his house and demand the deed. (Crowe 2000: 154–5)

This ghost has come back to communicate to his fellow soldiers and, of course, needs to be visible to them. The deed is eventually recovered and the family saved from penury. This episode is reminiscent of that of the female ghost who communicates with Corporal Q. Both ghosts need help and both need a live person to act for them. In Victorian times it was far more usual for a woman to need a man to act for her outside of the domestic space and the Victorian ideal for men is one of self-reliance and an ability to take responsibility for oneself. The ghost of this officer, though, requires physical help as he cannot impinge on the material world at all. He cannot act and he needs others to undertake the care of his family. This need of help resonates very differently for the figure of a dead wife than that of a soldier, placing this ghost figure in a feminised position of powerlessness and need.

The question of 'need' arises many times in relation to ghosts: the need for action to be taken, for recognition, or merely for the ghost to be witnessed by a living being. The ghost in 'Poor Pretty Bobby' appears before his lover as he needs to escape from his watery grave and come home. The eponymous poor pretty Bobby of Rhoda Broughton's story is feminised from the start. This is a relatively conventional story whereby our narrator Phoebe and her father's ward Bobby fall in love. Bobby serves at sea with his guardian, but finds him over-protective. He complains to Phoebe: '"Your father always takes a great deal too much care of me," he says with a slight frown and a darkening of his whole bright face. "I might be sugar or salt"' (Broughton 1995: 51). Britain is at war with France and although they capture several French ships, Bobby is not allowed to take any captured boats to shore on his own. He is not allowed to prove his mettle and his greatest fear is that his fellow officers '"conclude that my not being sent is my own choice; in short, that I am – *afraid*." (His voice sinks with a disgusted and shamed intonation at the last word)' (ibid.: 53, emphasis in original). When Bobby is eventually permitted to captain a captured French vessel back to port, the shackled French officers escape, take the ship and shoot Bobby, flinging his body over board.

Poor pretty Bobby is not allowed to embody any manly type of masculinity throughout the entire narrative. Before his death he falls ill with a fever, allowing Phoebe to 'nurse and cosset him' (ibid.: 51), and when he begins to recover they go out together, 'reversing the order of things – *he* leaning on *my* arm' (ibid.: 52, emphasis in original). Although he recovers from this fever, Bobby is set up to be apparitional. And in this story Phoebe too is connected with the ghostly. There is a questioning of who is the ghost and Phoebe associates herself with the ghostly several times. She says, 'I remember once standing with my back to a bright fire in our long drawing-room, and seeing myself reflected in a big mirror at the other end. I was so thinly clad that I was transparent, and could see through myself' (ibid.: 48). Just before she hears the phantom Bobby insistently knocking on the front door Phoebe says, 'I can see my own ghostly figure sitting up in bed, reflected in the looking glass opposite' (ibid.: 56). Phoebe's spectral presence contradicts and confuses the question of the ghost. But although she may be the more traditional female figure of the 'ghost in the noontide' (Dickerson 1996: 11), it is Bobby who becomes the actual ghost.

After his murder Bobby's ghost returns to Phoebe who apprehends her 'beautiful boy-lover' (Broughton 1995: 56):

> He stands there still and silent, and though the night is dry, equally free from rain or dew, I see that he is dripping wet; the water is running down from his clothes, from his drenched hair, and even from his eyelashes, on to the dry ground at his feet.
>
> 'What has happened?' I cry, hurriedly, 'How wet you are!' and as I speak I stretch my hand out and lay it on his coat sleeve. But even as I do it a sensation of intense cold runs up my fingers and my arm, even to the elbow. How is it that he is so chilled to the marrows of his bones on this sultry, breathless, August night? To my extreme surprise he does not answer; he stands there, dumb and dripping. 'Where have you come from?' I ask, with that sense of awe deepening. 'Have you fallen into the river? How is it that you are so wet?'
>
> 'It was cold,' he says, shivering, and speaking in a slow and strangely altered voice, 'bitter cold. I could not stay there.' (ibid.: 57)

Bobby is literally 'wet': he could not bear to stay where he had fallen and has attempted to come home. He is passive, minutely observed through Phoebe's feminine gaze. His ghost body freezes Phoebe's own body as she touches him, signifying not life and virility, but stagnation, immateriality and death. Phoebe tells us: 'a feeling of cold disappointment unaccountably steals over me – a nameless sensation, whose nearest kin is chilly awe' (ibid.: 56). Bobby cannot serve her now – this depleted figure of a man is a 'disappointment'. Tamar Heller, in a discussion about Broughton's earlier novels, looks at the way she allows her female characters to 'reveal the depth and desperation of their sexual passion' (Heller 2013: 12). Heller cites Margaret Oliphant's contemporary criticism of Broughton's work as epitomising 'this intense appreciation of flesh and blood, this eagerness of physical sensation' (ibid.: 12). Phoebe's sensual ambitions and longings are thwarted. Bobby is no longer 'flesh and blood' and coldness and 'chilly awe' are the only physical sensation he is able to impart. Allen Warren argues that the 'widely accepted' notion of manliness carried at its heart: 'the close connection between manliness and good health, both physical and moral [. . .] There was a widely held belief that a healthy physique was more important than a veneer of social culture' (Warren 1987: 199–200). Here, though, in Bobby's ghost body, we have the least healthy of all bodies: one which represents impotence, death and defeat; an insubstantial, ethereal body.

The Power of Will

The ghost that Sir Robert sees in Crowe's tale and Bobby's ghost are both needy and powerless to act for themselves. Bobby wants home, warmth and comfort, whilst the soldier's ghost needs someone to take care of his family for him. The ghost figure in the next story I want to turn to is slightly different. This is John Charrington, the main figure in E. Nesbit's famous ghost story 'John Charrington's Wedding'. The first line of the story reads: 'No one ever thought that May Forster would marry John Charrington; but he thought differently, and things which John Charrington intended had a queer way of coming to pass' (Nesbit 2015: 47). This opening of the story sets up the strength of John Charrington's will and the force of his determination to possess May Forster. M. Grant Kellermeyer states in his notes on the story: 'This ghost story, like so many others, is largely concerned with the trait of wilfulness. In this instance it is the power of a man's will to possess a woman' (Kellermeyer 2015: 47). When his friend jokingly ascribes the help of supernatural agency to his success with May to be due to 'mesmerism, or a love-potion', Charrington himself sites 'perseverance' (Nesbit 2015: 48). He refuses to be denied. Charrington is called away to see a dying man to whom it is suggested he is heir, but promises May that 'Nothing shall keep me' from their wedding day (ibid.: 50). However, when he arrives late at the church something is wrong. Our narrator's gardener describes how he looked:

> I never see Mr John the least bit so afore, but my opinion is he's been drinking pretty free. His clothes was all dusty and his face like a sheet. I tell you I didn't like the looks of him at all, and the folks inside are saying all sorts of things. You'll see, something's gone very wrong with Mr John [. . .] He looked like a ghost. (ibid.: 53)

This is, of course, a ghost story, and therefore we are pretty sure that John Charrington does not just 'look' like a ghost. The couple leave the church:

> John Charrington did not look himself. There was dust on his coat, his hair was disarranged. He seemed to have been in some sort of row, for there was a black mark above his eyebrow. He was deathly pale. But his pallor was not greater than that of the bride, who might have been carved in ivory – dress, veil, orange blossoms, face and all. (ibid.)

The bells ring and instead of 'the gay wedding peal, came the slow tolling of the passing bell' (ibid.). May seems horrified: 'The bride shuddered, and grey shadows came about her mouth, but the bridegroom led her on' (ibid.). They enter the wedding carriage and Charrington puts his head out of the window, crying to the driver, 'Drive like hell' (ibid.). The carriage returns some time later without Charrington but with May, almost spectral herself now: 'White, white and drawn with agony and horror' and with her hair turned 'white like snow' (ibid.: 56). John Charrington has returned from the dead to complete his wedding, as he declared before '*I shall be married, dead or alive*' (ibid.: 57, emphasis in original). The iron will of John Charrington has dragged May to hell, turned her into a white, ghostly figure, and within a week she too is dead. Was there a ghostly rape? It is, of course, impossible to say, but the ghost figure of Charrington – cold and wilful, cruel and determined – is not the more traditionally feminised figure of the returning phantom of a dead man. The dead soldier of Crowe's tale and poor pretty Bobby return through love; Charrington returns it seems merely because he is determined to possess May and will not break his word albeit that he breaks her body.

Nesbit's story is published later than Crowe's and Broughton's and John Charrington's ghost figure is not demasculinised, indeed it is more of a hyper-masculine figure whose spirit entirely masters both his own body and the laws of nature. There appears to be a movement from the feminised ghost figures of the early- to mid-Victorian period to a more robust and manly ghost figure in the later tales. Interestingly, this movement has been noted in relation to the female ghost figure, but not specifically the male. Diana Basham quotes Dorothy Scarborough from her 1917 essay 'Modern Ghosts' who argues for more 'muscular' Victorian ghosts as opposed to the helpless wraiths of before. She says where Gothic ghosts were as:

> fragile and helpless as an eighteenth century heroine when it came to a real emergency [later Victorian ghosts were] stronger, more vital; there seems to be a strengthening of ghostly tissue, a stiffening of supernatural muscle in these days. Ghosts are more healthy, more active, more alive than they used to be. (Basham 1992: 156)

Ghosts have become more robust, determined and disturbing over the period of the nineteenth century. Vanessa Dickerson looks at stories written by women towards the end of the century and says that 'female ghosts found in the stories by later writers are not only older but also less humble and more aggressive than their predecessors' (Dickerson 1996: 144). These female ghosts seek vengeance for their deaths. Ghosts in these stories, she argues, 'body forth the energies of the liberated, even if somewhat negatively liberated, women' (ibid.: 146). Dickerson's idea of purposeful, vengeful female ghosts seems to be suggesting a more 'manly' type of female ghost and in this way the female ghost body can be seen as liberated, radical and transformative.

However, in relation to masculinity this hardened, energetic ghost figure is not necessarily a good thing. In this case a more 'manly' ghost is a more disturbing ghost. In Nesbit's story there is strong criticism of John Charrington's robust ghost and his wilful disregard for May. The suggestion in 'John Charrington's Wedding Day' is that John *should not* have returned and he kills May by doing so. This is the ultimate 'shot gun' wedding and May has no volition or choice at all. There are echoes of Broughton's earlier story 'The Man with the Nose' (1873) here. In this story a new bride is permanently abducted by a mysterious mesmeric figure of a man with a most peculiar, distinctive (and phallic) nose. However, the suggestion is that this is an actual person (although he is apprehended by the poor bride in a dream as well), who has a real material presence. As a ghost it is Charrington who is the most active and destructive in his intentions and the execution of his ghostly will.

Conclusion

Speaking about people's encounters with ghosts and supernatural phenomena Crowe states that, 'there exists in one form or another, hundreds and hundreds of recorded cases in all countries, and in all languages, exhibiting that degree of similarity which mark them as belonging to a class of facts' (Crowe 2000: 142). People have always seen ghosts and the sighting of male ghosts is perhaps nothing extraordinary. However, the effect these visions have on Victorian gender politics is unexpected and powerful. Evoking and representing emotion – grief, loss, yearning and sometimes fear – the return of a dead man brings with it an inevitability of reflection and doubt. The male ghost figure of whatever sort embodies fragmentation and anxiety, undermining notions of the idealised, healthy, wholesome masculinity that Victorian society was so anxious to promote. Male ghosts cause *disruption* to gender norms: male ghost bodies are dis-engendered and dislocated in place and space.

This chapter has dealt with stories by just three Victorian women writers, but there were many more authors of ghost stories – both male and female – and many hundreds of tales. For all, though, the male ghost figure presents an anomaly. As it has no flesh or corporeal materiality, all that is left for the ghost is the visibility, the presence of the (insubstantial) body that needs to be witnessed in order for it to exist at all. Ghosts and men and men as ghosts appear to be something like oil and water: they cannot properly mix. Any male ghost body will, by its very presence (fictional or in 'reality') shake some of the bastions of Victorian philosophy and cultural expectations. Notions of the Kantian body/spirit split, questions of the body and materiality, of will, volition, agency and physical action are all shifted and destabilised by the most ephemeral of male ghosts and also by robust, active ghosts like John Charrington. Examining lesbian and gay versions of the ghost story in twentieth- and twenty-first-century tales, Paulina Palmer argues that the ghost, '[a]s well as evoking connotations of invisibility and fluctuations in visibility [. . .] can operate as an image for liminality and border-crossing' (Palmer 2012: 66). And while, when alive, the upper-class, white man in Victorian society may have signified the centre, as ghost-body he is now inevitably pushed into the margins, the liminal and border-spaces not intended for his occupation. The male phantom is dis-placed; all that his living body signified is re-placed, doubled and echoed, made transparent, ephemeral and temporary. Even a robust ghost like John Charrington is not a permanent fixture, albeit that his hold over May extends from beyond the grave. Death comes to us all, and the figure of the male phantom in Victorian tales acts as a memento mori, shaking the idea of patriarchal permanence and dismantling conventional conceptions of Victorian manliness.

Notes

1. I began to touch on this subject very briefly in an article entitled: 'Science, Ghosts and Vision: Catherine Crowe's Bodies of Evidence and the Critique of Masculinity', *Victoriographies*, 4: 1, pp. 46–61.
2. For discussion on women's education rights see Catherine Crowe, *The Story of Lilly Dawson* (2015), and on women's intuition and insight see *The Night Side of Nature* (2000).
3. William Hughes, *Tom Brown's School Days*, quoted in David Newsome, *Godliness and Good Learning* (Newsome 1961: 98). Newsome argues that Hughes painted Tom as 'the paragon of manliness' (ibid.: 98).

Works Cited

Barratt, F. [2001] (2008), 'The Organizational Construction of Hegemonic Masculinity: The Case of the US Navy', in Stephen Whitehead and Frank Barrett (eds), *The Masculinities Reader*, Cambridge: Polity, pp. 77–99.
Basham, D. (1992), *The Trial of Woman: Feminism and the Occult Sciences in Victorian Literature and Society*, Basingstoke: Palgrave Macmillan.
Bennett, G. (1987), *Traditions of Belief: Women, Folklore and the Supernatural Today*, Harmondsworth: Penguin Books.
Beynon, J. (2002), *Masculinities and Culture*, Philadelphia: Open University Press.
Briggs, J. (1987), *A Woman of Passion: The Life of E. Nesbit 1858–1924*, New York: New Amsterdam Books.
Broughton, R. [1872] (1995), *Rhoda Broughton's Best Ghost Stories and Other Tales of Mystery and Suspense*, Stamford: Paul Watkins Publishing.
Butler, J. (1990), *Gender Trouble: Feminism and the Subversion of Identity*, New York: Routledge.
Carroll, B. (2000), 'A Higher Power to Feel: Spiritualism, Grief and Victorian Manhood', *Men and Masculinities*, 3: 3, pp. 3–29.
Clough, P. and J. Halley (eds) (2007), *The Affective Turn: Theorizing the Social*, Durham, NC: Duke University Press.
Cox, M. and R. A. Gilbert (1991), *Victorian Ghost Stories: An Oxford Anthology*, New York: Oxford University Press.
Crowe, C. [1848] (2000), *The Night Side of Nature: Or Ghosts and Ghost-Seers*, Ware and London: Wordsworth Editions.

Crowe, C. [1848] (2015), *The Story of Lilly Dawson*, ed. Ruth Heholt, Brighton: Victorian Secrets Press.
Dickerson, V. (1996), *Victorian Ghosts in the Noontide: Women Writers and the Supernatural*, Columbia and London: University of Missouri Press.
Dyer, R. (1997), *White: Essays on Race and Culture*, London: Routledge.
Freeman, N. (2012), 'The Victorian Ghost Story', in Andrew Smith and William Hughes (eds), *The Victorian Gothic*, Edinburgh: University of Edinburgh Press, pp. 93–107.
Freeman, N. (2014), 'Sensational Ghosts: Ghostly Sensations', in Anne-Marie Beller and Tara MacDonald (eds), *Rediscovering Victorian Women Sensation Writers*, London and New York: Routledge, pp. 186–201.
Gordon, A. F. (2008), *Ghostly Matters: Haunting and the Sociological Imagination*, Minneapolis: University of Minnesota Press.
Hall, D. E. (1994), *Muscular Christianity: Embodying the Victorian Age*, Cambridge and New York: Cambridge University Press.
Heholt, Ruth (2014), 'Science, Ghosts and Vision: Catherine Crowe's Bodies of Evidence and the Critique of Masculinity', *Victoriographies*, 4: 1, pp. 46–61.
Heller, T. (2011), 'Rhoda Broughton', in Pamela K. Gilbert (ed.), *A Companion to Sensation Fiction*, Malden, MA: Wiley-Blackwell, pp. 281–92.
Heller, T. (2013), 'Introduction', in Rhoda Broughton, *Not Wisely But Too Well*, Brighton: Victorian Secrets Press, pp. 5–30.
Hendershott, C. (1998), *The Animal Within: Masculinity and the Gothic*, Ann Arbor: The University of Michigan Press.
Kellermeyer, G. M. (2015), *Man-Size in Marble and Others: The Best Horror and Ghost Stories of E. Nesbit*, Fort Wayne: Oldstyle Tales Press.
Landon, P. [1908] (1984), 'Thurnley Abbey', in J. A. Cuddon, (ed.), *The Penguin Book of Horror Stories*, Harmondsworth: Penguin Books, pp. 224–36.
Liggins, E. (2009), 'Introduction', in Rhoda Broughton, *Twilight Stories*, Brighton: Victorian Secrets Press, pp. i–vii.
Margree, V. (2014), The Feminist Orientation in Edith Nesbit's Gothic Short Fiction, *Women's Writing*, 21: 4, pp. 425–43.
Masters, Joellen (2015), 'Haunted Gender in Rhoda Broughton's Supernatural and Mystery Tales', *Journal of Narrative Theory*, 45: 2, pp. 220–50.
Nesbit, E. [1893] (2015), *Man-Size in Marble and Others: The Best Horror and Ghost Stories of E. Nesbit*, ed. M. Grant Kellermeyer, Fort Wayne: Oldstyle Tales Press.
Newell, Stephanie (2009), 'Postcolonial Masculinities and the Politics of Visibility', *Journal of Postcolonial Writing*, 45: 3, pp. 243–50.
Newsome, D. (1961), *Godliness and Good Learning: Four Studies on a Victorian Ideal*, London: John Murray.
Palmer, P. (2012), *The Queer Uncanny*, Cardiff: University of Wales Press.
Smith, A. (2010), *The Ghost Story 1840–1920: A Cultural History*, Manchester: Manchester University Press.

Tosh, J. (2005), *Manliness and Masculinities in Nineteenth Century Britain: Essays on Gender, Family and Empire*, New York: Pearson Education Limited.

Uglow, J. (1992), 'Introduction', in Richard Dalby (ed.), *The Virago Book of Victorian Ghost Stories*, London: Virago Press, pp. ix–xvii.

Wallace, D. (2004), 'Uncanny Stories: The Ghost Story as Female Gothic', *Gothic Studies*, 6: 1, pp. 57–68.

Warren, A. (1987), 'Popular Manliness: Baden-Powell, Scouting and the Development of Manly Character', in Andrew Mangan and James Walvin (eds), *Manliness and Morality: Middle-Class Masculinity in Britain and America, 1800–1940*, Manchester: Manchester University Press, pp. 199–219.

Part III

Unruly Bodies

Chapter 8

Aesthetics of Deviance: George du Maurier's Representations of the Artist's Body for *Punch* as Discourse on Manliness, 1870–1880

Françoise Baillet

As one of the most emblematic Victorian illustrated papers, *Punch* is famous for its coverage of topical events, political as well as social and artistic. With its stage-like setting and conventional system of language, the black-and-white image of the mid-Victorian era – the *Punch* vignette in particular – provides an interesting record of contemporary life. But beyond its denotative function, graphic art may also be considered for its ideological content. In an age when, as Martin Meisel suggests, different art forms – paintings, plays and novels – gradually adopted common styles and idioms in a way that cut across generic boundaries *Punch*'s widely circulated serialised vignettes seem to have played a significant role in the articulation of a cultural discourse (Meisel 1983: 3). '[A] shaping and defining mechanism' (Pointon 1993: 4), they offered a privileged space in which contemporary notions of class, rank and gender could be explored.

Punch's interest for moral, social and occupational 'types' existed from the magazine's earliest days. A legacy of the literary genre of the 'character' and of the graphic tradition of 'physiologies' – itself largely inspired by the writings of Johan Casper Lavater (1741–1801) – the depiction of 'types' assumed a Platonician equation between an individual's physical characteristics and their moral value. In the tradition of Rowlandson's *Characteristic Sketches of the Lower Orders* (1820), the *Punch* artists produced a visual archaeology of occupational types, providing a reassuring portrayal of an increasingly complex world. In this age of substantial economic, political and intellectual transformation, insecurities concerning income, prospects and more importantly status were common, generating a sharpening of class consciousness, a need among the Victorians to debate and discuss the social order 'with unprecedented urgency, intensity and anxiety' (Cannadine 1993: 62). And while social anxieties were keener among the middle-class groups, to which the magazine's readership largely belonged, *Punch*'s visual taxonomy allowed the (re)tracing of boundaries perceived as dangerously blurred. Bringing order into an ever-increasing variety of human types thus permitted a symbolic reordering of the Victorian society.

With his 'opposition [. . .] to social norms, fetishising artifice and individualism' (Hatt 1999: 249), the figure of the avant-garde artist was, from the beginning, a target of choice for the *Punch* cartoonists. From Leech's sporadic gibes at Pre-Raphaelite creeds to Sambourne's portraits, the persona of the vanguard painter or poet was increasingly read as the symptom of a social disease, becoming the subject of a debate on masculinity. Throughout the 1870s and early 1880s, while the craze for china, peacock feathers and sunflowers was reaching its apex, George du Maurier (1834–96) produced dozens of cartoons mocking famous individuals and ridiculing the indolence and affectations of their followers. The French-born illustrator, himself an artist trained under Gleyre in Paris (together with Poynter, Thomas Armstrong and James McNeill Whistler), had finally carved his initials in *Punch*'s mahogany table after Leech's death, in 1864. His familiarity with the leading figures of the movement, some of whom he knew well and met regularly (du Maurier 1952: 235), allowed him to deliver a scathing and yet hilarious criticism.

This chapter examines du Maurier's representations of the Aesthete's physical body for *Punch* as expressions of Victorian social anxieties about manliness. It will assess a selection of the numerous sketches produced in the late 1870s and early 1880s as a multi-faceted discourse on difference. Using the male body as a metaphor of society, du Maurier indeed explores the various accepted figures of the artist – the dandy, the secluded poet, the decadent avant-gardist, the degenerate Aesthete – pitting them against the dominant male constructions of the time, 'Carlyle's healthy hero, Spencer's biologically perfect man [. . .] and especially Kingsley's muscular Christian' (Haley 1978: 21). For Victorian masculinity, Stefan Dudink writes, 'was not a reassuringly fixed category that came with the possession of a male body' (Dudink 2004: 78). 'In a world transformed by industrialization and by *embourgeoisement*', it appeared rather as 'fluid and shifting, a set of contradictions and anxieties so irreconcilable within male life in the present as to be harmonized only through fictive projections into the past, the future, or even the afterlife' (Sussman 1995: 2–3). Hence the need, Sussman explains, 'to refashion the notion of manliness and of artistic manhood' (ibid.: 2).

With his 'power to fascinate, to puzzle, to travel, to persist and to figure in an ambiguous social situation in a revolutionary climate' (Moers 1960: 11–12), the nineteenth-century dandy will be examined first. As represented for *Punch* through a series of performative characters, du Maurier's nincompoop may be interpreted as a focus for a range of social, religious and mostly sexual concerns of the period. Beyond this ambiguous yet attractive character stands the more ominous figure of the degenerate aesthete, the focus of the second part of this chapter. Du Maurier's critical response to the avant-garde, as expressed through his recurrent characters of Maudle-the-painter and Postlethwaite-the-poet, stages the decadent male figure as symptom of a discourse on a gangrene undermining the social body. Using art as 'the embodiment or expression of national identity' (Tosh 2004: 62), the illustrator articulates a visual discourse on difference, quite literally drawing the line between deviance and respectability, danger and security, self and other.

'Culture, over-refinement and caprice' (Anon. 1877: 584): Du Maurier and the Dandy

As a newspaper written by Londoners for Londoners essentially, *Punch* drew much of its comic potential from the representation of the city. The early-Victorian swell, a 'demotic descendant of the Regency-era dandy' (Altick 1997: 507) and the London idler, a Baudelairian *flâneur* 'who assumed a different persona from week to week' (ibid.: 504), were familiar and recurrent figures of the early *Punch*. Both characters, English versions of Balzac's Brummell-inspired dandy, provided ample scope for satire, enabling *Punch* cartoonists to confront their extravagant targets to dominant constructions of manliness linked to work, production and restraint. And while Thackeray's gentleman – 'The Snobs of England, by one of themselves' appeared in fifty-three instalments, between 1846 and 1847 – and Jerrold's swell entertained the *Punch* reader on a weekly basis, they also flamboyantly explored, contradicted and indirectly reasserted the rising models of masculinity. Du Maurier's version of the Aesthetic dilettante, popularised during the 1870s, could belong to what Rhonda Garelick labels 'decadent dandyism' (Garelick 1998: 3). Largely inspired by Wilde, Whistler and Swinburne, he lives a self-absorbed life, challenging the mores of the Victorian bourgeoisie. He is 'one of those carefully controlled men whose goal [is] to create an effect, bring about an event, or provoke reaction in others through the suppression of the "natural"' (ibid.: 3). At a time when much of the debate around avant-garde art was staged around the representation of the human body, George du Maurier uses the Aesthete's physical appearance as a metaphor, singularising non-conformity and providing his readership with clearly decipherable signs of deviance.

One of the earliest vignettes of the series, 'Intellectual Epicures' (Figure 1) introduces the reader to the character of de Tomkyns, a dilettante 'steeped in aesthetic culture'. In a *Punch* issue largely devoted to the preparations of Queen Victoria's proclamation as Empress of India and to the parliamentary debates on Irish Home Rule, du Maurier's sketch brings a light yet highly critical touch, in line with the ideological posture of the magazine. Two years after the death of Shirley Brooks, a journalist who 'saw himself as a proponent of enlightened Conservatism' (Leary 2010: 122) and

Figure 1 Du Maurier, G. (1876), 'Intellectual Epicures'. (Source: *Punch*).

whose influence was still strongly felt through the editorship of his successor Tom Taylor, *Punch* had become the voice of the British establishment, expressing the prejudices of many of its middle-class readers. 'Intellectual Epicures' clearly illustrates this conservative editorial line, using de Tomkyns' weak frame and prostrate attitude as an inscription of deviant masculinity and offering insights into a number of contemporary anxieties.

Placed on either side of a symbolical partition, de Tomkyns (left) and Betsy Waring (right) adopt a similar attitude, standing alone in a room. In a mirror construction hinging upon the mantelpiece – richly decorated and adorned with bellows on one side, plain on the other – objects and items of furniture echo each other, underlining both social antagonisms and similar inclinations. And while de Tomkyns' delicate Japanese fan finds a ludicrous equivalent in Betsy's old saucepan, her own wicker chair becomes an elegant Louis XV armchair in the other half of the picture. In the background two collections of plates are visible: china for Ponsonby, earthenware for Betsy. Standing in the middle of their respective stages, the two characters strike the same languid pose, palm on cheek, drooping head and weary eyes. Tomkyns' knee breeches and velvet jacket clearly define him as one of du Maurier's many doubles of Oscar Wilde, whose velvet knickerbockers were often mocked. Uninterested by 'the events of the outer world', de Tomkyns is a dandy, 'clad in (imported) soft and shiny fabrics, overexcited by reading (French) novels' (Dudink 2004: 78), 'the epitome of selfish irresponsibility' (Moers 1960: 13). With his comfortable outfit which subtly dramatises the sinuosity of his body, marking his waist and delineating his hips (also emphasised by the unsteady pose he adopts), de Tomkyns visually contradicts the nineteenth-century construct of manly reserve, 'whose emblem [was] the buttoned frock of the Victorian gentleman' (Sussman 1995: 29). His left arm leaning against the mantelpiece and almost reduced to a misshapen form, Tomkyns adopts the 'cultivated slouch' of the du Maurier Aesthete, preferring 'inaction to action, passivity to assertion, all things decaying to those robust and healthy' (Freedman 1990: 147). A feminised figure uncontaminated by market forces and social demands, he finds in his seclusion the means to *be* rather than *do*, and experiences the 'ecstasy' Pater evoked in *The Renaissance* (Pater 1917: 236). With his 'artistic wall-papers, blue china, Japanese fans [and] mediaeval snuff-boxes', du Maurier's character adopts a Ruskinian posture, considering that 'his place is neither in the closet, nor on the bench, nor at the bar, nor in the library' and that '[t]he work of his life is to be two-fold only: to see, to feel' (Ruskin 1903: 49). Such a questionable choice thus likens him to an old woman for whom industrial and commercial development – railways and modern banking – are but figments of the imagination, as the caption suggests: 'I've often heard Rumours of Wars and Contumours [...] Steam-hingins a-bustin', and banks as folks trust in' (du Maurier 1876). And while Betsy's alienation from Victorian progress is presented as typical of her age, social condition and sex, de Tomkyns' appears as more contentious. Conforming to gendered notions of passivity, he is unmistakably deprived of his status as a nineteenth-century male: he is a 'non-man' (Moers 1960: 176). Finally, the title chosen for the picture, 'Intellectual Epicures', adds to its satirical intent, mocking the Aesthete's creeds and reducing them to a quest for pleasure and self-satisfaction. In a society influenced by Evangelical beliefs, themselves inspired from the Protestant tradition, complacency resulted in the erasure of masculinity, 'effeminacy and nonwork' being 'dialectically opposed to the masculine quality of work, which is strong and effective' (Barringer 2005: 55).

The same visual system prevails in 'Aesthetic Pride' (Figure 2), in which the supposed connection between avant-garde art and sexual deviance is emphasised. The poseur is here implicitly opposed to the manly artist, his self-centredness presented as an excuse for immorality. Du Maurier deconstructs the supposedly effeminate, idle and degenerate dandy, pitting him against dominant discourses linking manliness to work.

'Aesthetic Pride' depicts the dialogue between a '[f]ond mother' and her son, a '[y]oung genius (poet, painter, sculptor &c)' in the latter's studio (Figure 2). Sitting upright, her back against a flowery screen, which directly evokes James McNeill Whistler's Japanese decors, the worried mother attracts her son's attention to the fact that he lives 'too much alone' and should seek 'the society of his superiors'. The young man's name, Algernon, is a direct reference to Swinburne, one of du Maurier's favourite targets whose 'Ballad of Burdens' (Swinburne 1883) the illustrator had satirised as 'A Ballad of Blunders' in an earlier *Punch* issue. The association between creativity, genius and effeminacy is obvious: leaning towards his mother, his painter's palette in his left hand, Algernon appears as a frail and languid young man whose soft features and abundant hair – also reminiscent of Swinburne's – connote a deviant masculinity. Alienated and weak, the Aesthete refuses to confront the outside world, the Victorian quintessentially manly sphere, to remain in the company of a 'necessarily rather limited' circle of artists. With his somewhat contorted body – hands on his knees, right wrist almost dislocated and legs wide apart, generating a series of oblique and

Figure 2 Du Maurier, G. (1879), 'Aesthetic Pride'. (Source: *Punch*).

intersecting lines – Algernon, 'both artist and living art' (Fillin-Yeh 2001: 3), visually signifies the social disorder his artistic creeds could generate. The reference to a restricted circle of equals may be understood as an allusion to the homosexual practices of men such as Swinburne, Rossetti or Wilde, whose lifestyles not only represented 'a protest against the sexual mores of Victorian England' (Freedman 1990: 1–2) but also entailed an alienation from the wider middle-class public, whose values these artists ostensibly mocked and challenged. Rossetti in particular was famous for his seclusion, a choice Walter Pater had noted in his 1868 criticism of the poet's *Defence of Guinevere*. In this review, Pater had defined the poet as one 'who had something about him of mystic isolation' (Pater 1889: 228). At a time when, under the impulse of Charles Kingsley, the doctrine of Muscular Christianity largely informed the Victorian reaction to Aestheticism, this mystic isolation also brought with it connotations of Tractarianism which the *Punch* educated readership necessarily perceived. In contemporary minds, the distinction between the 'emaciated and effeminate pale young curates' (Vance 1985: 39) and the apathetic and secluded Aesthetic devotees was a slender one, both being suspected of perverted habits. Algernon's 'fastidious, die-away effeminacy' (Kingsley 1877: 249) thus connotes a threat to dominant sexuality. His disorderly shape seems to attest to a connection between moral and bodily health (Hatt 1999: 244), contradicting the Victorian (re)constructions of masculinity around the erect figure of the soldier (Vance 1985: 27). In the absence of 'the Colonel', du Maurier's recurring military character, visual contradiction is here provided through the upright figure of the mother, whose sober outfit and dignified features indicate her respectability. By advising her son to seek 'the society of [his] superiors', she expresses the dominant perception of what a successful artist should do. 'The no-nonsense climate of middle-class commercial society,' Altick remarks:

> had little time or tolerance of the 'mere' artist. To those of Evangelical persuasion, he was a wastrel, and very probably immoral [. . .] To those holding Benthamite values, the artist was a parasite, a non-producer except of luxury items; in no way did he contribute to the national wealth of physical well-being. (Altick 1973: 279)

Many commentators, among whom are Lorimer (1978), Adams (1995), Hall, McClelland and Rendell (2000), and, more recently, John Tosh (2004), have documented the construction of Victorian manliness which was 'understood as a strenuous psychic regimen, which could be affirmed outside the economic arena' (Adams 1995: 7), but also defined through the structure of gender relations, and particularly through power relations between different categories of others, men and women (Tosh 2004: 42). Unmarried and financially dependent, Algernon is unable to gain recognition and achieve the financial success which would define him as a man. His rather ludicrous conceit – 'My *what*, Mother? My superiors? Where are they!!!' (Figure 2) efficiently contradicts the concept of reserve, another central tenet of Victorian male identity.

Du Maurier's familiarity with the leading figures of the Aesthetic movement certainly informs the illustrator's long-lasting visual criticism of its creeds and affectations. Historians of the Victorian periodical press and of the Aesthetic movement also note that 'it became editorial policy to attack Aesthetes in *Punch* as much as it had previously dealt ruthlessly with the other movements and individuals' (Aslin 1969: 114). As early as 1868, a cartoon by Charles Keene had mocked the avant-garde 'Fadsby' who implored his landlady to remove the two Staffordshire chimney ornaments she had placed on the mantelpiece, describing them as 'fictile abominations'. Three years later, in 1871, Keene's 'Thing of Beauty' – a double reference to Keats' poetry and the cult of beauty – had staged a conversation between philistine uncle and Aesthetic nephew about the latter's new rug in a domestic interior filled with black furniture, Japanese fans and sunflowers. The other artist concerned with *Punch*'s anti-Aesthetic crusade was Linley Sambourne whose 'Fancy Portrait n°37' mocked Oscar Wilde, 'Aesthete of Aesthetes', depicting him as a drooping sunflower (Sambourne 1881). Sambourne was also the author of 'Sweet Little Buttercup' (1879), a sketch published in the very same issue as du Maurier's famous 'Refinements of Modern Speech', in which a young lady dressed in a William Morris dress is surrounded with Aesthetic embroidery. *Punch*, in a word, 'expressed the comfortable, middle-class attitudes of Victorian England, and if its humour was sometimes sharp and to the point, it never seriously questioned the values of the society to which it pandered' (Ormond 1969: 161).

This pictorial discourse becomes even more obvious in 'Nincompoopiana' (Figure 3), in which the dandy's body functions as a metaphor, and the connection between moral and bodily health is particularly emphasised. The *Punch* reader is here introduced to Prigsby and Muffington, followers of Maudle of Postlethwaite, an artistic pair 'based on Wilde and Whistler with a touch of Swinburne' (Aslin 1969: 112; Lambourne 1996: 116). Within the exclusive setting of 'Passionate Brompton', these characters live an Aesthetic life, expressing their admiration for their respective arts and finding a convenient stage in the living-room of another Aesthetic family, the Cimabue-Browns. 'Nincompoopiana' depicts Prigsby and Muffington as they discuss the merits of 'Little Bo Peep', a nursery rhyme Prigsby considers as 'freshah, loveliah, and more subtle than anything Shelley evah wrote' and whose music, Muffington confirms, surpasses everything 'Schubert [. . .] evah composed' (Figure 3). The names of Shelley (1792–1822) and Schubert (1797–1828) conjure up the figure of the Romantic dandy who, 'in all his ghostly elegance [. . .] haunted the Victorian imagination' (Moers 1960: 13), providing a cultural framework against which the avant-garde could be measured. And while the two nincompoops, standing in the middle of the room, adopt the familiar mannerisms of the Aesthete – slightly bent legs, drooping arms and expansive gestures, a supposed imitation of Pre-Raphaelite paintings – their all-male audience, four listeners in the foreground and another group behind them, look up to them, slouching in comfortable armchairs.

180 Françoise Baillet

Figure 3 Du Maurier, G. (1879), 'Nincompoopiana'. (Source: *Punch*).

In the background, the lavish decoration of the stage-like drawing-room – Morris 'Daisy' wallpaper and printed fabric and rugs, Sussex armchairs, blue china vase with almond blossom sprigs and small convex mirror – unmistakably defines performers and audience as 'martyr[s] to the decorative art of the 19th century' (Keene 1868), a phrase Keene had used in an early anti-Aesthetic cartoon. The aim here is to ridicule affectations widely seen as the hallmark of dandiacal Aestheticism. Barely two years before Gilbert and Sullivan's *Patience* (1881), Prigsby, Muffington and their ecstatic circle of devotees illustrate the quirks of the 'worship of the lily and the peacock's feather' (Lambourne 1996: 119). And the quirks, flaws and outright deformities are many. For beyond the efficiency of the caption which mocks the affected pronunciation of those 'surfeited with excess of *cultchah*' (Figure 3), du Maurier's line, here again, becomes the visible trace of the characters' deviance. With their apathetic figures, their entangled arms and intertwined legs, the listeners in the foreground visually embody deviousness. Stretched out on their chairs, they adopt that 'consummate attitude', 'lolloping [. . .]

in a tangle' (du Maurier 1881) and prefiguring both the illustrator's renowned Aesthete Tristram Moldwarp and Gilbert and Sullivan's fleshly poet Bunthorne. The clear-cut line around their deficient and almost dismantled shapes thus functions as a literal delineation of improbity. And in this picture full of references to Antiquity – a bust of Antinoüs, favourite of the Roman emperor Hadrian, is visible in the background while the audience is defined in the caption as a [Greek] chorus – deviousness, again, also means homosexuality, closely linked to Aestheticism in the public mind.

Du Maurier's critical response to the dandy, as expressed through his anti-Aesthetic series for *Punch*, therefore stages the male figure as symptom of, and discourse on, social deviance. His exclusive and apathetic dilettante articulates a physical and moral corruption which could undermine the social body. He stands – or rather, 'languishes' – as a dramatised image of an unhealthy art which, unchecked, could ultimately endanger the health of the nation. For beyond the ludicrous 'nincompoop' and his contorted admirers emerges the figure of the degenerate artist whose unrestrained masculinity and subversive creeds du Maurier represents as a sign of social disorder. At a time when the concepts of deviance and degeneration were constructed as matters of national concern, the image of a pathological and possibly contagious artistic avant-garde becomes all the more ominous as it conjures up images of decay and death.

Degeneracy, Decadence and the Body Politic

Punch's anti-Aesthetic crusade, and du Maurier's in particular, reached its climax between 1879 and 1881, at a time when many felt that painting, as showcased by Sir Coutts Lindsay's 'Palace of Art', the newly opened Grosvenor Gallery, 'was moving into a decadent phase' (Bullen 1998: 151). Many commentators, such as Leslie Stephen writing for the *Cornhill Magazine*, contended that there should be a relation between moral and creative excellence: 'If the artist should express every sentiment,' Stephen remarked, 'he certainly should not omit the noblest. He should provide utterance for the heroic, the patriotic, the social, and the religious, or his field will be limited indeed' (Stephen 1875: 95). With their tendency to focus on doom and decay and 'to exalt subjective individual experience at the expense of straightforward depictions of nature and reality' (Härmänmaa and Nissen 2014: 1), Victorian avant-garde movements represented a rebellion against the dominant moral standards of their times. Chamberlin and Gilman have documented the connection between the Victorian notion of progress, 'a structure [. . .] superimposed on human endeavor in order to provide it with shape and meaning' and the concept of degeneration, its 'necessary and antithetical structure' (Chamberlin and Gilman 1985: vii). More recently, Michael Foldy mapped out these concepts, replacing them in the specific context of Darwinian thought:

> The concepts of degeneration and decadence must be understood within the prevailing cultural and intellectual context, which was thoroughly dominated by a Spencerian world-view. Spencer's philosophy (which was influenced but not determined by Darwinian ideas) conceptualized human societies as living organisms that, like all other living beings, were subject to the natural processes of birth, death, decay, selection, and competition. (Foldy 1997: 71)

And at a time when cultural, social, medical and penal spheres were tightly intertwined, artistic decadence could undermine and contaminate the whole nation. Weak-bodied and subversive-minded Bohemians were therefore (re)written into national concerns. Hence, probably, this late nineteenth-century obsession with the supposed mental unbalance of non-conformist artists which commentators like Cesare Lombroso, Max Nordau and their British followers such as Henry Maudsley largely circulated and popularised. Both Lombroso's study on *The Man of Genius* (1891) and Nordau's *Degeneration* (1895) equate creative genius with moral insanity, warning their contemporaries against the 'complete absence of moral sense and of sympathy frequently found among men of genius' and observing that '[a]mong poets and artists, criminality is, unfortunately, well marked' (Lombroso 1891: 57). In a chapter devoted to 'Mysticism', Nordau even goes as far as reducing the Aesthetic choices of the avant-garde to deficient eyesight. 'The curious style of certain recent painters – "impressionists", "stipplers", or "mosaists", "papilloteurs", or "quiverers", "roaring" colourists, dyers in grey and faded tints', he writes,

> becomes all at once intelligible to us if we keep in view the researches of the Charcot school into the visual derangements in degeneration or hysteria [. . .] The degenerate artist who suffers from *nystagmus*, or trembling of the eyeball, will, in fact, perceive the phenomena of nature trembling, restless, and devoid of firm outline. (Nordau 1895: 27)

A few years before, in an article written for the *Art Journal* and entitled 'The Nemesis of Art; or, a Philistine Lecture', Harry Quilter had made the same analysis, suggesting that the 'enervating influence' of Pre-Raphaelite art was due to the Brotherhood's deliberate rejection, in its representation of life, of energy, freshness, and what may be called 'the unselfish emotions', and denouncing the 'unhealthiness of feeling' of an art which, 'while giving great pleasure to its admirers, does so in such a way as rather to injure their characters and depress their energies' (Quilter 1883: 135). In an interesting (and then commonplace) confusion between Pre-Raphaelitism, Aestheticism and what was yet to become Art Nouveau, Quilter insists above all on what he interprets as the decay of avant-gardism which he defines as a disease of the body, echoing Victorian reinterpretations of Juvenalian *mens sana in corpore sano* [a sound mind in a sound body].

'Nincompoopiana – The Mutual Admiration Society' (Figure 4) precisely illustrates this degeneracy discourse, opposing artistic perversion to martial rectitude. Possibly inspired by the growing popularity of Oscar Wilde, then recently arrived in London and already famous for his poetry published in reviews like *Kottabos* and the *Dublin University Magazine*, the scene takes place at Mrs Cimabue-Brown's (whose oxymoronic name evokes both pre-Renaissance Tuscan art and the average Englishman).

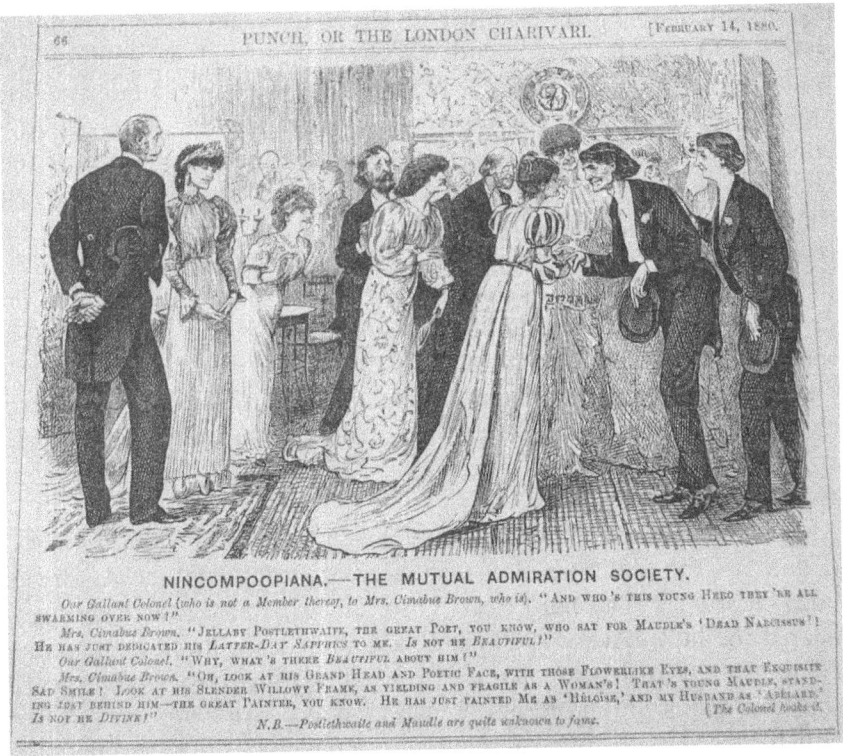

Figure 4 Du Maurier, G. (1880a), 'Nincompoopiana. The Mutual Admiration Society'. (Source: *Punch*).

The lions depicted are du Maurier's familiar *Punch* Aesthetes: Jellaby Postlethwaite 'the great poet' and Maudle 'the divine painter'. The question asked by 'our gallant colonel' – 'And who's this young hero they're all swarming over now?' – the literal quote of a remark made by Watts-Dunton during one of Whistler's celebrated Sunday breakfasts (Gaunt 1945: 104), renders du Maurier's point extremely clear. As often with the cartoonist, humour stems here from the blatant contradiction between the description made of Postlethwaite by the hostess (who mentions her guest's 'Grand Head and Poetic Face', 'Flowerlike Eyes' and 'Exquisite Sad Smile' before asking '*Is he not Beautiful?*') and the picture itself. With his gaunt face, hollow cheeks, thin frame and sunken eyes, Postlethwaite appears as a corpse, quite literally embodying the decay supposedly represented by his Aesthetic principles and way of life. His leanness and emaciation echo Lombroso's description of 'Genius and Degeneration' (Lombroso 1891: 7) while he presents several of Nordau's major physical signs of degeneracy (Codell 2003: 102). And even if the artistic pair sport abundant hair, the poet's scrawny neck and general atrophy – he is smaller than one of his female admirers, standing close to him – conspicuously evoke degeneracy, even morbidity. Barely standing on their 'Slender Willowy Frame[s], as yielding and fragile as a Woman's' (Figure 4), *Punch*'s Aesthetes articulate a major anxiety about disease and perversion, all the more clearly as the composition of the picture opposes them to the erect figure of the Colonel, an expression of normative manhood. In those years when the concept of health 'helped legitimize a moral approach to art by basing it on medical and physiological models' (Haley 1978: 67), they figure the toxicity of their artistic principles. As represented by du Maurier in the 'Nincompoopiana' series of the period 1879–81, the Aesthete is a figure of contagion, disease and death, a male equivalent of the prostitute, 'a sign of social disorder and ruin to be feared and controlled' (Nead 1988: 106). Because of their deviant and unrestrained social and sexual practices, both need to be separated from respectable society.

In a later sketch of the same series, 'The Mutual Admirationists' (Figure 5), the idea of a Bohemian toxicity reappears, the Aesthete's body figuring a national threat. Historians of the period have highlighted the link between the male body and the political, or national, community. 'British colonial rule,' Roper and Tosh argue, was partly justified by 'a conception of English manhood as a civilizing force' (Roper and Tosh 1991: 14). In a later essay, Tosh underlines the same national inscription of the male body, explaining that, 'In periods of emerging national identity or of national resistance, the dominant masculinity

Figure 5 Du Maurier, G. (1880b), 'The Mutual Admirationists'. (Source: *Punch*).

is likely to become a metaphor for the political community as a whole and to be expressed in highly idealised forms' (Tosh 2004: 49).

In du Maurier's vignettes, these idealised masculine forms are often symbolised by the towering figure of the Colonel, while the general dislocation of the Aesthete's body articulates the danger posed to the community by avant-gardism. This element of threat emerges quite clearly in a number of contemporary reviews of Pre-Raphaelite or Aesthetic works. Du Maurier himself, in a letter sent to his mother as a young man, had praised the 'clear, honest, wholesome, innocent, intellectual and most industrious British bohemia' (du Maurier 1898: 20) which he implicitly opposed to the unhealthy world of the avant-garde. Continental bohemia, to which British Aestheticism was associated, was perceived by many as 'politically or socially adversarial to bourgeois ambitions' (Codell 2003: 96).

In *Faces of Degeneration* (1989), Daniel Pick has convincingly demonstrated that the late Victorian discourse on the concept of degeneration essentially served an objective of social control. 'He who would find the centres of decay in a nation, still on the whole robust and active,' Pick argues, 'must seek for them at the points of social tension' (Pick 1989: 191). 'All the forces perceived as criminal or socially disruptive,' Foldy confirms:

> whether collective phenomena such as the socialist and feminist movements, or individual acts of subversion, such as Wilde's, which contested the hegemony of the dominant moral values, could be, and were, viewed by many as socially regressive, and labelled 'degenerate'. (Foldy 1997: 74)

Published in May 1880, 'The Mutual Admirationists' stages the artistic pair as they praise each other's art in front of an ecstatic female audience. And while Maudle, addressing 'Mrs Lyon Hunter and her Daughters', equates his friend's poetry to Shakespeare's, Postlethwaite describes the avant-garde painter as the new Velasquez under the fascinated gaze of 'the three Miss Bilderbogies' (Figure 5). In the background the upright figure of the Colonel is visible, standing next to the philistine Grigsby. Besides their conceit, the 'Mutual Admirationists' are, here again, remarkable for their improbable physical appearance. Slumped on a *méridienne*, Postlethwaite is looking at his audience, legs wound up on one another to the point of becoming almost indistinguishable and arms intertwined, forming a series of curves, sharp angles (elbows, knees) and broken lines. His lean and vacant face suggests the same unhealthiness as in the preceding sketch, here emphasised by the haggard look and consumptive frames of the three women he is facing. The main focus of the composition, the group formed by poet and admirers offers, besides, a visual commentary on the danger represented by a lack of emotional and sexual control. With their almost liquid bodies – Postlethwaite's undulating hair and back seem to be flowing away from the picture, echoing the fluid shape of the women's Aesthetic outfits – du Maurier's characters figure the uncontrolled outpouring of their emotions. By expanding out of their allotted space, they threaten to occupy – to contaminate – a collective space, albeit an already tarnished one. Unable to acquire true manhood by restraint and self-control, Postlethwaite and Maudle bespeak the inherent danger associated with their *risqué* choices, illustrating the 'spasmodic ramifications' and 'morbid deviations from healthy forms of life' Thomas Maitland [Robert Buchanan] was, nine years before, warning the *Contemporary Review* readers about in his diatribe against the 'Fleshy School of Poetry' (Maitland 1871: 334). And while Buchanan had stressed the need for the British art world to protect itself against 'the seeds of disease' that the 'unwholesome poet', D. G. Rossetti, was spreading 'wherever he [was] read and understood', du Maurier *re-presents* the omnipresence of that 'fleshy feeling' whose adepts 'bite, scratch, scream, bubble, munch, sweat, *writhe, twist, wriggle*, foam, and slaver, in a style frightful to hear of' (Maitland 1871: 343, my emphasis). The artist's line becomes the 'outward skin' protecting the body politic from the 'spasmodic, galvanic sprawlings' which, Carlyle explained in *Sartor Resartus*, could endanger it (Haley 1978: 76).

As expressed through his anti-Aesthetic series for *Punch*, du Maurier's critical response to the avant-garde therefore stages the male figure as symptom of and discourse on a gangrene undermining the social body. The illustrator's sinuous and contorted line becomes invested with an edifying mission, signalling dis-ease – these cramped positions – and confining its development. A 'focus for public and private pleasure, puzzlement and disquiet', (Bullen 1998: 1) the Aesthetic body becomes the means to distance and discuss the movement's social and moral implications. Placing the degenerate other under collective scrutiny through this visual discourse also has the effect of placing the *Punch* reader within the inner circle of proper society. 'The readers of the illustrated magazine,' Beegan argues, 'wanted to see who they were, and who their fellow Britons were, a desire not limited to press images' (Beegan 2008: 4). Belonging to this interpretive community allowed both du Maurier and his audience to define the Aesthetic avant-garde as a subject of mockery and thus to consolidate bourgeois identity.

Conclusion: An Intaglio Sketch of Artistic Respectability

In his contribution to *The Victorians and Race*, Tim Barringer examines the visual processes through which the notion of difference is assessed. 'The field of visual representation,' Barringer explains, 'offered a site for the production and dramatization of powerful distinctions between self and other, in which normative categories of body-type and behaviour could be presented in contrast to those of others, constructed as deviant' (Barringer 1996: 34–5). Far from being simple mirror-images of reality, pictures thus offered a privileged space for the articulation of a cultural discourse. The text-image relationship, as it was then played out in the pages of *Punch* and in the British periodical press at large, provided ample scope for this discursive practice which, as Peter Sinnema explains, was 'active in the production of truth(s), and engaged with a complex array of other discourses' (Sinnema 1998: 2). Du Maurier's Aesthetic stereotypes may thus be analysed as the expression of 'a shared set of assumptions operating between text and readers in the reading encounter' (ibid.: 3). By chuckling at the illustrator's weekly sketches, *Punch*'s middle-class readership took an active part in the expression of the dominant moral values.

Tracing the literal contours of (im)propriety also allowed du Maurier and the *Punch* cartoonists to deal with some of the most pressing artistic issues of the day. In spite of the increasing level of public interest for art and the large sums earned by a handful of artists among whom were W. P. Frith, Eastlake or Landseer and, to a lesser extent, George Elgar Hicks and William Mary Egley (Hoppen 1998: 406), the Victorian artist's status 'remained circumscribed' (Codell 2003: 18). And while some painter-professionals managed to achieve a remarkable rise in status, many others remained unacknowledged, sometimes respected but more often treated with disdain. The situation was even worse for graphic artists, whose art tended to be associated with the excesses of continental Bohemia, and thus remained outside the dominant constructions of masculinity. *Punch*'s 'official scorn of literary Bohemianism' (Leary 2010: 73), so obvious in later writings such as Marion Spielmann's history of the magazine, allowed it to cleanse itself from associations with disreputable circles. As an illustrated periodical relying on wood engraving, *Punch* was a part of the printing and publishing world and 'stood where artistic and journalistic bohemias met' (Fox 1988: 27). Little acknowledged by the art establishment, engraving remained generally scorned throughout the mid-Victorian years, often associated with the political activism of the early century. Despite the changes brought to graphic art by the advent of the Pre-Raphaelite Brotherhood which produced stronger, deeper and altogether more powerful illustrations – as in the Moxon edition of Tennyson's poems – Victorian graphic artists remained largely outside the dominant constructions of masculinity. Often trained as engravers only and involved in a 'lower' art, they were still, in the late nineteenth century, largely associated with the satire of the sexual scandals of the Regency.

Hence the need for *Punch*'s black-and-white artists – du Maurier in particular, who had collaborated with such artistic magazines as *Good Words*, *Once a Week* or the *Cornhill* – to rewrite themselves into respectable (art) producers. Tracing the contours of artistic propriety through the depiction of the deficient male body procured them social leverage, allowing them to claim normative Victorian manhood.

Works Cited

Adams, J. E. (1995), *Dandies and Desert Saints: Styles of Victorian Masculinity*, New York: Cornell University Press.
Altick, R. (1957), *The English Common Reader: A Social History of the Mass Reading Public 1800–1900*, Chicago: The University of Chicago Press.
Altick, R. (1973), *Victorian People and Ideas*, New York: Norton.
Altick, R. (1997), *Punch: The Lively Youth of a British Institution 1841–1851*, Columbus: Ohio State University Press.
Anon. (1877), 'The Grosvenor Gallery Exhibition', *The Athenaeum*, 79: 2584, pp. 583–4.
Aslin, E. (1969), *The Aesthetic Movement: Prelude to Art Nouveau*, London: Elek.
Barringer, T. (1996), 'Images of Otherness and the Visual Production of Difference: Race and Labour in Illustrated Texts', in S. West (ed.), *The Victorians and Race*, Aldershot: Ashgate, pp. 34–52.
Barringer, T. (2005), *Men at Work*, New Haven, CT and London: Yale University Press.
Beegan, G. (2008), *The Mass Image: A Social History of Photomechanical Reproduction in Victorian London*, Basingstoke: Palgrave Macmillan.
Bullen, J. B. (1998), *The Pre-Raphaelite Body*, Oxford: Clarendon Press.
Cannadine, D. (1993), *The Rise and Fall of Class in Britain*, New York: Columbia University Press.
Carlyle, T. [1843] (2005), *Past and Present*, Berkeley: University of California Press.
Chamberlin, J. E. and S. L. Gilman (eds) (1985), *Degeneration: The Dark Side of Progress*, New York: Columbia University Press.
Codell, J. (2003), *The Victorian Artist: Artists' Lifewritings in Britain, ca. 1870–1910*, Cambridge: Cambridge University Press.
Codell, J. (2009), 'Pre-Raphaelites from Rebels to Representatives: Masculinity, Modernity, and National Identity in British and Continental Art Histories, c. 1880–1908', in G. Michaela and T. Barringer (eds), *Writing the Pre-Raphaelites: Text, Context, Subtext*, Aldershot: Ashgate, pp. 53–79.
Cowling, M. (1989), *The Artist as Anthropologist: The Representation of Type and Character in Victorian Art*, Cambridge: Cambridge University Press.
Cowling, M. (2000), *Victorian Figurative Painting*, London: Andreas Papadakis Publisher.
Davidoff, L. and C. Hall (1987), *Family Fortunes: Men and Women of the English Middle Class 1780–1850*, London: Hutchinson.
Dawson, G. (1991), 'The Blond Bedouin', in M. Roper and J. Tosh (eds), *Manful Assertions*, London: Routledge, pp. 113–44.
Dudink, S. (2004), 'Masculinity, Effeminacy, Time: Conceptual Change in the Dutch Age of Democratic Revolutions', in S. Dudink, K. Hagemann

and J. Tosh (eds), *Masculinities in Politics and War: Gendering Modern History*, Manchester: Manchester University Press, pp. 77–95.

du Maurier, G. (1876), 'Intellectual Epicures', in *Punch*, 70, p. 33.

du Maurier, G. (1879a), 'Aesthetic Pride', in *Punch*, 77, p. 142.

du Maurier, G. (1879b), 'Nincompoopiana', in *Punch*, 77, p. 282.

du Maurier, G. (1880a), 'Nincompoopiana. The Mutual Admiration Society', in *Punch*, 78, p. 66.

du Maurier, G. (1880b), 'The Mutual Admirationists', in *Punch*, 78, p. 234.

du Maurier, G. (1881), 'Athlete and Aesthete', in *Punch*, 80, p. 122.

du Maurier, G. (1898), *Social Pictorial Satire*, New York and London: Harper and Brothers.

du Maurier, D. (ed.) (1952), *The Young George du Maurier. A Selection of his Letters, 1860–1867*, New York: Doubleday and Company Inc.

Ellegård, A. (1957), *The Readership of the Periodical Press in Victorian Britain*, Göteborg: Elanders Boktryckeri Aktiebolag.

Fillin-Yeh, S. (ed.) (2001), *Dandies: Fashion and Finesse in Art and Culture*, New York: New York University Press.

Foldy, M. S. (1997), *The Trials of Oscar Wilde: Deviance, Morality, and Late-Victorian Society*, New Haven, CT and London: Yale University Press.

Fox, C. (1988), *Graphic Journalism in England during the 1830s and 1840s*, London: Garland.

Freedman, J. (1990), *Professions of Taste: Henry James, British Aestheticism and Commodity Culture*, Stanford: Stanford University Press.

Garelick, R. K. (1998), *Rising Star: Dandyism, Gender, and Performance in the Fin-de-Siècle*, Princeton: Princeton University Press.

Gaunt, W. (1945), *The Aesthetic Adventure*, London: Jonathan Cape and the Book Society.

Gillett, P. (1990), *Worlds of Art*, New Brunswick, NJ: Rutgers University Press.

Gilman, S. L. (1991), *Inscribing the Other*, Lincoln and London: University of Nebraska Press.

Haley, B. (1978), *The Healthy Body and Victorian Culture*, Cambridge, MA: Harvard University Press.

Hall, C., K. McClelland and J. Rendall (2000), *Defining the Victorian Nation*, Cambridge: Cambridge University Press.

Härmänmaa, M. and C. Nissen (eds) (2014), *Decadence, Degeneration and the End*, New York: Palgrave Macmillan.

Hatt, M. (1999), 'Physical Culture: The Male Nude and Sculpture in Victorian Britain', in E. Prettejohn (ed.), *After the Pre-Raphaelites: Art and Aestheticism in Victorian England*, Manchester: Manchester University Press, pp. 240–56.

Hewitt, M. (ed.) (2000), *An Age of Equipoise? Reassessing Mid-Victorian Britain*, Aldershot: Ashgate.

Hoppen, K. T. (1998), *The Mid-Victorian Generation 1846–1886*, Oxford: Clarendon Press.
Keene, Charles (1868), 'Aesthetics', in *Punch*, 55, p. 87.
Kingsley, F. (ed.) (1877), *Charles Kingsley: His Letters and Memories of his Life*, vol. 1, London: C. Kegan Paul and Co.
Lambourne, L. (1996), *The Aesthetic Movement*, London: Phaidon Press Ltd.
Leary, P. (2010), *The Punch Brotherhood Table Talk and Print Culture in Mid-Victorian London*, London: The British Library.
Lombroso, C. [1891] (1984), *The Man of Genius*, New York and London: Garland.
Lorimer, D. A. (1978), *Colour, Class and the Victorians*, Bristol: Leicester University Press.
Maitland, T. [Buchanan, R.] (1871), 'The Fleshly School of Poetry', *The Contemporary Review*, 18, pp. 334–50.
Meisel, M. (1983), *Realizations*, Princeton: Princeton University Press.
Moers, E. (1960), *The Dandy: Brummell to Beerbohm*, London: Secker and Warburg.
Nead, L. (1988), *Myths of Sexuality: Representations of Women in Victorian Britain*, London: Basil Blackwell.
Nordau, M. [1895] (1920), *Degeneration*, London: William Heinemann.
Ormond, L. (1969), *George du Maurier*, London: Routledge and Kegan Paul.
Pater, W. (1889), *Appreciations, with an Essay on Style*, London: Macmillan and Co. Ltd.
Pater, W. (1917), *The Renaissance: Studies in Art and Poetry*, London: Macmillan and Co. Ltd.
Pick, D. (1989), *Faces of Degeneration: A European Disorder, c. 1848–c. 1918*, Cambridge: Cambridge University Press.
Pointon, M. (1993), *Hanging the Head Portraiture and Social Formation in Eighteenth-Century England*, New Haven, CT and London: Yale University Press.
Quilter, H. (1883), 'The Nemesis of Art; or, a Philistine Lecture', *The Art Journal*, new series 3, pp. 134–7.
Roper, M. and J. Tosh (eds) (1991), *Manful Assertions: Masculinities in Britain since 1800*, London: Routledge.
Ruskin, John (1903–12), *Works*, ed. E. T. Cook and A. Wedderburn, 39 vols, London: G. Allen, vol. XI, *The Stones of Venice*.
Sambourne, L. (1881), 'Punch's Fancy Portraits – N°37', in *Punch*, 80, p. 298.
Sinnema, P. (1998), *Dynamics of the Pictured Page: Representing the Nation in the* Illustrated London News, Aldershot: Ashgate.
Stephen, L. (1875), 'Art and Morality', *The Cornhill Magazine*, 32, pp. 91–101.
Sussman, H. (1995), *Victorian Masculinities*, Cambridge: Cambridge University Press.

Swinburne A. [1866] (1883), *Poems and Ballads*, London: Chatto and Windus.
Tosh, J. (1999), *A Man's Place: Masculinity and the Middle-Class Home in Victorian England*, New Haven, CT and London: Yale University Press.
Tosh, J. (2004), 'Hegemonic Masculinities and the History of Gender', in S. Dudink, K. Hagemann and J. Tosh (eds), *Masculinities in Politics and War: Gendering Modern History*, Manchester: Manchester University Press, pp. 41–58.
Vance, N. (1985), *The Sinews of the Spirit: The Ideal of Christian Manliness in Victorian Literature and Religious Thought*, Cambridge: Cambridge University Press.

Chapter 9

Suffering, Asceticism and the Starving Male Body in *Mary Barton*

Charlotte Boyce

> Nothing like the act of eating for equalizing men. Dying is nothing to it.
> (Gaskell 1995: 354)

> I never see the masters getting thin and haggard for want of food.
> (Gaskell 1996: 384)

On learning that John Thornton, the industrialist hero of Elizabeth Gaskell's *North and South* (1854–5), has recently opened a communal dining-room for his employees, Thornton's landlord Mr Bell signals his approval for the scheme by blithely declaring that there is 'nothing like the act of eating for equalizing men'; whereas men die differently according to their stations, Bell suggests, 'all eat after the same fashion' (Gaskell 1995: 354). This naive faith in the democratising power of consumption would not, in all likelihood, have been shared by Gaskell's early Victorian readers, for within the print culture of the period the 'act of eating' was consistently understood as a means by which to categorise and differentiate forms of masculinity. As the old weaver Job Legh astutely notes in Gaskell's earlier industrial fiction, *Mary Barton* (1848), 'I never see the masters getting thin and haggard for want of food' (Gaskell 1996: 384).

Dietary differences were a key theme in the raft of social investigations into the moral and physical condition of the manufacturing classes published during the 1830s and 1840s. Within these reports the white, working-class, male body was recurrently distinguished from its middle-class counterpart in terms of appetite: how, what and how much it consumed. Counter-intuitively though, within this discourse, those bodies with access to the least were typically constructed as the most gluttonous. Despite having to subsist on a meagre or, in many cases, inadequate diet during the periods of economic depression that haunted the '30s and '40s, industrial male labourers were invariably represented in terms of alimentary voracity by social commentators. Figured as the possessors of an excessive, animalistic – and sometimes quasi-cannibalistic – hunger, working-class men were positioned in overt ideological opposition to the bourgeois manly ideal, which was celebrated in early Victorian culture for its exemplary qualities of self-discipline and control.

Perhaps unsurprisingly, assumptions about the unruly character of working-class male appetites frequently slipped over from social discourse into contemporary fiction, such as Gaskell's own. In *North and South*, for instance, the self-denying rigour that underpins John Thornton's entrepreneurial success stands in direct contrast to the improvidence and immoderation displayed by labourers such as Nicholas Higgins (a man who, by his own admission, is 'given to drink') and John Boucher, the unemployed father of eight whose very name suggests the French word for 'mouth' (*bouche*) and whose frenzied hunger impels him to join the mob of 'men, gaunt as wolves, and mad for prey', who riot against Thornton's mill (Gaskell 1995: 319; 176). As Herbert Sussman explains in his influential study of nineteenth-century masculinity, the ability to properly regulate the body and its desires was an integral component of the Victorians' class-based conceptions of manliness (Sussman 1995: 11). Therefore, while Thornton's capacity to sublimate physical appetite into productive forms of industry marks him out as a model of bourgeois manhood, the rioters' 'demoniac desire [. . .] for the food that is withheld from [their] ravening' associates them instead with 'working-class *un*manliness': that is, the untamed, 'unregulated flow of male energy' that threatens to derange individual psyches and damage the social order (Gaskell 1995: 175; Sussman 1995: 65, my emphasis).

For critics such as Tamara Ketabgian, 'bestial and automatic instincts' similarly 'define the symbolic contours of working-class habit' in *Mary Barton*, the *Tale of Manchester Life* on which this essay concentrates (Ketabgian 2011: 71). Certainly, the novel's descriptions of starving weaver Ben Davenport snatching 'with animal instinct' at a jug of tea intended for his weary wife, and of hungry trades union members seizing eagerly at the opportunity to indulge in 'tobacco and drink', seem to participate in the pervasive cultural conflation of brutish cravings with working-class masculinity (Gaskell 1996: 62; 185). However, to focus narrowly on such examples of apparent intersection with popular stereotype is to miss what Lisa Surridge recognises as *Mary Barton*'s key difference from *North and South*: the former novel's 'emphatic identification' of 'exemplary manliness' with its lower-class characters (Surridge 2000: 333). Although Gaskell appears, at times, to reproduce culturally entrenched ideas about proletarian excess in her earlier novel, she also complicates such easy ideological assumptions via a series of representations in which hungry male workers demonstrate the kind of stoical self-denial more usually associated with middle-class manhood.

In particular, John Barton (the character whom Gaskell originally intended to be the eponymous hero of her novel)[1] comes to cultivate an abstemious relationship to food during the course of the text. This rigorous and ethically motivated practice of renunciation recalls the *askesis* valorised in the classical education typically enjoyed by Victorian gentlemen; notably, however, the working-class Barton's asceticism is self-taught. Having been schooled in the visceral pangs of hunger since childhood, as an adult he repeatedly denies the cravings of his body so that he can nourish others, whose need for food he deems to be greater than his own. This determined subdual of physical appetite is characterised as inherently ennobling, not least because to refuse food when it is scarce conceivably requires a greater effort of self-will than to do so when it is plentiful. As Lesa Scholl points out, 'the ability to moderate (or regulate) one's own appetite is a luxury that few can afford'; those who 'have the capacity to choose when, how much, and what they eat' usually enjoy a level of social agency that liberates them from the 'fear that what they currently have will not be renewed' (Scholl 2016: 4).

If asceticism works to elevate and ennoble working-class masculinity within Gaskell's novel on the one hand, it also has the potential to damage, or even obliterate, the self-denying male body on the other. In a vivid demonstration of Sussman's point that overly intensive forms of masculine self-discipline threaten to 'distort the male psyche and deform the very energy that powers and empowers men' (Sussman 1995: 3), Barton's continued suppression of appetite comes to be shadowed by a monomaniacal obsession with social inequality that eventually erupts into murderous violence; following the masters' rejection of the workers' appeal for higher wages, Barton shoots and kills Harry Carson, the playboy son of a local factory-owner, who has previously shown a callous disregard for the working men's plight. As well as such externally directed violence, Barton's asceticism is also imbricated with the self-destructive tendencies exhibited by proto-anorexic female characters in early Victorian literature; from the time of the murder, his previously stoical self-denial slips into a more masochistic form of self-starvation, finally reducing him to a 'phantom likeness' of himself (Gaskell 1996: 347). In light of this semantic instability, I shall argue in this essay that going without food works ultimately to unsettle Victorian cultural constructions of gender and class in *Mary Barton*, at once masculating and feminising the starving male body and eroding the ostensibly fixed, but in fact only too permeable, grounds of distinction between working- and middle-class manhood.

Categorising Masculine Appetite(s)

In the spring of 1837, as a period of economic depression loomed, an article in the Tory *Blackwood's Edinburgh Magazine* reconfigured the coming crisis in terms of a national crisis of masculinity:

> No more heavy curse could be visited on a nation than [. . .] with an industrial crash imminent, to have men in the supreme direction of affairs mentally, morally, physically moreover, incapable of rising, not above only, but to the level of circumstances which surround them. (Mallalieu 1837: 554)

The signal fear articulated here – that British masculinity might not be up to the task of meeting the challenges imposed by a new industrial age – was one that reverberated throughout the 1830s and 1840s, as a number of critics have pointed out.[2] Back in 1831, Thomas Carlyle had fretted that 'the old ideal of Manhood has grown obsolete, and the new is still invisible to us, and we grope after it in darkness' (Carlyle 1831: 373). In Alfred Mallalieu's *Blackwood's* essay, this anxious struggle to locate and formalise a neoteric pattern of manhood seems still to be on-going. Clearly though, the modern masculine ideal on which industrial Britain's future depended was not to be found in the kind of aristocratic masculinity embodied by the then Whig Prime Minister, Lord Melbourne, of whom Mallalieu complains, 'a life of luxurious ease [. . .] has wasted whatever of vigour might once have been his in the heyday of the blood [. . .] it is not in his nature to be energetic' (Mallalieu 1837: 554). Implicit in this focus on Melbourne's lack of manly dynamism (tell-tale symptom of an enervating, class-based repletion) is the notion that what Britain requires to succeed in the industrial age is not the leadership of a languid and satiated aristocracy but the activity of a new breed of male striver, motivated by a robust and vitalising hunger.

One of the potent wellsprings of energy that drove masculinity, hunger was conceived of as a powerful but potentially chaotic force in Victorian culture. On the one hand, it could work in positive ways to fuel ambition, stimulate ingenuity and invigorate social progress; a spur to activity, hunger could function as a necessary corrective to the bodily and mental torpor that was assumed to afflict upper-class masculinity. On the other hand, it could manifest itself in dangerous or disruptive forms, exciting men to acts of violent rebellion or driving them to states of mental derangement. Carlyle, for instance, attributed the eruption of 'delirious Chartism' amongst working people in the late 1830s to the 'black mutinous discontent' with their conditions of existence that 'devour[ed] them' from within (Carlyle 1840: 3; 34). Similarly, in 1848 – the notorious 'year of revolutions' – British newspapers anxiously reported that the security of several European cities was under threat from 'masses of unemployed workmen, entertaining wild views, and urged by hunger into violence' (Anon. 1848: 4).

If hunger was to facilitate activity that was socially, culturally and economically useful, it had to be carefully harnessed and channelled into appropriate forms of endeavour: disciplined and converted into productive physical or intellectual labour. Helpfully, the ancient and medieval past furnished Victorian men with a variety of role models from whom they could learn the ascetic self-practice necessary to the sublimation of bodily appetite. As Lee Behlman suggests, the exemplary Stoicism of Roman leaders such as Marcus Aurelius provided a valuable paradigm of 'self-discipline and moral authority' that could be used to 'guide British manhood' through the trials and tribulations of modernity (Behlman 2011: 1).[3] Alternatively, as Sussman notes, the 'productive repression' of the medieval monk presented Victorians with 'the very model of a new form of manhood', suitable for adoption by the nineteenth-century male (Sussman 1995: 27; 16). A notable example of this endorsement can be found in *Past and Present* (1843), where Carlyle co-opts the historical figure of Abbot Samson – a 'stoical monastic man' who was 'in the highest degree indifferent' to alimentary matters – as an archetype of manliness, owing to his ability to reconcile the twin demands of 'self-denial and strenuous effort' (Carlyle 1918: 88; 87; Sussman 1995: 25).

Importantly, though, the Victorian male's capacity to replicate such historical ascetics' successful transmutation of hunger into productive, orderly activity was not seen as universally achievable across the class spectrum. As James Eli Adams explains, the self-control that denoted proper manliness was enmeshed in systems of 'symbolic' as well as economic 'capital', forming part of the Victorians' 'urgent preoccupation' with delineating 'new hierarchies of authority' (Adams 1995: 4; 5). A commodious marker of social status, appetitive discipline helped to distinguish bourgeois masculinity from both its upper- and working-class counterparts. While aristocratic masculinity was commonly associated with luxurious self-indulgence, as we have seen, the proletarian male appetite was popularly conceived of as voracious and undiscriminating. Indeed, alongside a wealth of statistics and reportage testifying to the abject impoverishment and chronic starvation to be found in British manufacturing districts, Victorian print media disseminated many censorious accounts of working men's alimentary excesses, habitual intemperance and utter thraldom to the demands of the stomach.

Although the inflexible timetable that structured the working day in nineteenth-century factories, mills and workshops placed severe restrictions on *when* labouring men were able to eat, it failed to elicit correspondingly disciplined modes of consumption, according to a range of social commentators, who contrasted the strict regularity of the factory bell with the unruly behaviour that typically followed its announcement of the breakfast or dinner hour. An 1849 piece for the *Morning Chronicle* suggested that 'as the chimes sound, all the engines pause together, and from every workshop [. . .] the hungry crowd swarms out' to dinner (Reach 1849: 5). Elsewhere, physician James Kay claimed that the labourer 'has neither moral dignity nor intellectual nor organic strength to resist the seductions of appetite' following his exertions at work, when 'a meal of the coarsest food is prepared with heedless haste, and devoured with equal precipitation' (Kay 1832: 11). As Ketabgian points out, in such accounts of factory life, 'working-class regularity and irregularity emerge as closely intertwined forces' (Ketabgian 2011: 79). Artificially suppressed by the mechanistic rhythms of the working day, the industrial operative's visceral hunger goes on to erupt with brute force during his leisure hours, reverting to what is tacitly seen in middle-class reportage as its 'natural' state.

Strikingly, these accounts provide little sense of a lack of available food in lower-class communities, or, perhaps more importantly, of a lack of income with which to purchase it. Rather, they tend to coincide with what historian John Burnett calls 'one of the most widely held attitudes about working people' in circulation in the early Victorian period: namely, 'that they were extravagant and improvident, [and] that their incomes would be quite adequate for their needs if only they were laid out economically and not squandered on expensive foods and drink' (Burnett 1989: 48). In his *Philosophy of Manufactures*, for instance, Andrew Ure confidently attests to the lavish tastes of the proletariat, claiming that it is not hunger but 'nervous ailments', the result of 'a diet too rich and exciting for their in-door occupations', that form the prevailing cause of ill-health among factory workers (Ure 1835: 298).

Where Victorian commentators do acknowledge the hunger of working-class men, it tends to be in ways that, once again, emphasise the animality (and, hence, the alterity) of lower-class masculinity. In his study into *Cases of Death by Starvation*, John Lhotsky declares that those affected by hunger sometimes '[dilacerate] the arms and other parts of their body with their teeth, for the sake of satisfying, in some degree, the cravings of a ravenous, and as it were, beastly appetite' (Lhotsky 1844: 3). The suggestion, here, that bestial hunger gives rise to autophagous impulses is paralleled by other writers' implication that the poor engaged in practices that were quasi-anthropophagic. In *Past and Present*, Carlyle recalls a case in which two parents were found guilty of poisoning their children in an attempt to defraud a burial-society, and subtly figures this act of filicide in cannibalistic terms:

> What shall we do to escape starvation? [. . .] Our poor little starveling Tom, who cries all day for victuals, who will see only evil and not good in this world: if he were out of misery at once; he well dead, and the rest of us perhaps kept alive? It is thought, and hinted; at last it is done. And now Tom being killed, and all spent and eaten, is it poor little starveling Jack that must go, or poor little starveling Will? (Carlyle 1918: 4)

The concatenation of killing and eating, here, is suggestive of human sacrifice; the Stockport parents have (metaphorically) fed off their children, Carlyle implies, heightening the impression by means of a sinister allusion to paternal cannibalism in Dante's *Inferno*: 'Yes, in the Ugolino Hunger-tower stern things happen; best-loved little Gaddo fallen on his Father's knees!' (ibid.: 4).

Such extreme representations of proletarian appetite in narratives intended for middle-class readers can, of course, be interpreted in terms of their defensive psychological function. As Scholl points out, 'the fear of being forced to acknowledge connection to – and therefore responsibility for' – the 'unhuman, animalistic, irrational corporate body' 'motivates the need for imaginative distance' in a variety of early Victorian texts dealing with the poor (Scholl 2016: 52). By erecting class-based barriers between civilised self and unruly other, such texts participate in the task of protecting middle-class consciousness, while concomitantly deflecting wider questions about social inequality, moral injustice and ethical accountability.

Yet, it is important to recognise that it was not only in conservative discourse that the industrial male body was constructed in terms of alimentary 'otherness'. The image of the worker as bestial and voracious was also deployed in more radical texts, though 'with quite different ends in mind', as Macdonald Daly observes (Daly 1996: xxvii). In his *Condition of the Working Class in England* (1844), socialist writer Friedrich Engels deplores the animal excesses of Manchester labourers, but attributes their behaviour to capitalist exploitation; when working men are used for their labour and then 'abandon[ed] [. . .] to starvation' once trade stalls, it is hardly 'to be wondered at' that they should 'give [themselves] over blindly and madly' to the few 'sensual pleasures' available to them, he suggests (Engels 1993: 10; 139). A similar sympathy for proletarian indulgence emerges in the poetry of the radical writer Robert Nicoll, where raucous festivity performs both an analgesic and amnestic function. The working-class speaker of 'A Bacchanalian' explains:

> From misery I freedom seek –
>   I crave relief from pain;
> From hunger, poverty, and cold –
>   I'll go get drunk again! (Nicoll 1853: 185)

Oral excess is again here presented as a defensible response to the misery of exigency. Crucially, though, while the purpose and sentiment of this kind of empathetic representation of proletarian ravenousness may differ from the more disapproving examples deployed by advocates of the factory-system, its essential effect is the same: in radical and conservative discourse alike, hungry working-class men are reduced to mere stomachs – all appetitive impulse, no self-control.

'Daddy, a bit of bread!': Manly Nurturance and Heroic Self-Denial

At a superficial level, Gaskell's *Mary Barton* appears to coincide with a number of the assumptions about male appetite outlined in the section above. In particular, the novel rehearses familiar claims about the uneconomical habits of labouring men, which cause their patterns of consumption to veer wildly between hedonistic overindulgence and extreme privation. In keeping with James Kay's suggestion that spendthrift workmen '[debase themselves] beneath the animals whose instincts teach them to lay up stores for the season of need', Gaskell's narrator accuses the factory operatives to whose thoughts and feelings she claims to give sympathetic voice of a 'child-like improvidence' that induces them to 'forget all prudence and foresight' when trade is brisk and work plentiful (Kay 1832: 28; Gaskell 1996: 24). Among these workers apparently careless of the future is John Barton. Despite having first-hand knowledge of the suffering that may result from 'the scanty living consequent upon bad times' (his mother, we are told, died from starvation), Barton spends all of his earnings with 'the confidence [. . .] of one who was willing, and believed himself able, to supply all his wants by his own exertions' – a confidence that may also be labelled 'improvidence', the narrator observes, in a strong hint that the distresses of the poor can be attributed as much to deficiencies in *domestic*, as to downturns in national, economy (ibid.: 7; 24).

Yet, if *Mary Barton* fails to escape entirely from hegemonic constructions of undisciplined and extravagant working-class appetite, it nevertheless serves to complicate them. As a number of critics have noted, Gaskell's novel is replete with examples of sober, manly nurturance, whereby labouring men voluntarily defer or dismiss their own bodily wants in order to supply the alimentary needs of children or strangers.[4] In some cases, these acts of nurturance are relatively straightforward expressions of familial love or kindness. For instance, at the homely tea-party that takes place in the second chapter of the novel, George Wilson nurses one of his sickly twin sons, trying 'vainly to quieten [the boy] with bread soaked in milk' in an act of quasi-maternal care that is mirrored later, in Chapter 9, when Job Legh recalls how he and his neighbour Jennings hand-reared their orphaned infant granddaughter Margaret on their journey from London to Manchester (ibid.: 18). The description of the two compassionate but clumsy men trying awkwardly to coax a mixture of bread and milk into the hungry child's uncooperative mouth – 'it made its mouth like a square, and let [the mixture] run out at each o' the four corners'– represents a rare moment of light-hearted humour in Gaskell's novel (ibid.: 105). However, as Lisa Surridge cautions, the 'triumphant comedy' of this anecdote should not blind us to its political significance (Surridge 2000: 336). The story's close proximity to John Barton's more solemn evocation of 'many a little one clemming [starving] at home' ties it to *Mary Barton*'s bleaker political themes, as well as to the novel's culturally subversive investment in the ideal of the nurturing working-class man who is capable of rising above mere animal instinct (Gaskell 1996: 101). Notably, we are told that, on the journey to Manchester, Legh and Jennings were obliged to forego their own meals at a coaching-inn, having selflessly devoted the short time allowed to them before their vehicle's departure to their attempts to satisfy baby Margaret's hunger. This solicitous, self-renouncing tendency is also demonstrated in Gaskell's novel by the 'manly' Jem Wilson who devotes his wages to feeding his unemployed family and gives up his break-time to go and buy oranges for his ailing younger brothers, and by the Chartist delegates to London in Chapter 9, who 'eat but little' of the hearty breakfast provided for them because they cannot stomach it knowing that their 'wives and little ones' back at home have 'nought to eat' (ibid.: 44; 100).

In addition to its abundant representations of familial nurturance by working-class men, *Mary Barton* also supplies some striking examples of what might be termed 'disinterested self-denial', in which the beneficiaries of masculine abnegation are strangers rather than kin. This type of altruistic behaviour is exhibited most frequently in the novel by John Barton. Like George and Jem Wilson and Job Legh, Barton is keen to do all he can to ameliorate the hungers of his family: as a boy he frequently 'told the noble lie, that "he was not hungry, could not eat a bit more"' at mealtimes, so that his meagre portion of food might be distributed among his younger siblings, while later, as a father, all of the bodily pain he experiences from famishment during a period of unemployment is 'swallowed up in anxiety' for his starving son, Tom (ibid.: 114; 25). Crucially, though, Barton's ethos of humanitarian care is not restricted to his immediate household. When George Wilson tells him of the desperate situation of Ben Davenport, a fellow factory-worker dying of fever, whose family has 'ne'er a stick o' fire nor a cowd [cold] potato' to sustain them, Barton takes a charitable interest in the Davenports' welfare despite the fact that he is not personally acquainted with them and has barely enough food and money with which to support himself and his daughter Mary (ibid.: 59). He generously gifts the wretched family the sparse fare he has put aside for his supper – 'bread, and a slice of cold fat boiled bacon'– and the small portion of oatmeal he has in the house (ibid.). More benevolently still, he pawns his few possessions of value (a coat and a silk pocket-handkerchief) for the sum of five shillings and uses the money to purchase the Davenports meat, bread, candles and coal: the human necessities of 'food, light, and warmth' (ibid.: 61). Barton's status as a selfless, manly nurturer is further cemented in an affecting scene in which he nurses back to consciousness the semi-lifeless Mrs Davenport, who has collapsed from lack of food. After hastily preparing some gruel, made from the donated oatmeal 'with the useful skill of a working man', Barton tenderly spoon-feeds the feeble, starving woman until eventually she revives (ibid.: 62).

As well as underpinning such particularised examples of masculine altruism, disinterested self-denial also structures more generally Barton's trades unionist activities and Chartist politics, as Gaskell's narrator makes clear:

> what perhaps more than all made him relied upon and valued [by the bodies of men to whom he belonged] was the consciousness which every one who came in contact with him felt, that he was actuated by no selfish motives; that his class, his order, was what he stood by, not the rights of his own paltry self. (ibid.: 170)

This lack of regard for his 'own paltry self' is repeatedly emphasised in the text via both words and deeds. As Patsy Stoneman points out, it is noticeable that all of Barton's radical political speeches make 'mention of starving children' whereas, on his own account, he 'would be glad and thankful to lie down and die out o' this weary world'. Barton has a sense of obligation to live on and fight for fair wages so that 'them little ones' might have their 'daily bread' (Stoneman 2006: 47; Gaskell 1996: 188). In similar vein, the 'really pure gladness of heart' he feels on being chosen as a Chartist delegate to London in 1839 stems not from a self-interested wish to improve his own material circumstances but from the hope that he might help to secure 'some grand relief' for his fellow beings (Gaskell 1996: 86). Indeed, despite having to bear 'his share of [. . .] bodily sufferings', Barton repeatedly plays down his own experience of physical hunger, at one point assuring Job Legh and Mary that he felt 'fat and rosy' by comparison with the other 'thin, wan, wretched-looking chaps' who made up the Chartist delegation (ibid.: 114; 100). He also refuses any pecuniary assistance from his trade union during a period of sustained unemployment, having a 'stern determination' to 'bear it all' without aid (ibid.: 115). Though the union would willingly have supported him, we are told, thinking 'it better to propitiate an active, useful member, than to help those who were more unenergetic', Barton demurs, insisting that they instead lend their assistance to Tom Darbyshire ('a backbiting enemy' of his), who has 'more need of it', owing to his large family of seven children (ibid.: 116).

Significantly, then, Gaskell's novel suggests that if hard times give rise to desperate impoverishment and bestial forms of hunger, they also occasion demonstrations of disinterested 'self-denial, among rude, coarse men, akin to that of Sir Philip Sidney's most glorious deed' (ibid.: 58). The 'glorious deed' alluded to here is Sidney's fabled refusal of water as he lay dying on the battlefield of Zutphen so that refreshment might be given to another injured soldier, whose need he deemed to be greater than his own. The narrator's attribution of equivalent acts of noble self-sacrifice to lower-class men works pointedly to disrupt the class-based assumptions about stoical masculinity and appetitive self-control explored in the previous section of this essay. Whereas labouring men were commonly conceived of in the first half of the nineteenth century as unthinking and insatiable 'machines that eat', Gaskell characterises them instead as 'being[s] not altogether sensual', who possess the intangible quality of 'soul' more usually associated with socially elevated forms of masculinity (Sherman 2001: 10; Gaskell 1996: 170).

Certainly, the sympathetic 'heart-service' rendered to those in need by men such as John Barton is figured as 'of far more value' to the poor than the mechanical acts of charity performed by middle-class characters such as Harry Carson (Gaskell 1996: 61). As Surridge notes, the latter's casual donation of five shillings to help the suffering Davenport family is dwarfed in significance 'by the enormous generosity of John Barton's gift of the same sum', which could only be realised by the pawning of precious possessions (Surridge 2000: 337). Similarly, Barton's genuine acts of altruism lay bare the falseness of Carson's pretentions to self-sacrifice during his proposal to Mary. Here, Harry declares himself willing 'to sacrifice a good deal' – to brave the disappointment of his family and the 'ridicule' of wider society – for her love (Gaskell 1996: 137). However, his pompous romantic posturing and egoistic preoccupation with what he is 'ready to give up' – tellingly, he refers to his proposal as a 'sacrifice' no fewer than three times – expose the hollowness of his claims to selflessness; unlike the authentically stoical and unselfish John Barton, the middle-class Harry Carson is a man unable to rise above the interests of 'his own paltry self' (ibid.: 137; 170).

Of course, Harry's class position in many respects insulates him from the kinds of urgent ethical choices faced by men like John Barton, which encourage acts of true self-renunciation. The first time we meet him, Harry is enjoying a leisurely breakfast in his father's 'luxurious' library, 'lazily' picking over the meal that has been 'nicely prepared' for him by the Carsons' kitchen staff (ibid.: 68). The contrast between his privileged, well-nourished existence and that of the working-class men who are obliged to choose between feeding themselves and feeding others is rendered starkly apparent by the emergence of the 'gaunt, pale' George Wilson within the Carsons' sumptuously appointed home (ibid.: 70). Having not eaten since the previous day, Wilson (who has come to request an infirmary order for Ben Davenport) is tortured by the sight and smell of food to which he has no access: 'altogether the odours were so mixed and appetising, that Wilson began to yearn for food to break his fast' (ibid.: 67). However, no one in the household recognises his famishment – 'not feeling hunger themselves, [they] forgot it was possible another might' – and, as a result, his 'craving [turns] to sickness' (ibid.). As Scholl notes, there is a cruel disjunction here between the sensory experiences of olfaction and gustation: 'the nose promises a taste that will not be experienced' by the mouth and this lack of sensory unity helps to convey the starving man's 'lack of social agency' (Scholl 2016: 61).

Wilson's hunger is eventually assuaged when the Carsons' cook perceives his pale, emaciated look and presents him with a handful of bread and meat. Elsewhere in *Mary Barton*, though, hungry working-class men are brought into painful proximity with the food that is withheld from them and their families with no hope of accessing it. In a scene that is pivotal to the development of John Barton's radical politics, the desperate, jobless weaver stands at the window of a grocer's shop, feasting his eyes on the unobtainable luxuries within – 'haunches of venison, Stilton cheeses, moulds of jelly' – while haunted by the knowledge that, back at home, his son Tom is dying from a lack of proper nourishment (Gaskell 1996: 25). Barton's bitter consciousness of the correlation between social and dietary inequality is further exacerbated when he sees Mrs Hunter, the wife of the factory-owner who has recently made him redundant, emerge from the shop 'loaded with purchases for a party' (ibid.: 25). The motif of the hungry male cruelly separated from the food that would sustain him and his family emerges again, later in the novel, when Job Legh recites a poem by Samuel Bamford in which a 'famished lad' wanders along a high street, stopping to peer through the transparent barrier of each shop window at the abundant provisions within (ibid.: 111). The tortuous effect of looking without tasting in these examples accentuates the heroic character of masculine self-sacrifice in *Mary Barton*; the narrative coupling of visual overload with gustatory deprivation renders the ability of working-class men to exercise appetitive self-discipline in the interests of others all the more laudable. Yet if acts of familial nurturance and disinterested self-denial serve to ennoble working-class masculinity in Gaskell's novel, these self-sacrificing behaviours are also invested with a problematically destructive potential. While depriving himself of food, John Barton, in particular, allows himself to be eaten up with anger at the injustices of the Victorian class system, and this corrosive flow of negative energy has devastating consequences, eventually venting itself in an act of extreme violence which inflicts damage on both the bourgeois male body and the hungering proletarian self.

'Learning to do without food': Asceticism and Masculine (Self-)Destruction

If John Barton's ability to discipline corporeal appetite is prized in *Mary Barton* as a sign of noble manly character, his *askesis* is not of the patient, uncomplaining kind that Gaskell associated with Christian forbearance. Though able to brave the debilitating pangs of physical hunger with an almost 'Spartan endurance', Barton cannot bear his and his fellow workers' sufferings with meek submission, owing to his heightened political and class consciousness; that would be 'too much to expect', the narrator notes (Gaskell 1996: 171: 115). His fixation on the great (and apparently divinely sanctioned) gulf that separates rich from poor emerges in the very first chapter of the novel via a series of emotively charged rhetorical questions that focus specifically on issues of access and entitlement to food:

> If my child lies dying (as poor Tom lay, with his white wan lips quivering, for want of better food than I could give him), does the rich man bring the wine or broth that might save his life? If I am out of work for weeks in the bad times [. . .] and the thin bones are seen through the ragged clothes, does the rich man share his plenty with me, as he ought to do, if his religion wasn't a humbug? (ibid.: 10–11)

This preoccupation with questions of social and dietary injustice surfaces once again in Chapter 6 of the novel. When George Wilson praises the Christ-like docility preached by Ben Davenport in the days before his illness – 'It were as good as Bible-words [. . .] a' about God being our Father, and that we mun bear patiently whate'er He sends' (ibid.: 65) – Barton protests that the entrenched inequalities in the current social order work to countermand such unquestioning faith and passive resignation:

> [The masters have] screwed us down to th' lowest peg, in order to make their great big fortunes, and build their great big houses, and we, why we're just clemming, many and many of us. Can you say there's nought wrong in this?' (ibid.: 66)

Such bitter thoughts of social injustice continue to trouble Barton's psyche following the rejection of the Chartist petition to Parliament. The humiliation he feels as a result of the government's failure to recognise the urgent reality of working-class hunger manifests itself in a kind of aphasia; denied the material sustenance he sees as his class's right, he instead swallows down his words about what happened at Parliament House, telling Job Legh, 'If you please, neighbour, I'd rather say nought about that [. . .] I canna tell of our down-casting [. . .] I'll not speak of it no more' (ibid.: 102). Notably, Barton's 'deep mortification' is accompanied by a particularly intensive episode of self-abnegation: after his return from London he undergoes 'a long period of bodily privation', which he attempts to bear with his usual 'stoical indifference', persuading himself that he cares little about mere physical needs (ibid.: 168). On this occasion, however, he is unable to quell entirely hunger's insurrectionary force. In one of a series of narratorial observations linking famishment and radical politics with ontological fragmentation, we are told that 'the body took its revenge for its uneasy feelings' by impairing Barton's psychological state; his 'mind became soured and morose, and lost much of its equipoise. It was no longer elastic, as in the days of youth, or in times of comparative happiness' (ibid.: 169). Disfigured by the effects of malnourishment, Barton's consciousness comes to be possessed by a single 'overpowering thought': the iniquitous and seemingly insuperable disparity between the classes in contemporary society (ibid.).

Tellingly, this mental fixation is described by Gaskell in terms of a condition particularly associated with bourgeois masculinity in Victorian literature.[5] Once again unsettling the distinction between class-based iterations of manliness, the narrator explains that 'the same state of feeling which John Barton entertained, if belonging to one who had had leisure to think of such things, and physicians to give names to them, would have been called monomania' (ibid.). Defined by psychiatrist Jean-Étienne Esquirol as an 'intellectual disorder' involving the overvaluation of 'a single object' or idea (Esquirol 1845: 320), monomania constituted one of the morbid distortions of mental energy that threatened the integrity and stability of nineteenth-century masculinity. If manhood was understood in terms of a vital but unruly force, then its security was deemed to be continually at risk, capable of slipping 'into the gender-specific mental pathology that the Victorians saw as male hysteria or male madness' (Sussman 1995: 13). Anxieties about the task of managing the natural energy that fortified manliness – of keeping it in healthy equilibrium – circulated in particular around those exemplary figures of middle-class masculinity, the men of business and industry. According to the medical practitioner Charles Turner Thackrah, the same single-mindedness that enabled such men to achieve success in the commercial sphere also endangered it, for their tenacious focus on matters of 'calculation, speculation, and commercial arrangement' often resulted in 'vital energy' being 'drawn from the operations for which nature designed it', thus weakening male power (Thackrah 1831: 84; 85).

Significantly, Barton's monomaniacal tendencies follow a similarly destructive pattern to the putative middle-class businessman's 'excessive application of mind' (ibid.: 86). As we have seen, an overwhelming conviction that 'it's the poor, and the poor only, as [cares] for the poor' induces Barton to severely restrict his already limited consumption in the interests of others; however, this extreme alimentary denial causes him to be consumed by 'diseased thoughts', which (exacerbated by the opium he takes to deaden his cravings for food) eventually sap both bodily and mental vigour (Gaskell 1996: 11; 169). His daughter Mary is among the first to identify the change that takes place in his mien and character; she perceives the effects of inanition 'in his shrunk, fierce, animal look' and recognises a new animosity in his previously affectionate attitude towards her (ibid.: 115). Indeed, on one occasion, we are told, 'in his passion he had even beaten her', this sudden outburst of male violence functioning as a proleptic warning of what is to come in the novel (ibid.: 117). Fuelled by the twin potencies of hunger and anger, Barton rejects the course of peaceful protest and, at a meeting of trades union members, persuades his peers to redirect their aggression away from the strike-breakers of their own class, who in desperation 'mun choose between vitriol and starvation', and channel it instead towards 'the masters as has wrought this woe' (ibid.: 189; 190). Inflamed by his words, the union men engage in a murderous conspiracy which culminates in Barton drawing the lot that binds him to a deadly purpose: the assassination of the affluent and carefree Harry Carson, the novel's stock representative of insouciant bourgeois masculinity.

In an interesting textual elision, the violent deed that results in Harry's death is figured only indirectly in the novel, the act itself having taken place outside of the main narrative. The reader, like the distraught members of the Carson family, must retrospectively reconstruct the fatal event from the trace it leaves behind: the small, blue spot on Harry's left temple that speaks of a gunshot fired purposefully and at close range. Yet while occluding the precise moment in which class-based male hostility erupts with murderous force, Gaskell dwells in some detail on the damage this violence wreaks on the body and psyche of the perpetrator. Revealingly, on the day of the murder, Barton's asceticism takes on a more radical and masochistic form than it has previously. When Mary offers to prepare her haggard-looking father a meal, he replies solemnly that he is 'larning to do without food' and later rejects the dish she cooks for him: 'If thou'rt doing that for me, Mary, thou mayst spare thy labour. I told thee I were not for eating' (ibid.: 196). Although Barton's refusal of sustenance here may be conceived of as part of a behavioural continuum, there is a qualitative difference between the acts of disinterested self-denial performed earlier in the text and the extreme self-starvation now being practised. Whereas previously Barton's food refusal was communally orientated – always undertaken for others – it now constitutes a form of private, individual penance for the murder he has sworn to commit; devoured by guilt, he embarks on a regime of total abstemiousness that seems to be more about self-punishment than noble manly asceticism.

Yet, although Gaskell intended her hero's story to demonstrate that 'violating the eternal laws of God, would bring with it its own punishment of an avenging conscience far more difficult to bear than any worldly privation', Barton's self-mortification can be read in a political as well as a penitential light, owing to its affinity with the practice of hunger strike, a strategy of resistance that has historical associations with civil protest against disempowerment (Chapple and Pollard 1997: 74).[6] Maddened by a social order that permits its citizens to starve, Barton directs his anger outwards, towards an oblatory representative of that society, but also inwards, against the abject body that society fails to value. In doing so, he aligns himself with the proto-anorexic female characters found in early Victorian novels such as Charlotte Brontë's *Shirley*, who, starved of purpose by 'a dysfunctional society', 'internalize that dis/order as self-starvation'

(Lashgari 1992: 141). Indeed, the masochistic food-refusing behaviours and pathological psychical states exhibited by Barton in the later parts of *Mary Barton* can be seen as analogous with the 'complex of psychoneurotic symptoms' that Sandra M. Gilbert and Susan Gubar famously identify with 'female feelings of powerlessness and rage' in Emily Brontë's *Wuthering Heights* (Gilbert and Gubar 1979: 284). In light of this overlap with feminine-coded somatic protest, it is interesting to note that Barton's self-abnegation was first learnt from his mother, whom he regularly saw 'hide her daily morsel' in order to 'share it among her children' when food was scarce (Gaskell 1996: 114). Imitating this renunciative maternal behaviour later in life, Barton comes to resemble what Gail Turley Houston calls 'the mythic figure of the self-denying, always nourishing' domestic woman, while in the extreme stages of physical mortification he takes on the character of her more destructive twin, the self-immolating female anorexic (Houston 1994: 155).

As well as destabilising the boundary between middle- and working-class forms of masculinity, then, Barton's starving body also unsettles gendered subject positions owing to its tacit feminisation in the text. Locus of competing and contradictory subjectivities, it works to reveal the fragility and fallibility of Victorian conceptions of gender and class. Perhaps unsurprisingly, Gaskell's narrative is ultimately unable to sustain the weight of the ideological tensions exposed by Barton's conflicting identities. Notably, the author removes Barton from diegetic view for a significant portion of the second half of the novel and when he does re-emerge he is figured in terms that are conspicuously non-human. It seems that 'the inward gnawing of [. . .] remorse', together with his on-going pursuit of a punishingly ascetic regime ('how body and soul had been kept together [. . .] no one can say'), have combined to reduce Barton to a mere spectre (Gaskell 1996: 352; 354):

> A footfall was heard along the pavement; slow and heavy was the sound [. . .] a form [. . .] glided into sight; a wan, feeble figure [. . .] It went before Jem, turned up the court at the corner of which he was standing, passed into the broad, calm light; and there, with bowed head, sinking and shrunk body, Jem recognised John Barton.
> No haunting ghost could have had less of the energy of life in its involuntary motions than he. (ibid.: 345–6)

As the lexis of spectrality and use of the neuter pronoun here imply, at the very point of his rematerialisation in the novel John Barton is rendered in immaterial terms and thus extricated from the discourses of class and gender that have previously delimited his person. This retreat into Gothic language is accompanied by a secondary set of images of dehumanisation that generate similar effects; as well as a ghost, Barton is figured as one of the machines that the masters consider their workers to be. His 'automaton body' lacks any kind of sentience or volition, mechanically performing small daily tasks 'from mere force of habit', while his metronomic movement is characterised as a 'measured clockwork tread' (ibid.: 354; 346).

This deployment of the language of the ghost and the machine cleverly absolves Gaskell from the responsibility of resolving the gender and class-based ambiguities that have previously inflected her representation of John Barton. The novelist's evasive semiotics enable her to circumvent the representational problems set up in the novel, while also preparing the narrative ground for Barton's ultimate demise. Indeed, it is telling that the novel ends not with the character whom Gaskell originally intended to be the hero of her work, but with Mary's now-husband, the hale and hearty Jem Wilson – a man who, while sharing some of Barton's nurturing traits, represents an altogether less complicated version of working-class masculinity. It seems that the starving male body, as personified by John Barton, is just too socially and culturally disruptive a force to be allowed to endure in *Mary Barton*. Site of slippage between manly asceticism and feminine nurturance, stoical endurance and violent insurgence, he testifies in his unruliness to the tensions and fluidities inherent in Victorian constructions of gender and class.

Notes

1. In an 1849 letter to Mrs Greg, Gaskell explained '"John Barton" was the original title of the book. Round the character of John Barton all the others formed themselves; he was my hero, *the* person with whom all my sympathies went' (Chapple and Pollard 1997: 74).
2. See, for instance, Adams 1995, Sussman 1995 and Surridge 2000.
3. Behlman nuances this point with the observation that the Victorians' understanding of Roman Stoicism was subject to 'historical remodelling', so as to render it more compatible with contemporary ideals (Behlman 2011: 2).
4. See, for instance, Surridge 2000 and Stoneman 2006.
5. In *Lady Audley's Secret*, for instance, the barrister Robert Audley twice questions whether he might be suffering from monomania as he investigates the disappearance of his friend George Talboys, and is later

accused of being a monomaniac by Lady Audley herself (Braddon 1987: 146; 254; 287). Louis Trevelyan, the jealous husband at the centre of Trollope's *He Knew He Was Right*, is another gentlemanly figure who demonstrates monomaniacal tendencies, although his obsession isn't explicitly labelled as such.

6. Although James Vernon suggests that the hunger strike originated with the early twentieth-century suffragette movement (Vernon 2007: 43), Caroline Walker Bynum points to a much longer history of fasting as political protest, drawing attention to the medieval practice of 'fasting to destrain' and the '1774 fast of the Massachusetts and Virginia colonists to express dissatisfaction with England' (Bynum 1987: 192).

Works Cited

Adams, J. E. (1995), *Dandies and Desert Saints: Styles of Victorian Manhood*. Ithaca and London: Cornell University Press.

Anon. (1848), 'Alarming Position of France. Lesson to be Derived from it', *The Leeds Mercury*, 22 April 1848, p. 4.

Behlman, L. (2011), 'The Victorian Marcus Aurelius: Mill, Arnold, and the Appeal of the Quasi-Christian', *Journal of Victorian Culture*, 16: 1, pp. 1–24.

Braddon, M. E. (1987), *Lady Audley's Secret*, ed. David Skilton, Oxford: Oxford University Press.

Burnett, J. (1989), *Plenty and Want: A Social History of Food in England from 1815 to the Present Day*, 3rd edn, London: Routledge.

Bynum, C. W. (1987), *Holy Feast and Holy Fast: The Religious Significance of Food to Medieval Women*, Berkeley and London: University of California Press.

Carlyle, T. (1831), 'Characteristics', *The Edinburgh Review*, 54: 108, pp. 351–83.

Carlye, T. (1840), *Chartism*, London: James Fraser.

Carlye, T. (1918), *Past and Present*, ed. A. M. D. Hughes, Oxford: Clarendon Press.

Chapple, J. A. V. and Arthur Pollard (eds) (1997), *The Letters of Mrs Gaskell*, New York: Mandolin.

Daly, M. (1996), 'Introduction', in Elizabeth Gaskell, *Mary Barton*, London: Penguin, pp. vii–xxx.

Engels, F. [1845] (1993), *The Condition of the Working Class in England*, ed. David McLellan, Oxford: Oxford University Press.

Esquirol, J. É. (1845), *Mental Maladies. A Treatise on Insanity*, trans. E. K. Hunt. Philadelphia: Lea and Blanchard.

Gaskell, E. [1855] (1995), *North and South*, ed. Patricia Ingham, London: Penguin.

Gaskell, E. [1848] (1996), *Mary Barton: A Tale of Manchester Life*, ed. Macdonald Daly, London: Penguin.
Gilbert, S. M. and S. Gubar (1979), *The Madwoman in the Attic: The Woman Writer and the Nineteenth-Century Literary Imagination*, New Haven, CT and London: Yale University Press.
Houston, G. T. (1994), *Consuming Fictions: Gender, Class, and Hunger in Dickens's Novels*, Carbondale and Edwardsville: Southern Illinois University Press.
Kay, J. P. (1832), *The Moral and Physical Condition of the Working Classes Employed in the Cotton Manufacture in Manchester*, London: James Ridgway.
Ketabgian, T. (2011), *The Lives of Machines: The Industrial Imaginary in Victorian Literature and Culture*, Ann Arbor: University of Michigan Press.
Lashgari, D. (1992), 'What Some Women Can't Swallow: Hunger as Protest in Charlotte Brontë's *Shirley*', in Lilian R. Furst and Peter W. Graham (eds), *Disorderly Eaters: Texts in Self-Empowerment*, University Park: Pennsylvania State University Press, pp. 141–52.
Lhotsky, J. (1844), *On Cases of Death by Starvation, and Extreme Distress among the Humbler Classes, Considered as One of the Main Symptoms of the Present Disorganization of Society; With a Preparatory Plan for Remedying these Evils in the Metropolis and Other Large Cities*, London: John Ollivier.
Mallalieu, A. (1837), 'The Whigs – the Radicals – the Middle Classes – and the People', *Blackwood's Edinburgh Magazine*, 41: 258, pp. 553–72.
Nicoll, R. (1853), *Poems by Robert Nicoll, with a Memoir of the Author*, Providence, RI: George H. Whitney.
Reach, A. (1849), 'Labour and the Poor', *Morning Chronicle*, 22 October 1849, p. 5.
Scholl, L. (2016), *Hunger Movements in Early Victorian Literature: Want, Riots, Migration*, Abingdon and New York: Routledge.
Sherman, S. (2001), *Imagining Poverty: Quantification and the Decline of Paternalism*, Columbus: Ohio State University Press.
Stoneman, P. (2006), *Elizabeth Gaskell*, 2nd edn, Manchester and New York: Manchester University Press.
Surridge, L. (2000), 'Working-Class Masculinities in *Mary Barton*', *Victorian Literature and Culture*, 28: 2, pp. 331–43.
Sussman, H. (1995), *Victorian Masculinities: Manhood and Masculine Poetics in Early Victorian Literature and Art*, Cambridge: Cambridge University Press.
Thackrah, C. T. (1831), *The Effects of the Principal Arts, Trades, and Professions, and of Civic States and Habits of Living, on Health and Longevity: With a Particular Reference to the Trades and Manufactures of Leeds: And Suggestions for the Removal of Many of the*

Agents, which Produce Disease, and Shorten the Duration of Life, London: Longman, Rees, Orme, Brown, and Green.

Trollope, A. [1869] (1985), *He Knew He Was Right*, ed. John Sutherland, Oxford: Oxford University Press.

Ure, A. (1835), *The Philosophy of Manufactures: Or, an Exposition of the Scientific, Moral, and Commercial Economy of the Factory System of Great Britain*, London: Charles Knight.

Vernon, J. (2007), *Hunger: A Modern History*, Cambridge, MA and London: The Belknap Press of Harvard University Press.

Chapter 10

Fosco's Fat: Transgressive Consumption and Bodily Control in Wilkie Collins' *The Woman in White*

Joanne Ella Parsons

There has been much written on women, food and bodily control in both the Victorian period and beyond, but with the rise of fat studies and scholarly research into masculinity academia has begun to recognise that there is also a discourse that is deeply embedded in men's relationship to food and the body.[1] This relatively new field of scholarship has produced many insightful and highly pertinent readings of the fat male body. In the Victorian period, in particular, one focus has been on that Dickensian favourite, Joe from the *Pickwick Papers* (Dickens 1837). Fat boy Joe is easily categorised partly due to the fact that sleep apnoea was latterly entitled Pickwickian syndrome by Burwell et al., which helped to align the reading of his corpulent form with a medicalised interpretation of his fat (Burwell et al. 1956). In addition to this type of reading, critics such as Sander L. Gilman have dwelt on Joe's indolence and dubious voyeuristic sexuality (Gilman 2004: 159–60). Jos, the 'fat *gourmand*' from Thackeray's *Vanity Fair* has also received critical attention because his indulgence in dubious foreign foodstuffs, such as curries, is written on his corpulent form (Thackeray 1968: 93). Scholars, such as Annette Cozzi, have attributed his fat as being due to both the dangers of empire and his unrestrained appetite (Cozzi 2010). Both Jos' and fat boy Joe's weight can be said to be gained from over-indulgence and a lack of will, but Fosco's fat is less easy to attribute to lack of self-control and regulation. Collins' corpulent Count is instead a wearer of 'fat drag' which Huff considers to be both exploitative of, and 'disrupt[ive] of dominant narratives of fatness' (Huff 2010: 93; 104). I wish here to extend this argument further, as I will consider how Fosco's fat engages with discourses of power and gender, through both its performativity and his transgressive consumption of feminine treats.

The first accurate weighing scales were developed in the eighteenth century, but increased in popularity and use in the nineteenth century, due to the contemporary obsession with quantification and categorisation (Rogers 1993: 172). Rogers comments on how

> [a]s the nineteenth century proceeded, new quasi-scientific theories would supply a new buttress for traditional sizism, but also ways of confusing the simple readings of the body: this was the period in which endomorphs, ectomorphs and pynik types began to be catorgorized. (ibid.: 181)

It has been often recognised in scholarly and non-scholarly circles that the Victorian era was defined and policed by the compulsion to control. Discipline over the body was perceived as essential in fulfilling the strict boundaries of prescribed manliness, and failure to adhere to dietary and bodily restrictions meant a rejection of the privileged contemporary categories of social acceptability. By the 1860s insurance companies were capitalising on this and began to devise height and weight charts in order to both prescribe acceptable norms and also indicate deviation. Huff considers that '[t]he corpulent body was seen as particularly resistant to normalization, because it was visibly individuated; it would not resolve itself into the supposedly universal body defined as average' (Huff 2001: 48). This individuated body showed its visible rejection of Victorian standards in two ways: firstly physically – the corpulent body is conspicuous through its sheer consumption of physical space – and secondly through the rejection of dietary rules which, again, was written on the body of the fat man. In an era where, in essence, the central core of manliness was defined by discipline and self-control, it stands that Count Fosco's fat exists as a visible symbol of lack of gastronomic control and therefore tends to act as an indicator of other undesirable traits, which serves to reinforce the boundaries of acceptable dietary consumption.

Clyde K. Hyder informs us that 'Collins gave [Fosco] a Falstaffian physique, because, [as he himself had noted] the popular notion [was] that a fat man could hardly be villainous' (Hyder 1939: 302). If Collins considered it to be unusual to create a corpulent criminal mastermind, then he could be playing into longstanding existing discourses on the transgressive nature of the fat body. Broadly, the perception of the corpulent male body falls into two distinct categories; firstly that of the jolly fat man as indicated by William Wadd in his 1816 preface to the third edition of *Cursory Remarks on Corpulence*, who apologises for the prior 'imperfect state' of the previous edition and resubmits this amended edition to the 'corpulent, good-humoured part of the community' (Wadd 1816: iv). This text is one of many that reference the good humour of the larger gentleman. One such example is the gentle and well-regarded Daniel Lambert, who Wadd refers to as 'prodigy of clogged machinery' (ibid.: 9). Lambert was born in 1770 and died in 1809 weighing between fifty-two to fifty-six stone, depending on which report is consulted, despite claiming to drink only water and consume very little food. Although he died at the beginning of the nineteenth century he was an important figure for the Victorians, as Huff states, '[Lambert's] legend was preserved and transmitted throughout the nineteenth century, and, in the process, it was fragmented, revised and made to serve a multiplicity of purposes' (Huff 2008: 39). Indeed, Lambert was often referred to in weight management books during the Victorian period. Contemporary reports indicate that not only was he good natured, compassionate and sincere but that he was also known for 'acts of great heroism and strength' (ibid.: 38). Secondly, there is the man whose excessive frame enables him literally to throw his weight about, which can manifest itself in a particular type of domineering, excessive and transgressive consumer, who could crave power and control over others. This may be read as an indicator of over-indulgence, which has been associated with lack of control over food and the body. As David Haslam, in his sweeping survey of literary fat men and women throughout the ages, states:

> It would seem that, in many instances, in literary terms, for men to be 'big' is commendable, powerful, rich and influential, but to be grossly big, obese or corpulent is to be set apart from the normal, and such men's habits and other attributes are more gross. Fat men in literature are extremes, and if not jolly or villainous are extremely weak-willed or socially inept. (Haslam and Haslam 2009: 231)

Count Fosco is undoubtedly villainous, but he is additionally a bodily mass of contradictions and, as Meckier states, he is 'the novel's staunchest proponent of duplicity' (Meckier 1982: 115). Indeed he is not only duplicitous in his criminal activity, but also through his body since his fat does not fit his inner self. His exteriority is at odds with his interiority. Fosco is said to be 'silent and sensitive, and ready to sigh and languish ponderously (as only fat men can sigh and languish), on the smallest provocation' (Collins 1973: 263). The outward emotions that Fosco displays through sighing and languishing are feminised, but his silence indicates that his true nature is concealed from others. It is important to note that 'languishing' on sofas was indicative of moral collapse.² At other times, Fosco can be extremely active in the text and 'his movements are astonishing light and easy' (ibid.: 197) like a woman's, but despite his 'great, big body' (ibid.: 198) he manages to creep up on people with his disturbingly quiet footfalls, 'his horribly silent tread' (ibid.: 261). Fosco is able to be both the lazy, gluttonous sloth and perform the role of the cheery fat man, while, at the same time, infiltrating society and managing his true role of criminal mastermind.

Marian Halcombe has a complex relationship with Fosco, and her masculinised femininity is mirrored in his feminised masculinity. She openly admits her prior prejudices towards fat individuals:

> Before this time, I have especially disliked corpulent humanity. I have always maintained that the popular notion of connecting excessive grossness of size and excessive good-humour as inseparable allies, was equivalent to declaring, either that no people but amiable people ever get fat, or that the accidental addition of so many pounds of flesh has a directly-favourable influence over the disposition of the person on whose body they accumulate. I have invariably combated both these absurd assertions by quoting examples of fat people who were as mean, vicious, and cruel, as the leanest and the worst of their neighbours. (ibid.: 196)

But despite these prejudices, Marian says the Count became 'established in my favour, at one day's notice, without let or hindrance from his own odious corpulence. Marvellous indeed!' (ibid.). Marian is very confused by her attraction to the Count, which is in opposition to her aversion and rational repugnance of 'corpulent humanity' (ibid.). In order to try to understand this, she attempts to analyse her positive inclination towards the Count, which goes beyond his 'remarkable likeness' to the 'Great Soldier', Napoleon (ibid.). This connection reinforces the extent of the Count's control in the text as he is literally wearing the mask of the French dictator. Napoleon, like Fosco, is an ambiguous figure, as he is read in a variety of different ways: he is feared, admired, and an object of ridicule.

Marian's description concludes by describing his 'unfathomable grey eyes [. . .] [which] have at times a cold, clear, beautiful, irresistible glitter in them, which forces me to look at him, and yet causes me sensations, when I do look, which I would rather not feel (ibid.: 197). These sensations indicate both the strength and the potential sexual nature of her attraction to him. His eyes have a mesmeric quality, indicating their power; it is also surely significant that hypnotism was frequently performed publicly in the nineteenth century, thereby constructing Fosco as a piece of theatre.[3] The desirability and seductive qualities that the corpulent body exudes was not unknown in Victorian culture, but as Joyce Huff elaborates,

> It has frequently been noted that the corpulent body was sometimes presented as desirable in nineteenth-century erotic painting and literature. But its presentation was framed in such a manner that even in its desirability, corpulence maintained a stigma. The fat body could not represent normative sexuality for the mid-Victorians. It must represent an excess that was taboo. The eroticizing gaze that the nineteenth century directed at the corpulent body was thus also an exoticizing one. (Huff 2001: 50)

Fosco is, of course, exoticised; he is clearly and unashamedly foreign despite his 'unusual command of the English language' (Collins 1973: 197); he strolls 'backwards and forwards across the grass' in Nankeen trousers and 'purple morocco slippers' exaggerating and embracing the foreign, and therefore, the exotic which may be coded for the reader as threatening (ibid.: 205). Marian says that '[h]e is as fond of fine clothes as the veriest fool in existence' (ibid.: 199) and this statement acquires extra resonance when the reader later learns of Fosco's financial problems. Fosco's expensive and gaudy dress is a significant indicator of his fiscal greed so, in a sense, his clothes act as a marker of his immorality, in the same way as he stands out because of his fat and his eating habits.[4] Fosco reflects Eastern excess, in his feminine exotic clothes, as his 'blue blouse, with profuse white fancywork over the bosom, covered his prodigious body' (ibid.: 205). This body is so 'immensely fat' (ibid.: 196) that it transgresses gender boundaries, as his bosom manoeuvres his body into feminine territory. As he suns himself on the grass, he sings 'Figaro's famous song in the Barber of Seville [. . .] like a fat St Cecilia masquerading in male attire' (ibid.: 205), thereby displaying his abnormal sexuality and transgressive gender unashamedly. The opera proudly and loudly proclaims his Italian nationality. It is also surely significant that he is not likened to one of the celebrity tenors circulating at the time, and is instead compared to the Roman martyr and patroness of musicians; the irony being that, while feminised, Fosco is no martyr. Huff summarises that '[w]hen fat is enticing it is the lure of something out of bounds, the excitement of slumming among the marginal' (Huff 2001: 50), and Fosco's sexuality *is* marginalised and forbidden due to his transgression of gender boundaries. It is made clear in the text that it is Marian, with her own transgressive gender status, and Madame Fosco, an 'impertinent' (Collins 1973: 171), 'vain and foolish' (ibid.: 194) woman, who are attracted to the Count, not Laura who is an idealised portrayal of appropriate Victorian femininity.

To a great extent, *The Woman in White* is about the compartmentalisation of the sexes. D.A. Miller states clearly that the novel concerns itself with

> enclosing and secluding the women in male 'bodies', among them institutions like marriage and madhouses. And the sequestration of the woman takes for its object not just women, who need to be put away in safe places or asylums, but men as well, who must monitor and master what is fantasized as the 'woman inside' them. (Miller 1986: 112)

This notion has been commented on by other critics, such as Tamar Heller, who perceives that when Walter Hartright encounters Anne Catherick at the crossroads outside of London what he fears most is the 'infection of her femininity, which he symbolically catches from her along with her, and Laura's nervousness' (Heller 1992: 125). But the Count, who is the driving force behind the attempt to erase Laura's identity and secure her femininity first within the boundaries of marriage and latterly within an asylum, demonstrates absolutely no inclination to master the 'woman inside' himself. Instead, he actively ingests femininity and therefore partakes of its nature, symbolically infecting himself, while at the same time continuing to enclose the feminine within his own male body. Fosco's corpulence has not been gained through overindulgence in a manly diet, rich in meat. In their famous book of English dietary habits through the ages, Drummond and Wilbraham state 'one can clearly trace the belief [. . .] that the eating of meat arouses and stimulates the animal passions' (Drummond and Wilbraham 1991: 396), and this belief was put into practice throughout the nineteenth century, as women were told to avoid protein and meat in their diets, while it was positively encouraged in men's consumption. Bourdieu in his study of class and consumption patterns insists that '[m]eat, the nourishing food par excellence, strong and strong-making, giving vigour, blood, and health, is the dish for the men, who take a second helping [. . .] men, the natural meat-eaters' (Bourdieu 2005: 75). However, there were still limits to its suitability for consumption, as even in men's diets meat was seen to be harmful in excess because it was perceived to '"turn the blood", overexcite' (ibid.: 75).[5]

So, Fosco does not indulge in manly appetites with regard to gustatory consumption and instead prefers to greedily swallow sweet treats and quench his thirst with 'eau sucrée' -sugar and water – rather than the brandy that Percival offers (Collins 1973: 295). As he is 'devouring' a fruit tart and cream (ibid.: 263) he declares to Marian 'in his softest tones and tenderest manner', that '[a] taste for sweets is the innocent taste of women and children. I love to share it with them – it is another bond, dear ladies, between you and me' (ibid.). This uncomfortable statement indicates that the Count aligns himself with the feminine through food. Soft and tender tones and manners are associated with women and it is through his masquerade of ideal feminine qualities that he proves to be most repugnant and at his most dangerous. Eating brings us back into a close connection with our bodies, as the act of consumption forces the consumer to focus upon the tastes, sensations, smells and feelings of satisfaction or discomfort that the gastronomic experience provides. It is an essentially corporeal experience. Elspeth Probyn, reflecting on the corporeality of eating and sex states, 'the point of which is the opening up of the body to reveal a multitude of surfaces that seek out contact with other surfaces near or far' (Probyn 2000: 61). But Count Fosco goes beyond 'seek[ing] contact with other surfaces' as he opens up his bodily experience to symbolically consume and control women and children. He literally ingests their innocence and this, rather than creating the bond that he suggests, actually serves to render them powerless in the face of his cannibalistic consumption. Fosco does not merely eat his food, he instead, 'devours pastry as I have never seen it devoured by any human beings but girls at boarding schools' (Collins 1973: 201), consuming it aggressively and greedily; his sexual deviance and feminised status explicitly displayed through his appetite. The reference to 'girls at boarding schools' implies secretive behaviour and the yet to be controlled prodigious and unfeminine appetites of young girls.

Count Fosco is a voracious consumer of sugar and luxury foods and, as has been pointed out in Judith Flanders' excellent discussion of Victorian domesticity, '[i]t was notable that expensive foods, or ones that tasted good enough to be consumed from desire rather than hunger, were often considered the most unwholesome' (Flanders 2003: 45). He delights in foods that are meant to be occasional treats, such as sugar-plums. Sugar-plums were actually comfits, rather than the usually assumed sugared plums, so they are essentially a hard sugar sweet with no connection to the fruit (Mason 2004: 120). This 'false' naming reflects Fosco's 'false' presentation, and it is another clear example of how his true character is revealed through the food that he ingests and gives to others. Mason discusses how comfits had a history of adulteration, and quotes Frederick Accum, who published his famous *A Treatise on Adulterations of Food and Culinary Poisons* in 1820, and found that 'the white comfits, called sugar pease, are chiefly composed of a mixture of sugar, starch and Cornish Clay' (qtd ibid.: 131). These sweets proved to be not what they seemed and their participation in the great food adulteration scandal connects them to questions of unhealthy food as well as foodstuffs that literally poison, which foreshadows Fosco's later use of drugs to subdue and control.

These sugary indulgences stand as symbol of his debts and his extravagant habits, which in Victorian terms are indicative of his immorality. According to Flanders, 'Extravagance was immoral; thrift was moral; the greatest good was knowing one's place and living up to it precisely' (Flanders 2003: 132). Despite his titled nobility, Fosco does not know his place: he lives beyond his means and his immoral greed and extravagance is written on both his clothes and his body. He stands as a spendthrift in the field of food, shamelessly gorging and feasting upon sugar-plums, pastries and tarts, but he is not an indiscriminate consumer, as he targets food that is unwholesome, lacking in nourishment and decadent.

It has been advocated since the eighteenth century that refined foods and sugar should be avoided and the consumption of these is linked to a lack of the discipline and control that marks acceptable Victorian masculinity. George W. Burnap in his *Lectures to Young Men on the Cultivation of the Mind and the Formation of Character and the Conduct of Life* (1840) instructs, 'It is in vain that you nourish the body with the greatest variety of the most luxurious food. Sickness will be produced not health, weakness not strength' (Burnap 1840: 19). Therefore Fosco's pursuit of shameless pleasure in the sweet foods he consumes transgresses strict Victorian dietary codes.[6] His focus should have instead been on abstinence and control as evidenced in Wadd's *Cursory Remarks on Corpulence* where he insists that, 'the only certain and permanent relief [from corpulence], is to be sought in a rigid abstemiousness, and a strict and constant attention to diet and exercise' (Wadd 1816: 31).

Fosco also transgresses the strict boundary of ideal Victorian manliness in his interactions with his pets, and is a perverse, lascivious, monstrous image of corrupted maternity. The Count bestows parental care onto mice and a 'vicious cockatoo' (Collins 1973: 203) who can merely 'ruffle his clipped wings' in protest against his unnatural mothering. While his relationship with his wife remains barren, the Count houses his 'poor-little-harmless-pretty-Mouseys' in a 'little pagoda of gaily-painted wirework' and 'feeds his white children' (ibid.: 207; 198; 207) as a mother tends her young. Pamela Gilbert states that 'food is primarily associated with the female body and breast' (Gilbert 1997: 20) and in feeding his aberrant 'white children', Fosco once again transgresses the acceptable limits of Victorian gender codes.

The Count possesses an extraordinary power over animals, as he is able to silence a 'savage' bloodhound and inspire devotion in his 'treacherous' cockatoo (Collins 1973: 198-9) but he is, however, not above using animals as vehicles for unprovoked spite. When he gives up his own lunch to a 'little shrivelled up monkey' in the street (ibid.: 528) it is, according to Harvey Peter Sucksmith 'an empty gesture of capricious malice' because he feeds the monkey not from kindness but instead to punish the organ grinder (Sucksmith 1973: xix). The other motivation behind the Count's willingness to share food is that he perceives its value as a mechanism for manipulation and control. Fosco, when talking quietly to his mouse, declares, 'Ah, nice little Mousey! come kiss me. What is your own notion of a virtuous man, my pret-pret-pretty? A man who keeps you warm, and gives you plenty to eat' (Collins 1973: 211). This could also be a description of his relationship with his wife, as there are examples in the text of Fosco feeding her like a pet (ibid.: 200). By treating his wife in the same manner as his mice, it serves to demean her position. Marian states that his 'management of the Countess [. . .] is a sight to see' although she qualifies this with the parenthesis 'in public' suggesting either the limitations of his control, or, perhaps, the use of more violent methods, since she also states that his 'private rod' of iron is 'always kept upstairs' (ibid.: 200). But, in public, he controls her with kind words, calling her 'my angel' and feeds her with the same sugar-plums that he consumes, 'which he puts into her mouth playfully, from a box in his pocket' placating her jealousy and ensuring her silence (ibid.). Nicholson, in his comprehensive survey of the power relations that exist with regard to the control of food, perceives that sweet foods are often used to lure others into danger, as they are what he terms 'compulsive foods' and as such are connected with obsession and enslavement (Nicholson 1992: 46). It is no surprise Nicholson writes that sweet foods are frequently associated with deception, which means they, therefore, serve as an overt signifier of the Count's dishonesty, literally marking his body with duplicity (ibid.: 46).

Fosco's act of feeding his wife also illuminates the irregular nature of their relationship, since typically, '[t]he woman offers cooking in exchange for sex; the man offers sex in exchange for cooking. It follows that women "receive" sex as men are "fed" food. Eating can be spoken of as synonymous with the sex act itself' (Visser 1991: 273). Fosco upsets the order of natural matrimony: he supplies the food and he mothers his pets while she remains barren, sitting childlike beside him engaged in the submissive and yet ambiguously masculinised role of rolling his cigarettes (Collins 1973: 240). However, he retains his masculine control and dominance in the relationship because, as Marian states, he

> looks like a man who could tame anything. If he had married a tigress, instead of a woman, he would have tamed the tigress. If he had married me, I should have made cigarettes as his wife does – I should have held my tongue when he looks at me, as she holds hers. (ibid.: 195)

Madame Fosco, who prior to her marriage, 'was always talking pretentious nonsense, and always worrying the unfortunate men with every small exaction which a vain and foolish woman can impose on long-suffering male humanity', has been transformed into a 'civil, silent, unobtrusive woman' although Marian does question how much she 'really is reformed [. . .] in her secret self' which is suggestive of limitations to the corrupt power that the Count wields (ibid.: 194; 195).

Margaret Visser reveals that, '[f]ood is a female concern, and often one of the main sources of a woman's power in the household' (Visser 1991: 276). She elaborates,

> Because food and drink usually reach the family through the woman's hands, fear of women usually translates into suspicion that they are poisoners [. . .] Poison [. . .] is a secretive, sneaky way of killing anyone, in addition to which it is often liquid and administered in food – all of which makes poison a peculiarly 'female' weapon, certainly in the folklore and mythology of all races, and possibly in fact as well. Fear of poison can strengthen the pressure upon men not to rove, but stay with their families: they might eat only what is prepared for them by their wives or mothers, or by women otherwise in their control. (ibid.: 277–8)

Fosco, in an additional expression of his transgressive gender status, administers a poisonous substance to Laura when she arrives in London. He offers her water that 'had so strange a taste that it increased her faintness', which leads her to take the smelling salts that have been laced with either toxic ether or chloroform, and 'her head become giddy on the instant' (Collins 1973: 393). In his later narrative and confession, Fosco extols the virtues of chemistry and in doing so he transforms this female method of murder into man's noble pursuit of science and art. Reframing it as 'scientific knowledge', Fosco claims that he was 'indebted to [his] Art' of using noxious drugs on only two occasions: on the maid carrying Marian's letters so that they could be intercepted by Madame Fosco and when he rendered Lady Glyde unconscious so that she could be secured in an asylum (ibid.: 561). However, the Count has proved to be an unreliable narrator and the reader is left unable to fully trust his proclamations. He assumes a god-like status when talking about his chemical prowess as he argues:

> Mind, they say, rules the world. But what rules the mind? The body. The body (follow me closely here) lies at the mercy of the most omnipotent of all potentates – the Chemist. Give me – Fosco – chemistry; and when Shakespeare has conceived Hamlet, and sits down to execute the conception – with a few grains of powder dropped in his daily food, I will reduce his mind, by the action of his body, till his pen pours out the most abject drivel that has ever degraded paper. Under similar circumstances, revive me the illustrious Newton. I guarantee that, when he sees the apple fall, he shall *eat it*, instead of discovering the principle of gravitation. (ibid.: 560, emphasis in original)

Here, Fosco clearly indicates that even for great minds such as Shakespeare and Newton, the drugged body is stronger than the natural will. He asserts that 'it is lucky for society that modern chemists are, by incomprehensible good fortune, the most harmless of mankind' (ibid.: 561) thereby undermining his argument since we know that Fosco, the chemist, is far from 'harmless' and is, instead, a force to be reckoned with.

The danger he poses is also revealed in the fact that his power is not exerted only over women. Fosco governs English nobility in the form of Sir Glyde in an equally forceful manner, and so Madame Fosco is not the only character in the text that Fosco treats like one of his animals. For instance, a word from the Count can temper Sir Percival's reaction in the face of Laura's female resistance, making him submit like a 'tamed animal' when she refuses to sign the legal document so that Percival can borrow money: 'They both looked at each other. Sir Percival slowly drew his shoulder from under the Count's hand; slowly turned his face away from the Count's eye [. . .] and then spoke, with the sullen submission of a tamed animal' (ibid.: 222). The Count as well as exerting an inordinate amount of control in the text also dominates the textual space in the novel. Descriptions of his gargantuan physical appearance consume Marian's diary entries which becomes a space that is, in turn, invaded by Fosco and, in doing so, he commits what Miller perceives to be a metaphorical textual rape (Miller 1986). Elizabeth Anderman has since expanded upon this and has discussed how this feeling of rape is made more explicit due to the layout of Marian's narrative, because its 'disjointed nature and breathy dashes' indicate her inability to control her narrative voice, which in turn excites the senses of the reader:

> The reader rushes through the dashes and gaps hoping to discover that Marian has overcome her body. The lines run together as the reader tries to make sense of the repetitive language and circular images. So, like Marian the reader is breathless and agitated – embodied. Therefore when Fosco inserts himself into the pages of the diary, he enters a written space where both Marian and the reader are focussed upon their bodies, making his transgression overtly physical. (Anderman 2009: 86)

This is an extension of the theme of the troublesome female body being controlled and contained by the male. Fosco is not merely content with the theft of Laura's identity in exchange for financial reward, but he penetrates Marian's personal thoughts and private textual space. He also invades the space of the reader as we discover that he has also crept up on us with his 'horribly silent tread' and has stood reading over our shoulder as he has previously intruded upon his fellow characters and, as Anderman states, the focus at this point in the text is upon bodies, which makes his intrusion more transgressive and sexual in nature. Fosco's penetration of Marian's diary is not just a simple exertion of his very masculine force but because he is so closely connected with the feminine his act is rendered all the more perverse.

While Fosco has forcibly and bodily intruded upon Marian's private space, it is also Marian with whom he identifies. He toasts her with his feminine sugar and water:

> Can you look at Miss Halcombe, and not see that she has all the foresight and the resolution of a man? With that woman for my friend, I would snap these fingers of mine at the world. With that woman for my enemy, I, with all my brains and experience – I walk, in your English phrase, upon egg-shells! And this grand creature – I drink her health in my sugar and water – this grand creature, who stands in the strength of her love and her courage, firm as a rock between us two, and that poor flimsy pretty blond wife of yours – this magnificent woman, whom I admire with all my soul, although I oppose her in your interests and mine. (Collins 1973: 296)

In this speech Count Fosco acknowledges that Marian's virtuous masculinity complements his corrupt feminised sexuality and he recognises her superiority to other women. Marian is, indeed, worthy of his admiration although she helps to cause his downfall. She comes closer to understanding the Count than any other character in the novel. It is Marian who observes the Count in his guise of a 'Man of Sentiment'; she writes in her diary that she feels that this facet of his character was 'not assumed for the occasion' and so, if this is, as she suspects, a revealing moment where she is able to detect some genuine feeling within the Count then surely it is significant that this is also the evening where '[h]e ate little or nothing' (ibid.: 260). This indicates that Fosco is a conscious eater rather than a man who is subject to chaotic disordered consumption.

In *Fat Boys: A Slim Book* Sander Gilman discusses how by the mid-nineteenth century psychology began to focus on diseases of the will, which became categorised as 'abulia' (Gilman 2004: 100–1). This pathological condition meant that 'there is no ability to move from motive and desire to execution', and obese men were often said to suffer from abulia (ibid.: 101). This was an affliction that was considered to affect more men than women, and 'it was in the promise of execution, of being able to act, that the fat man now showed his masculinity': so by overcoming obesity through manly action masculinity was restored (ibid.). However, this category of abulia may not be conveniently imposed upon Fosco as there are indications in the text that his considerable mass has been gained, not through the lack of will, but because of it. Hartright reflects on the Count's ability to avoid detection after Pesca fails to recognise him at the opera:

> It was easy to understand why that recognition had not been mutual. A man of the Count's character would never risk the terrible consequences of turning spy without looking to his personal security quite as carefully as he looked to his golden reward. The shaven face, which I had pointed out at the Opera, might have been covered by a beard in Pesca's time; his dark brown hair might be a wig; his name was evidently a false one. The accident of time might have helped him as well – his immense corpulence might have come with later years. (Collins 1973: 538–9)

While Hartright attributes the Count's 'immense corpulence' to an 'accident of time', the evidence in the text, such as his inability to eat as the stereotypically emaciated 'Man of Sentiment' and the manner in which he eats, suggests otherwise: Fosco 'devours' his food as if his life depended on it (ibid.: 201). However, Rachel Ablow points out that his 'attempts to disguise himself by becoming enormously fat can be foiled by the red mark on his arm that proves his membership in, and betrayal of, an Italian secret society' (Ablow 2003: 170). While the Count has attempted to hide his criminality under a great visible mass, and his tattoo under his flamboyant clothes, he is still unable to disguise certain aspects of himself, which hint towards the truth of the man beneath the masquerade.

Despite his superficial mastery of his bodily disguise it is Laura, with 'the child's subtle faculty of knowing a friend by instinct' who instantly recognises an enemy in him, and so renders him conspicuous by failing to mention him in her letters home to Marian, thereby rendering him the rather large elephant in the room (Collins 1973: 181). Her 'strange silence' and instinctive dislike, while being a significant indication of his later textual dominance, serves to illustrate the limitations to his disguise and influence (ibid.). However, this is not the only chink in his armoury of control, as the Count participates in what Daly refers to as the '[c]ommunity of nervousness' in the text (Daly 1999: 463). *The Woman in White*, as previously discussed, is partially concerned with the fear of 'infection' from femininity (Heller 1992: 125), so the Count, who actively ingests femininity through his diet, is also infected with the feminine nervousness that pervades the text. While Hartright believes that the Count was 'born without nerves' (Collins 1973: 324), Fosco actually 'starts at chance noises as inveterately as Laura herself' (ibid.: 198) throughout the novel and as Miller elaborates, 'nervousness is not so much missing as mastered' (Miller 1986: 109). Eventually it is this feminine nervousness that triumphs when he sees the Brotherhood so that, '[a] mortal dread had mastered him, body and soul' (Collins 1973: 531).

This feminine triumph has been indicated earlier in the novel when Marian suffers a strong reaction observing Fosco's unnatural children, his 'pretty mouseys', climbing over his body. She declares that

> [t]hey are pretty, innocent-looking creatures; but the sight of them creeping about a man's body is, for some reason, not pleasant to me. It excites a strange, responsive creeping on my own nerves; and suggests hideous ideas of men dying in prison, with the crawling creatures of the dungeon preying on them undisturbed. (ibid.: 208)

Marian's repulsion at the sight of the Count foreshadows his later death when the corpulent consumer becomes the consumed cadaver. The femininity within himself that the Count transgressively embraced has gained control over him, so, like a woman, he falls victim to male dominance, when the power of the masculine

Brotherhood overwhelms him and punishes his corrupted and feminised masculinity, leaving him to be discovered in the Paris morgue. Words are not able to reveal the truth at the heart of the Count; his wife's biography of him, published after his death, remains a closed book by maintaining the illusion he created, throwing 'no light whatever on the name that was really his own, or on the secret history of his life' (ibid.: 582). His confession is merely another version of whatever 'truth' he is choosing to present.

It appears that the only hope of revealing the true Count is through his body lying naked in what Dickens later termed the 'obscene, little Morgue' after he has been found in the Seine (Dickens 2014: n.p.). This is a reading that has appealed to Vicky Greenaway as she argues that the exposed Count's body strips him of his outer disguises and, in doing so, unmasks him, thus ironically reducing him to his corpulent transgressive body, which is laid bare for consumption by others. She suggests that

> Fosco's death is similarly an excision of his capacity to dissemble and proliferate. His murder ruthlessly localises his identity to the locale of the fixed and unchanging corpse. Fosco's body on the Paris morgue slab is a naked and transparent object open to the voyeuristic consumption of the Paris mob: 'There he lay [. . .] exposed.' His clothes are hung above his naked body: there will be no more disguises or dissimulations. (Greenaway 2008: 50)

However, I contend that the text actually provides a less neat conclusion to his masquerade, which is evident in the scene where Hartright joins the crowd to observe the body of the Count:

> There he lay, unowned, unknown; exposed to the flippant curiosity of a French mob! There was the dreadful end of that long life of degraded ability and heartless crime! Hushed in the sublime repose of death, the broad, firm, massive face and head fronted us so grandly, that the chattering Frenchwomen about me lifted their hands in admiration, and cried in shrill chorus, 'Ah, what a handsome man!' The wound that had killed him had been struck with a knife or dagger exactly over his heart. No other traces of violence appeared about the body, except on the left arm; and there, exactly in the place where I had seen the brand on Pesca's arm, were two deep cuts in the shape of the letter T, which entirely obliterated the mark of the Brotherhood. (Collins 1973: 581)

And it is this complex final reaction that undermines Greenaway's assessment. Fosco remains closed and his body is able to transform itself, even in death, to a 'handsome man': awesome in his sublimity and grandeur (ibid.). His last transformation is to both the honourable Hartright and more morally dubious voyeuristic Frenchwomen. So it is made clear that Fosco will never be fully 'exposed' and this is underpinned by location. The Paris morgue is considered to be a 'spectacle of the real' but, as Schwartz argues, it is also a place of theatre as the real bodies lead to a creation of a drama of mystery and uncovering for the greedy spectators (Schwartz 1998: 48).[7] Fosco participates in this theatre, as his audience tries to uncover meaning in his form, thereby indicating that until the moment his body becomes subject to the gradual dissolution of the flesh from the bone which death will bring and is no longer able to transform and deceive, he will continue to defy explanation and understanding.

Notes

1. For scholarly work on women's consumption and bodies see A. Krugovoy Silver (2002), *Victorian Literature and the Anorexic Body*, Cambridge: Cambridge University Press; and L. Talairach-Vielmas (2007), *Moulding the Female Body in Victorian Fairy Tales and Sensation Novels*, Aldershot: Ashgate.
2. For more information on languor and languishing and its connections to moral collapse, particularly with regard to masturbation see D. Mason (2008), *The Secret Vice: Masturbation in Victorian Fiction and Medical Culture*, Manchester: Manchester University Press.
3. For a detailed discussion on mesmerism in the nineteenth century, see W. Hughes (2015), *That Devil's Trick: Hypnotism and the Victorian Popular Imagination*, Manchester: Manchester University Press.
4. Extravagant, inappropriate clothes and the fat man is a recurring trope in the literature of this period. *Vanity Fair*'s Jos Sedley is one such example of a man marked by his absurd clothing. Although this, of course, is framed somewhat differently as the focus has mainly been on his ridiculous performance as a dandy.
5. I have already discussed extensively the connection between meat and 'over-excitement' in my article on Surtees (Parsons 2014). Roast beef in particular is associated with the English, and John Bull is often seen in illustrations and caricatures consuming vast quantities of this British staple.
6. See Charlotte Boyce's chapter in this volume.
7. See P. Vita (2010), 'Returning the Look: Victorian Writers and the Paris Morgue', *Nineteenth-Century Contexts*, 25: 3, pp. 241–55, as well as Schwartz 1998 for more information on the Paris morgue and its 'theatrical' qualities.

Works Cited

Ablow. R. (2003), 'Good Vibrations: The Sensationalization of Masculinity and *The Woman in White*', *Novel*, 37: 1/2, pp. 158–81.

Anderman, E. (2009), 'Hysterical Sensations: Bodies in Action in Wilkie Collins's *The Woman in White*', in Marilyn Brock (ed.), *From Wollstonecraft to Stoker: Essays on Gothic and Victorian Fiction*, Jefferson, NC: Jefferson McFarland and Co., pp. 79–88.

Bourdieu, P. (2005), 'Taste of Luxury, Taste of Necessity', in Carolyn Korsmeyer (ed.), *The Taste Culture Reader: Experiencing Food and Drink*, New York: Berg, pp. 72–8.

Burnap, G. W. (1840), *Lectures to Young Men on the Cultivation of the Mind and the Formation of Character and the Conduct of Life*. Baltimore: John Murphy.

Burwell, C. et al. (1956), 'Extreme Obesity Associated with Alveolar Hypoventilation – A Pickwickian Syndrome', *The American Journal of Medicine*, 21, pp. 811–18.

Collins, W. [1860] (1973), *The Woman in* White, Oxford: Oxford World's Classics, Oxford University Press.

Cozzi, A. (2010), *The Discourses of Food in Nineteenth-Century British Fiction*, New York: Palgrave Macmillan.

Daly, N. (1999), 'Railway Novels: Sensation Fiction and the Modernization of the Senses', *ELH*, 66: 2, pp. 461–87.

Dickens, C. [1837] (1986), *Pickwick Papers*, Oxford: Oxford University Press.

Dickens, C. [1863] (2014), 'Some Recollections of Mortality', in *The Uncommerical Traveller*, The University of Adelaide Library. Available at: <https://ebooks.adelaide.edu.au/d/dickens/charles/d54ut/chapter19.html> (last accessed 28 May 2017).

Drummond, J. C. and A. Wilbraham (1991), *The Englishman's Food: Five Centuries of English Diet*, revd edn, London: Pimlico.

Flanders, J. (2003), *The Victorian House: Domestic Life from Childbirth to Deathbed*, London: Harper Perennial.

Gilbert, P. K. (1997), *Disease, Desire and the Body in Victorian Women's Popular Novels*, Cambridge: Cambridge University Press.

Gilman, S. L. (2004), *Fat Boys: A Slim Book*, Lincoln: University of Nebraska Press.

Greenaway, V. (2008), 'The Italian, the Risorgimento and Romanticism in *Little Dorrit* and *The Woman in White*', *Browning Society Notes*, 33, pp. 40-57.

Haslam, D. and F. Haslam (2009), *Fat, Gluttony and Sloth: Obesity in Medicine, Art and Literature*, Liverpool: Liverpool University Press.

Heller, T. (1992), *Dead Secrets: Wilkie Collins and the Female Gothic*. New Haven, CT: Yale University Press.

Huff, J. L. (2001), 'A "Horror of Corpulence": Interrogating Bantingism and Nineteenth-Century Fat Phobia', in Jane Evans Braziel and Kathleen

LeBesco (eds), *Bodies Out of Bounds: Fatness and Transgression*, Berkeley: University of California Press, pp. 39–59.

Huff, J. L. (2008), 'Freaklore: The Dissemination, Fragmentation, and Reinvention of the Legend of Daniel Lambert, King of Fat Men', in Marlene Tromp (ed.), *Victorian Freaks: The Social Context of Freakery in Britain*, Columbus: Ohio State University Press, pp. 37–59.

Huff, J. L. (2010), 'Fosco's Fat Drag: Performing the Victorian Fat Man in Wilkie Collins's *The Woman in White*', in Elena Levy-Navarro (ed.), *Historicizing Fat in Anglo-American Culture*, Columbus: Ohio State University Press, pp. 89–108.

Hughes W. (2015), *That Devil's Trick: Hypnotism and the Victorian Popular Imagination*, Manchester: Manchester University Press.

Hyder, C. K. (1939), 'Wilkie Collins and *The Woman in White*', PMLA, 54: 1, pp. 297–303.

Krugovoy Silver, A. (2002), *Victorian Literature and the Anorexic Body*, Cambridge: Cambridge University Press.

Mason. D. (2008), *The Secret Vice: Masturbation in Victorian Fiction and Medical Culture*, Manchester: Manchester University Press.

Mason, L. (2004), *Sugar-Plums and Sherbet: The Prehistory of Sweets*, Devon: Prospect Books.

Meckier, J. L. (1982), 'Wilkie Collins's *The Woman in White*: Providence against the Evils of Propriety', *The Journal of British Studies*, 22: 1, pp. 104–26.

Miller, D. A. (1986), 'Cage aux Folles: Sensation and Gender in Wilkie Collins's *The Woman in White*', *Representations*, 14, pp. 107–36.

Nicholson, M. (1992), 'Magic Food, Compulsive Eating, and Power Poetics', in Lilian R. Furst and Peter W. Graham (eds), *Disorderly Eaters: Texts in Self-Empowerment*, Philadelphia: Pennsylvania University Press, pp. 43–60.

Parsons J. E. (2014), 'Eating Englishness and Causing Chaos: Food and the Body of the Fat Man in R. S. Surtees' *Jorrocks's Jaunts and Jollities*, *Handley Cross*, and *Hillingdon Hall*', *Nineteenth-Century Contexts*, 36: 4, pp. 335–46.

Probyn, E. (2000), *Carnal Appetites: Food, Sex, Identities*, London: Routledge.

Rogers, P. (1993), 'Fat is a Fictional Issue: The Novel and the Rise of Weight-Watching', in Marie Mulvey-Roberts and Roy Porter (eds), *Literature and Medicine during the Eighteenth Century*, London: Routledge, pp. 168–87.

Schwartz, V. (1998), *Spectacular Realities: Early Mass Culture in Fin-de-Siècle Paris*, Berkley and Los Angeles: University of California Press.

Sucksmith, H. P. (1973), 'Introduction', in Harvey Peter Sucksmith (ed), *The Woman in White*, Oxford: Oxford World's Classics, Oxford University Press, pp. v–xx.

Talairach-Vielmas, L. (2007), *Moulding the Female Body in Victorian Fairy Tales and Sensation Novels*, Aldershot: Ashgate.

Thackeray, W. [1848] (1968), *Vanity Fair*, London: Penguin.
Visser, M. (1991), *The Rituals of Dinner: The Origins, Evolution, Eccentricities and Meaning of Table Manners*. New York: Grove Weidenfeld.
Vita, P. (2010), 'Returning the Look: Victorian Writers and the Paris Morgue', *Nineteenth-Century Contexts*, 25: 3, pp. 241–55.
Wadd, W. (1816), *Cursory Remarks on Corpulence or Obesity Considered as a Disease with a Critical Examination of Ancient and Modern Opinions Relative to its Causes and Cure*, 3rd edn, London: J. Callow.

Chapter 11

Sensationalising Otherness: The Italian Male Body in Mary Elizabeth Braddon's 'Olivia' and 'Garibaldi'

Anne-Marie Beller

Mary Elizabeth Braddon is best-known as a prolific sensation novelist, whose immensely popular novels in the second half of the nineteenth-century shocked conservative critics as much as they delighted her vast readership. Many deprecators of Braddon's sensation fiction focused on the perceived immorality of her depictions of criminal femininity and, indeed, characters such as Lady Audley have come to be seen as typifying the genre's preoccupation with transgressive women. However, sensation fiction arguably focuses an equivalent attention on the construction of Victorian masculinity, exploring ideas of approved and deviant versions of 'manliness'; Braddon's plot trajectories frequently trace the socialisation of the hero into an appropriate version of masculinity. Indeed, sensation fiction's representations of what Lyn Pykett termed the 'Improper Feminine' are equally dependent on a corresponding engagement with contemporary ideas of what a *man* should be (Pykett 1992). As Richard Nemesvari has recently suggested in relation to sensation fiction of the 1860s:

> novelistic depictions of proper/improper femininity can *only* take place in the context of carefully delineated proper/improper *masculinity*, as male characters take up their own assigned melodramatic roles of seductive cad, social-climbing adventurer, or stalwart husband. Increasingly, therefore, discussions of the sensation novel recognise the need to explore how depictions of *maleness* contributed to its controversial status, and to its complex mixing of cultural critique with status quo conformity. (Nemesvari 2015: 88, emphasis in original)

In this chapter, I argue that Braddon's interest in, and exploration of, forms of masculinity in crisis was evident from the very beginning of her writing career, before the success of *Lady Audley's Secret* bought her fame and notoriety in equal measure. I examine the two lead poems from her first published book, *Garibaldi and Other Poems* (1861), with a particular focus on 'Olivia', to demonstrate the ways in which Braddon negotiates contemporary stereotypes of masculinity and nationality, and often undermines them. My contention is that the male body in Braddon's early poetry operates as the site upon which tensions are played out surrounding British anxieties regarding 'manliness' and nation in the mid-Victorian period. The first section of this chapter explores Victorian images of Italy, with a particular focus on nation and masculinity. I then proceed to examine these ideas in Braddon's poetry, before offering a final consideration of homosociality and the ways in which both poems privilege homosocial bonds over heteronormative relationships.

Although she achieved fame as a novelist, Braddon began her writing career as a poet. Her first published book was a collection of poetry entitled *Garibaldi and Other Poems* (1861), which she wrote at the request of her patron, John Gilby. Gilby dictated the subject matter of the lead poem in the collection, which was to be an account in verse of Giuseppe Garibaldi's recent Sicilian campaign, a topic of widespread popular interest in Britain at the time. In contributing to the 'Garibaldimania' of the early 1860s, Braddon joined the company of established poets, such as Elizabeth Barrett Browning and Walter Savage Landor, who offered similarly admiring accounts of the current military events in the peninsula.[1]

Considering that Braddon was an unknown poet, *Garibaldi and Other Poems* was extensively reviewed, and favourably for the most part. The *Athenaeum*, for instance, perceived in Braddon's writing a 'clear evidence of poetical ability' and 'a talent which deserves encouragement' (Braddon 1861: 259). Most reviewers, however, considered the choice of topic for the lead poem a mistake, or even a cynical attempt to cash in on the current popularity of the Italian general with the British public. Several critics (for example, in the *Athenaeum*, *The Literary Gazette* and the *National Magazine*) praised 'Olivia', the second poem of the collection, and the shorter lyric poems, as better examples of the new poet's skill. Certainly, the other poems are more typical of Braddon's style and interests and, in many ways, foreground and anticipate the themes that would characterise her career as a novelist. Braddon herself acknowledged that the subject matter of the 'Garibaldi' poem was not one that she relished, and she later wrote of her frustration as she 'pored and puzzled over Neapolitan revolution and Sicilian campaign': 'How I hated my own ignorance of modern Italian history' (Braddon 2003: 28). Despite Braddon's apparent reluctance to write about the Risorgimento, she returned to Italian settings and characters in subsequent works, most immediately in the second poem of the *Garibaldi* collection – 'Olivia'. Together, the two poems reflect on the construction of Italian masculinity at a key moment in British perceptions of both Italy and Italians. Moreover, these constructions are used to reflect on the corresponding constructions of British 'manliness' in the period, as a way of negotiating anxieties around shifting gender roles and ideologies. As John Tosh has argued in relation to nineteenth-century masculinities: '[a]ny identity, and especially an insecure one, is partly constructed in juxtaposition to a demonized "other" – an imagined identity composed of all the relevant negatives, and pinned onto its nearest approximation in the real world' (Tosh 2005: 49). In Braddon's early poems, such Othering is examined and, as I argue, ultimately destabilised.

'Garibaldi' recounts the remarkable Sicilian campaign of 1860 in 159 Spenserian stanzas. The poem paints Garibaldi and his 'Thousand' in unambiguously heroic and chivalric terms and, in this way, reflects the prevailing admiring view of the Italian General in Britain at this time. As Marcella Sutcliffe suggests,

> Garibaldi's aura as national 'hero' – with all the qualities of manliness and gentleness attributed to him by the popular press – was also emphasised by the romantic image of Italy as a gendered nation, a beautiful woman who had been wronged and violated by invaders and who needed to be rescued. (Sutcliffe 2014: 6)

Sharing the Italian setting, but eschewing the political themes, 'Olivia' is a long verse narrative about a young English nobleman's bewitchment by a beautiful, duplicitous woman in Naples. Like 'Garibaldi', it offers useful insights into the ways in which Italy figured in the mid-Victorian popular and literary imagination. Read in conjunction with one another, 'Garibaldi' and 'Olivia' present an interesting perspective on changing British representations of Italian masculinity, in the light of political and military developments in the peninsula at this period. In 'Garibaldi', we are presented with the Italian male as military hero, in contrast to the more romantic focus of 'Olivia', which deals with masculinity in more complex and, arguably, more interesting ways. Nevertheless, there are overlaps and parallels in the treatment of Italian masculinity across the two poems. In effect, read in relation to one another, the poems analyse the political body and the physical body respectively, and each work to complicate, and even subvert, dominant existing stereotypes.

Victorian Images of Italy

Before discussing the differing representations of Italian masculinity in Braddon's two poems, it is necessary to highlight mid-Victorian attitudes to both Italy and Italians in the nineteenth century. As recent scholarship has demonstrated, Italy held a fascination for the Victorians, eliciting complex and paradoxical responses. As Alessandro Vescovi, Luisa Villa and Paul Vita have summed it up:

> To the Victorians, Italy was what the Orient is to Europeans of the twentieth century, a mixture of attraction and repulsion: attraction for the ancient civilization and for Italy's contemporary struggle to put an end to a period of political and economic subjugation and, at the same time, repulsion to its chaotic roads, dirty inns, stinky slums, crime and depravation. (Vescovi et al. 2009: 8)

Matthew Reynolds has also considered nineteenth-century British perceptions of Italy as possessing similarities to Orientalism, to the extent that he coins the term 'Italianism'. Reynolds argues that Italy was habitually depicted as 'past, southern, feminine, gentle, egalitarian, fanciful; Britain as future, northern, masculine, blunt, hierarchical, practical' (Reynolds 2001: 84). Such oppositions are clearly evident in Braddon's poems, as will be discussed in due course. However, the idea of Italy as an 'anti-image' of Britain is one that is ultimately destabilised, particularly in 'Olivia'. In enacting such a destabilisation, Braddon arguably substantiates the arguments of Kathryn Walchester, who suggests that Victorian women writers were positioned in a more complex way to the stereotypes discussed by Reynolds than their male contemporaries. As she explains:

> In their writing about Italy, women travel writers manipulate and disrupt a number of established representations of Italy and the role of the woman writer. What I am suggesting is that the ambiguous nature of both the status of the woman author and Italy in these texts complicate a series of binary oppositions, which for example had set Italy and femininity against Britain and masculinity. (Walchester 2007: 2)

Walchester argues that '[w]omen writers challenge "Italianism" in that, although they present the region as an "anti-image" to Britain, they do not always identity themselves with the "self" of Britain in opposition to the "other" of Italy' (ibid.: 9). Although Walchester's argument is about early nineteenth-century women travel writers, I would suggest that her claims may feasibly be extended to later Victorian female novelists and poets, Braddon included. Walchester argues convincingly that the woman writer is able to 'erode' the binary opposition between Britain and Italy, as defined by critics such as Reynolds, partly through the way that they conflate another binary – that of the public and the private – by writing about Italian politics as women (ibid.: 8–9).

The ambivalent perception of 'Italianness' discussed by these scholars played a crucial role in the wider mid-Victorian construction of an English identity, whereby perceived differences of national character contributed to the shaping of nineteenth-century constructions of the self through the process of 'Othering'. In Braddon's poems, the Italian male body becomes the site for the exploration of these tensions and ambiguities, representing alternately the physical body, the political body, the 'foreign' body and the national body.

Neither 'Garibaldi' nor 'Olivia' are serious political or philosophical reflections on the Risorgimento, in the way that Barrett Browning's 'Casa Guidi Windows' or even Clough's *Amours de Voyages* can be claimed to be. 'Olivia' is more typical of Braddon's subsequent sensation novels in its preoccupation with the themes of crime, passion and madness. Unlike 'Garibaldi', which attempts to provide a faithful (if idealised) account of contemporary political and military affairs, 'Olivia' appropriates a more romantic tradition of writing about Italy and, in doing so, offers insight into Victorian assumptions and perceptions at the more popular level. However, what I want to argue is that Braddon doesn't simply recycle such representations in a straightforward manner. In 'Olivia' she both appropriates and subverts contemporary English stereotypes about Italians, exploring (and ultimately deconstructing) a series of binary oppositions, including many of the binaries identified by Reynolds and others, discussed above.

As the poem progresses, these binaries – between men and women; England and Italy; reason and passion; health and disease; realism and sensation – bleed into each other and, in doing so, suggest the innate instability of such constructions. Braddon's exposure of cultural representations as inherently unstable seems to illustrate Homi Bhabha's argument regarding the perceived fixity of stereotypes. In *The Location* of *Culture*, and more specifically in the third chapter of that book, 'The Other Question', Bhabha argues that colonial discourse is contingent on the 'concept of "fixity" in the ideological construction of otherness' (Bhabha 2004: 18), and that this fixity is the 'sign of cultural/historical/racial difference' (ibid.: 18). Because this fixity, though, is illusory, it facilitates, to quote Bhabha, a 'productive ambivalence'; Otherness is 'at once an object of desire and derision' (ibid.: 9) and thus a space from which to question colonial discourse.

Nineteenth-century Italy was not, of course, colonially subject to Britain. Nevertheless, dominant Victorian representations – cultural, literary and artistic – were predicated on a language of power, hierarchical distinction and even primitivism, familiar from colonial discourse, so that postcolonial theories of otherness can provide a useful framework for analysing the circulation and invocation of, as well as resistance to, popular cultural perceptions of Italy. The binaries around which Braddon constructs her poem are typical of mid-Victorian conceptions of Italy. As Annemarie McAllister suggests, the 'trope of contrast between paradisiacal natural environment and degraded inhabitants, or indeed contrast between perceived characteristics of England and Italy, was a key feature of the discourse about Italy and Italians in the mid-nineteenth century' (McAllister 2007: 20).

Braddon challenges the fixity of cultural stereotypes in 'Olivia' by imbuing them with a fluidity, whereby assigned national characteristics are seen to shift between the English and the Italian characters. Initially, Italy and women are associated with sensation, passion, instability and diseased states, in opposition to an English identity that is implicitly male, rational and healthy. However, such binaries are ultimately collapsed, as the narrative's attempts to sensationalise and 'other' the Italian male body are resisted. As the poem progresses, the chief Italian protagonist becomes increasingly imbued with typically 'English' characteristics, whereas the English nobleman is infected by 'Italian' passion and irrationality. Braddon's poem, therefore, offers a fruitful text for the analysis of popular mid-Victorian negotiations of the 'foreign body' and its implicit role in the construction of a healthy national identity.

'Garibaldi' and 'Olivia'

Since Braddon's poetry remains under-researched and relatively unknown, I will first offer a brief summary of the respective narrative content of the two poems under consideration, before demonstrating in more detail how these ideas work in the texts. 'Garibaldi' follows the hero's campaign from the shores of Calabria where he first landed with his small army, through various incidents up to the assault on Palermo, on to Garibaldi's retirement from the war, and ends on 'a vigorous and impetuous harangue to Victor Emmanuel' (Anon 1861d: 547). It focuses on the themes of freedom from oppression, masculine courage and male bonds. In 'Garibaldi', the central male body is represented wholly in heroic terms – as a soldier, a national saviour. The old-fashioned epic form and fixed rhyme scheme of the Spenserian stanza evoke an established tradition of heroic manhood. By contrast, the freer structure of 'Olivia' is more modern, fittingly for a poem that complicates traditional stereotypes of masculinity and nationality.

The first person speaker of 'Olivia' is twenty-year-old Avonly, the eldest son of an English earl, who is travelling in Naples with a tutor. He meets, and is instantly captivated by, a beautiful woman (three years his senior). Olivia lives with her father, a disreputable adventurer who makes a living by cheating at cards, and from the outset it is clear that she is as untrustworthy as she is dazzling. While he is in Italy, Avonly receives news of his father's death and consequently his own succession to the title and estates. Despite knowing in his heart that Olivia is cold and mercenary, the young nobleman is infected by what he describes as his 'life's great madness' (Braddon 1861: l. 112) in his passion for her, and marries her regardless. Enter Carlo Angelo, a handsome opera singer, with whom Olivia has previously had some form of (at this stage) unspecified relationship. After this meeting, the action shifts to London, with Olivia holding court in the highest echelons of English society, while Avonly is treated by her as a 'favourite footman' (ibid.: l. 721). At a party one night, Carlo Angelo makes an unexpected appearance and Avonly is gripped by suspicion and jealousy of the singer. Some weeks later, returning to London from a visit to his estates, Avonly overhears Olivia and Angelo in conversation. It becomes clear that the singer is his wife's long-standing lover and, to make matters even worse, she is currently attempting to persuade her paramour to murder her English husband. Angelo meets Avonly on the stairs and realises he has heard everything. They arrange to fight a duel, during which Angelo is accidentally killed. When Avonly returns to break the unwelcome news to his wife that *he* is alive and her lover dead, he finds her entertaining her latest victim, a sixty-year old duke. On hearing the news that Angelo is dead, Olivia has a fit of hysterics, and Avonly leaves her forever. A trial clears him of murder and the young earl takes Angelo's body back to Naples, where he remains in self-imposed exile from the country of his birth.

In a condensed summary such as this (the poem is nearly 1,800 lines in length), the melodramatic and clichéd elements are obvious. However, Braddon's poem assembles the basic ingredients of melodrama and proceeds to infuse them with new complexity, blurring the traditional significations so that stock characters lose their habitual meanings. Readerly expectations are continually undercut, in a way that encourages a re-evaluation of familiar cultural stereotypes and assumptions.

The first of these subversions of expectation occurs in relation to Olivia herself. From the start of the poem, the narrator, Avonly, repeatedly associates the loveliness of Olivia with the beauties of the Italian landscape, thus encouraging the reader to identify femininity with Italy. Olivia, we are told, has 'all the Naples sunlight in her face' and a 'glory in her eyes [which] shone back that other sun in the low skies' (Braddon 1861: ll. 71; 94). This association of Olivia with Italy also echoes Victorian perceptions of Italy as a compelling juxtaposition of transcendent beauty and degradation, since Avonly's narration makes it clear that Olivia's dazzling beauty is matched by a degraded and corrupt moral character: she is one 'On whom all worldliness had left its taint, / Who held each virtue as a kind of paint / to hide the native vices of the earth' (ibid.: ll. 163–5).

However, just as we begin to sense that we know where this is going, Braddon upsets these initial connections by revealing that Olivia is not in fact Italian and that her nationality is a matter of some indeterminacy. Avonly has initially dwelt extensively on Olivia's physical appearance: 'Her waving hair upon the southern breeze / Floated a *golden* veil that reached her knees; / Her eyes a scintillating *blue*, / Had every look, and not one true' (ibid.: ll. 64–7, my emphasis). Olivia's blonde-haired, blue-eyed beauty not only anticipates Lady Audley, Braddon's most famous duplicitous *femme fatale*, but also evokes a conventionally English notion of beauty. Next we are told of Olivia and her father: 'They were French – German – Spanish, as some said. / It was his will in Naples to give out / They came of a high Norman race' (ibid.: ll. 137–9). This deliberate ambiguity about the precise nature of Olivia's 'otherness' is interesting. The poem's trajectory, which moves towards a validation of Italianness, demands that Olivia's nationality be 'other', due to her undeniable status as morally and sexually beyond the pale. But Braddon also frustrates Victorian readers' ability to specifically culturally stereotype Olivia (as either French, German, Spanish, etc.), and though she remains 'foreign' and thus both exotic and potentially untrustworthy, she is an unspecified other, whose otherness ultimately is inferred to reside in her femininity.

Another effect of Olivia's indeterminate nationality is that Carlo Angelo, the opera singer who is in love with her, becomes the central Italian figure. Expectations that Angelo will embody the role of the clichéd Italian villain are gradually demolished (as discussed below) until, finally, he emerges as the most noble and tragic character in the poem. This was a point completely missed by most contemporary reviewers, whose own adherence to cultural stereotypes are apparent in remarks such as those of an *Athenaeum* critic, who describes Angelo as 'a super-refined, unpleasant opera-singer' (Anon. 1861a: 259). This comment is far more revealing of the reviewer's prejudices than it is an accurate description of Angelo's characterisation as it develops through the poem. Indeed, Braddon encodes the respective virtues and traits of her two male protagonists in the names bestowed on them: Angelo emerges as the true angel of the poem – a pure spirit – whose death enables him to transcend social constructions of gender. Significantly, angels are ambiguous in their gender. In the Judeo-Christian Bible, angels appear as men, as women, as well as on occasion appearing to change gender or to have no discernible gender at all. Thus, Angelo's name reflects both his status as angel and his indeterminate relation to gender stereotypes – oscillating as he does between the traditional traits ascribed to both men and women. This ambiguity also relates to Angelo's occupation of opera singer, as discussed below. Avonly, on the other hand, evokes ideas of Englishness in its semantic allusion to Avalon, the legendary island of Arthurian legend. Avon is also the old Celtic word for river, thus reinforcing the associations between Avonly's character and the history and legends of Britain.

Initial representations of Angelo evoke familiar mid-Victorian stereotypes, while simultaneously undercutting them through the inclusion of the attributes of the English upper classes. For instance, Angelo is described by Avonly as 'Coldly grave / And dignified, the frigid bow he gave – / Cold as an *Englishman*'s' (Braddon 1861: ll. 579–81, my emphasis). Angelo himself refers to England as 'A noble land [...] the proud and free / antithesis of trampled Italy' (ibid.: ll. 584–5), an assessment which can only be read ironically, when England, not Italy, becomes the site of his own *ignoble* murder and Avonly's disgrace. Moreover, repeated references to Angelo being 'tall and *proud*' and possessed of 'reckless beauty, reckless *pride*' (ibid.: ll. 834; 1482, my emphasis) work to recall and question his previous stereotypical assessment of the respective countries. It is also notable that Braddon's poem continually works to undermine the idea that England and Italy are in fact antithetical – and she calls into question the attributes assigned to each in Angelo's statement. If

Italy is 'trampled' by the historical oppression of France and Austria, Braddon also shows it, through Angelo, to be 'proud' and 'noble'. In contrast, by the end of the poem, Lord Avonly (representative of England) is neither 'proud', 'noble' or 'free', but an exile from his own country, enslaved by his past.

Angelo repeatedly resists the attempts of both Olivia and Avonly to frame him within cultural stereotypes. When Olivia assumes his compliance in her plan to have Avonly murdered, he replies:

> You've read of Southern villains in your books,
> And peopled Italy with villainies.
> You think I hide a dagger in my breast,
> And murder skulks beneath my silken vest;
> You have read wrong – we do not kill – we fight,
> And hold our only foes the foes of right.
> I will not slay your fair-haired boy, nor be
> One blot the more on fallen Italy. (ibid.: ll. 1047–54)

Angelo directly confronts national stereotypes here, and rejects them. Note that Angelo says that Olivia has '*read* wrong' – the implication being that literary representations of Italians are partially responsible for propagating such stereotypes. Reynolds points out that one of the features of what he terms 'Italianism' was 'that there was considerable cultural circulation between the representers and the represented. The English fuelled their imaginings of Italy with reading of Italian writers' (Reynolds 2001: 82). Just as Angelo accuses Olivia of judging him by her reading practices, elsewhere too he is repeatedly connected to certain forms of anti-realist literature, predominantly melodrama. After his impassioned speech quoted above, wherein Angelo refuses to 'slay' her husband, Olivia retorts: 'Who talked of slaying him? you choose your phrase / From old Minerva novels and stage-plays' (ibid.: l. 143). The links to melodramatic literature, and its associations with women and foreigners (both popularly stereotyped by mid-Victorians as excitable and irrational) anticipates the debates over the sensation novel that were to dominate 1860s literary discourse, and in which Braddon was to play a major part. The connections between national characteristics and reading practices also gestures to the power of literary stereotypes in promoting xenophobic cultural beliefs. Indeed, as McAllister astutely observes: 'To contain Italians within the boundaries of the page was to establish the superiority of the reader by the controlling gaze, yet also, paradoxically, to allow readers to participate in Italian Otherness' (McAllister 2007: 25).

Angelo's speech also conflates a number of mid-Victorian popular assumptions about Italians, while simultaneously repudiating their veracity. The line 'we do not kill – we *fight*' (ibid.: l. 1051, my emphasis) would have resonated strongly with English readers in 1861, with Garibaldi's Sicilian campaign still a matter of popular topical debate, not to mention being the subject of the poem immediately preceding 'Olivia'. Angelo's words here thus work to deny the stereotype of Italian degradation and lawlessness and replace it with a more noble and honourable image. In 'Garibaldi', similarly, images of Italian masculinity as effeminate and emotional are displaced by manly, independent and heroic representations. In a typical passage, the omniscient speaker of the poem recounts one of Garibaldi's rousing and patriotic speeches to his men:

> And thus he answers them: – 'Italia's sons,
> Ye glorious remnants of old battles fought,
> Your wrongs are mightier than your master's guns,
> United, all things – disunited, nought; –
> Ye need no foreign help, too dearly bought,
> No, – let your children to their children tell
> Alone their father's death, or freedom fought,
> Alone they conquered, and alone they fell,
> Their war-cry this – "Italia and Emmanuel!"'
> (ibid. 'Garibaldi': stanza 21)

Mariaconcetta Costantini has recently argued that Braddon's 'heroicization of the *condottiero* bears evidence of a widespread tendency to use Garibaldi as a trigger of self-criticism and a valorous alternative to the sceptic materialism of Victorian society' (Costantini forthcoming: 2). Hence, 'Garibaldi' may be seen as a covert critique of British values and, in relation to my specific argument, British masculinity, in a similar way to 'Olivia'. As the quotation makes clear, there is an emphasis on male relationships and male behaviour that contribute to a particular mode of masculinity: a critique of British values inevitably involves a different set of values in opposition to them.

Despite her conscientious attempt to present an accurate account of the Sicilian campaign, Braddon's poem contains a considerable quantity of romanticised oratory and hyperbole. One reviewer gently mocked Braddon for the 'vast amount of oratorical blaze and crackle about "Italia" and "Sicilia"', and appeared equally amused and exasperated by the fact that she 'actually makes Garibaldi improvise a song (words and melody), after the manner of an operatic hero' (Anon. 1861b: 2). Braddon's artistic licence in presenting her Italian general in such a manner provides a link between Garibaldi (as Braddon imagines him) and Angelo, the opera singer in 'Olivia', thereby tying both poems to the romantic tradition of writing about Italy. As Sutcliffe points out (2014), such romanticising of Italy was clearly evident in the British constructions of Garibaldi during the early 1860s. Moreover, the figure of the opera singer in itself conjures connotations of specific forms of masculinity. In dominant British thinking about manliness, the male operatic singer was considered effeminate and exotic, while simultaneously being the focus of admiration for women. This was in part a consequence of the history of the male opera singer. Elizabeth Abbot in her book, *A History of Celibacy*, notes that 'until the late eighteenth century, Italian opera and castrati were indistinguishable concepts, and 70 percent of male opera singers were castrati' (Abbot 1999: 333). This trend decreased (though did not entirely come to an end) with the introduction of female opera singers by the beginning of the nineteenth century; yet the stigma of effeminacy remained evident. As Pierre Dubois also notes of the castrati: 'they were not real men because they had been emasculated, and this consequently constituted a threat to the nation's masculinity' (Dubois 2015: 22). These associations have implications for reading both Angelo in 'Olivia' and Garibaldi. In some respects, they render Braddon's characterisation of Garibaldi a paradox; he is simultaneously associated with the hyper-manliness of the soldier and military commander and also the traditionally emasculated and effeminised figure of the Italian opera singer. Suzanne Aspden has also discussed the ways in which opera 'came to be seen as music's pre-eminent contributor to nationalism' (Aspden 2012: 276). In this way, Braddon's use of the figure of the Italian male opera singer functions as a useful short-hand for both the theme of national identity and for a specific form of admired, yet simultaneously marginalised and effeminised masculinity. In 'Olivia', Avonly's direct representations of Angelo are more interesting still. In addition to the cultural stereotyping ascribed to Olivia, the young earl also draws on more overt racial signifiers, which effectively 'Orientalise' Angelo. Oscillating between images of black and white, Avonly describes 'his hair – of inkiest hue, / So black, his pale face by the contrast shone / White as a mask' (Braddon 1861: ll. 506–7); 'the foreign beauty of his face', we are told, is 'More *Eastern* than Italian – those dark eyes' (ibid.: ll. 520–1, my emphasis). The mask metaphor could be read as Avonly's half-conscious subscribing here to primitivist discourses about Italians and their 'racial' inferiority, which Angelo's Caucasian appearance merely veils. Avonly lingers almost obsessively on Angelo's physical form, finding him at once beautiful and Other, and the repetitions of the words 'foreign' and 'beauty' are revealing: 'But I could every line and feature trace / That made the foreign beauty of his face' (ibid.: ll. 513–14).

At the moment when Avonly overhears his wife together with Angelo, he emphasises more overtly still this racial otherness: 'As then I saw that man I see him yet; / Still see the young, the pale Italian face, / With that dark something of an Eastern race / Darkening its beauty' (ibid.: ll. 1212–15). The repetition of 'Eastern', together with the suggestion that this 'darkens' his beauty, reinforces Vescova, Villa and Vita's association between Victorian representations of Italy and twentieth-century depictions of the Orient. Both practise a form of exoticism, which Brett Berliner sees as a 'form of relativism where an other is exalted or denigrated as a means of defining the self [. . .] [T]he exotic is constructed as a distant, picturesque other that evokes feelings, emotions, and ideals in the self that have been considered lost in the civilizing process' (Berliner 2002: 4). This exoticism takes on a homosocial, even homoerotic, form in Braddon's poem, as Avonly constantly talks of Angelo's beauty, as discussed above. Moreover, at the end of the poem, after the Italian's death in England, Avonly takes his body back to Naples and remains there, tending his grave, a point to which I will return.

From the beginning of Avonly's infatuation with Olivia, the characteristics that define him as a typically Victorian, English, upper-class male begin to fragment and are replaced by many of the attributes that Angelo evokes as being Italian. Similarly, once the action shifts to London, the healthy, rational body of England itself is increasingly infected by 'Italian' passion and sensationalism. When Angelo arrives in London, Avonly is immediately transported back in memory to the Neapolitan landscape: 'Italy – Naples – all the summer scene [. . .] Flashed back' (Braddon 1861: ll. 832–4). And from this point on, descriptions of England evoke earlier images of Italy. When Avonly overhears his betrayal by Olivia, as he stands on the stairs, he observes: 'the glimpse of garden through the hall, / With orange trees that never blew, and flowers / That withered slowly through the hot noon hours' (ibid.: ll. 939–41), which is arguably a more Italian than English image.

It is significant that the duel between Avonly and Angelo takes place in England rather than Italy. Duelling had long been outlawed and was largely out of fashion by the mid-nineteenth century, so it strikes the reader as an un-English thing to be happening, or at least anachronistic. It is almost as if Olivia and Angelo have 'infected' respectable English society with their 'foreign ways'. But Angelo's suggestion that they should use pistols rather than swords – 'let us fight / In the old English fashion' (ibid.: ll. 1276–7) – reminds his opponent that duelling is as much an English tradition as a Continental one, thereby collapsing distinctions between the two nations again. When Avonly arrives at the duel, Angelo is 'lying at the foot / Of a great oak-tree's gnarled and rugged root' (ibid.: ll. 1427–8), the Italian's association with the oak – a quintessentially English symbol and the national tree – again emphasising the way in which Italian and English signifiers in relation to the descriptions of scenes and scenery are increasingly blurred throughout the poem.

The duel climactically brings together the questions of honour, nobility and the reversal of stereotypes that the poem has progressively explored. Angelo nobly and bravely fires in the air, whereas Avonly refuses to do so and, though he swears he meant to miss his opponent, a slight malfunction with his pistol leads to the Italian being shot through the heart.

> One folded arm beneath his ruffled hair,
> The thin smoke curling in the balmy air,
> One idle hand entwined in the long grass
> On which the breezes tremble as they pass;
> His drooping eyelids shutting out the skies
> Kept the dark secrets of his eastern eyes.
> Handsome, insouciant, in the dying day,
> Upon the brink of night and death he lay.
> (ibid.: ll. 1433–40)

Avonly's description of Angelo's dying body focuses simultaneously on his beauty ('handsome') and his otherness ('eastern eyes'). At the moment of his death, they are reconciled in their mutual hatred of Olivia, the 'dreadful creature, miscalled woman' (ibid.: l. 1508), who has apparently been the cause of all this tragedy. Finally, Braddon's poem allows national differences to be elided in male homosocial bonds. The Italian's dead body, cradled in the arms of his erstwhile English rival, becomes the site where cultural difference is bridged. Othering is displaced from race and nation onto gender, Italian honour is restored, English pride is humbled, and Woman is positioned as the ultimate Other.

Queer theory has provided us with a mode of analysis and a language through which to identify and discuss instances of gender transgression in literary texts. As Eve Kosofsky Sedgwick notes: 'in any male-dominated society, there is a special relationship between male homosocial (*including* homosexual) desire and the structures for maintaining and transmitting patriarchal power' (Sedgwick 1985: 25, emphasis in original). In 'Olivia', the heteronormative resolution is excluded, the poem eliminating the disruptive female and concluding with bonded masculinity. The ultimate coupling of the poem involves the two male rivals, albeit separated by death.

> By the Naples shore,
> Where I drag out the remnant of my days,
> There is a grave, wild myrtles trailing o'er,
> 'Tangled with arbutus flowers; the grass
> White with spring's snow, the wood anemone.
> (Braddon 1861: ll. 1651–5)

The flower symbolism is significant here: in Greek and Roman mythology respectively, myrtles were sacred to Aphrodite and to Venus, the goddesses of love; they are widely understood as representing love and are the Hebrew symbol for marriage. Similarly, arbutus means 'Thee only do I love' and, as such, arbutus trees and flowers are also symbolic of love and devotion. The final flower that Braddon mentions as adorning Angelo's grave is the anemone, which, according to Greek mythology, sprang from Aphrodite's tears as she mourned the death of Adonis; the anemone also symbolises unfading love. Braddon thus concludes her poem about male rivalry with the suggestion of male love and devotion.

A superficial reading of this resolution to 'Olivia' might see the representative of Italian masculinity vanquished in combat by its English counterpart, yet Avonly's exile in Naples and the insistence on specific flowers suggest to the reader that Braddon is offering a more complex picture. Avonly's devotion can only be expressed after the death of Angelo and beyond the geographical perimeters of England, but his behaviour nonetheless demonstrates a form of homosocial relationship, which complicates notions of heteronormative and national masculinities. Although now an absent presence, Angelo, as the Italian male body, dominates the poem's ending, taking on a significance for the narrative and for Braddon's interrogation of gendered behaviour that it is unable to fill during the rest of the poem.

As can be seen in these readings of 'Garibaldi' and 'Olivia' offered in the light of notions of masculinity and the Other, Braddon's representation of the Italian male body plays with, if not actually subverts, some of the predominant associations of masculinity and nationality from the period in which she is writing. It is perhaps not surprising that Braddon should comply with her patron's request in paying attention to the figure of Garibaldi, nor that, given the focus on Italy, these two poems should appear side by side. Of more interest, and perhaps more surprisingly given the contrasting subject matter and narrative, both poems are nonetheless concerned specifically with the Italian male body. Both poems show Braddon's awareness of, but also willingness to question, prevalent opinion and cultural representations of this subject matter. It is only by reading them in parallel, as it could be argued that Braddon intended, that the reader appreciates the extent to which these poems offer a thoroughgoing engagement with questions of masculinity and nationality through their focus on the Italian male body.

Note

1. On 'Garibaldimania' and the British construction of Garibaldi in the 1860s, see Sutcliffe 2014, Beales 2002, Davis 1982 and Riall 2007, among others.

Works Cited

Abbot, E. (1999), *A History of Celibacy*, New York: Scribner.
Anon. (1861a), 'Garibaldi; and Other Poems', *Athenaeum*, 1739 (23 Feb.), p. 259.
Anon. (1861b), 'Literature', *Daily News*, issue 4647 (3 April), p. 2.
Anon. (1859a), 'England and Italy', *Bell's Life in London and Sporting Chronicle* (17 April), p. 3.
Anon. (1859b), 'Garibaldi', *The Lady's Newspaper*, issue 629 (15 Jan.), p. 33.
Anon. (1861c), '*Garibaldi, and Other Poems*, by M. E. Braddon', *National Magazine*, 9: 53 (Mar.), p. 278.
Anon. (1861d), '*Garibaldi and Other Poems*', *The British Quarterly Review*, 66 (April), p. 547.
Aspden, S. (2012), 'Opera and National Identity', in Nicholas Till (ed.), *The Cambridge Companion to Opera Studies*, Cambridge: Cambridge University Press, pp. 276–97.
Beales, D. (2002), *The Risorgimento and the Unification of Italy*, London and New York: Routledge.
Berliner, B. A. (2002), *Ambivalent Desire: The Exotic Black Other in Jazz-Age France*, Amherst, MA: University of Massachusetts Press.
Bhabha, H. (2004), *The Location of Culture*, London: Routledge.
Braddon, M. E. (1861), *Garibaldi and Other Poems*, London: Bosworth.

Braddon, M. E. [1860] (2003), 'My First Novel', in Chris Willis (ed.), *The Trail of the Serpent*, New York: Modern Library, pp. 415–27.

Costantini, M. (forthcoming), 'M. E. Braddon's Literary Apprenticeship: Heroism, Madness and Sensation in Garibaldi and Three Times Dead', *Women's Writing*.

Davis, John A. (1982), 'Garibaldi and England', *History Today*, 32, pp. 21–6.

Dubois, P. (2015), *Music in the Georgian Novel*, Cambridge: Cambridge University Press.

McAllister, A. (2007), *John Bull's Italian Snakes and Ladders: English Attitudes to Italy in the Mid-Nineteenth Century*, Newcastle: Cambridge Scholars Publishing.

Nemesvari, R. (2015), 'Manful Sensations: Affect, Domesticity and Class Status Anxiety in *East Lynne* and *Aurora Floyd*', in Phillip Mallett (ed.), *The Victorian Novel and Masculinity*, Basingstoke: Palgrave Macmillan, pp. 88–115.

Pykett, L. (1992), *The 'Improper' Feminine: The Women's Sensation Novel and the New Woman Writing*, London: Routledge.

Reynolds, M. (2001), *The Realms of Verse, 1830–1870: English Poetry in a Time of Nation-Building*, Oxford and New York: Oxford University Press.

Riall, L. (2007), *Garibaldi: Invention of a Hero*, New Haven, CT: Yale University Press.

Sedgwick, E. K. (1985), *Between Men: English Literature and Male Homosocial Desire*, New York: Columbia University Press.

Sutcliffe, M. (2014), *Victorian Radicals and Italian Democrats*, London: Royal Historical Society.

Tosh, J. (2005), *Manliness and Masculinity in Nineteenth Century Britain: Essays on Gender, Family, and Empire*, Harlow: Pearson.

Vescovi, A. L. Villa and P. Vita (2009), *The Victorians and Italy: Literature, Travel, Politics and Art*, Milan: Polimetrica.

Walchester, K. (2007), *Our Own Fair Italy: Nineteenth Century Women's Travel Writing and Italy 1800–1844*, Oxford and Bern: Peter Lang.

Contributors

Françoise Baillet is currently a Senior Lecturer in British Studies at the University of Cergy-Pontoise, France, where she has taught history and art since 2004. Her research addresses British cultural history in the nineteenth century, and focuses in particular on *fin-de-siècle* painting, the Victorian press and the text-image interplay in illustrated literature. She is the author of a doctoral thesis (2002, Paris-Sorbonne) on George du Maurier's pictorial criticism of Pre-Raphaelitism and Aestheticism, and has published articles on Victorian painters and black-and-white artists. She is currently working on a book project entitled *Visions and Divisions. Punch's Cultural Discourses and the Victorian Social Order (1850–1880)* which examines the visual discourse of the magazine (with caricature as its central aesthetic code) as a way of maintaining social, gender and artistic borders in Victorian England. Her latest articles deal with the representation of workers and paupers in *The Illustrated London News* and *The Graphic*.

Joanne Begiato is Professor of History and Head of History, Philosophy and Culture at Oxford Brookes University. She specialises in the history of masculinities, family and marriage. She has published many articles and chapters on subjects as diverse as wife-beating, fatherhood, pregnancy, married women's status under the law and tearful sailors. Her books include *Unquiet Lives: Marriage and Marriage Breakdown in England 1660–1800* (Cambridge University Press, 2003), *Parenting in England 1760–1830: Emotions, Identity and Generation* (Oxford University Press, 2012) and *Sex and the Church in the Long Eighteenth Century: Religion, Enlightenment and the Sexual Revolution* (I. B. Tauris, 2017) with William Gibson. She is currently working on a monograph called *Materialising Manliness in Britain c. 1760–1901: Bodies, Emotions, and Objects* (Manchester University Press, forthcoming 2019) and three edited volumes:

Law and Litigants in Early Modern English Society: Essays in Memory of Christopher W. Brooks (Cambridge University Press, forthcoming 2019) with Michael Lobban and Adrian Green; *Martial Masculinities: Experiencing and Imagining the Military in the Long Nineteenth Century* (Manchester University Press, forthcoming 2019) with Michael Brown and Anna-Maria Barry; and *A Sailor's Progress? Negotiating Masculinities and Modernity in the Maritime World 1815–1940* (Palgrave Macmillan, forthcoming 2019) with Karen Downing and Steven Gray.

Anne-Marie Beller is Senior Lecturer in English Literature at Loughborough University. She is the author of *Mary Elizabeth Braddon: A Companion to the Mystery Fiction* (McFarland, 2012), *Mary Elizabeth Braddon: Writing in the Margins* (Routledge, forthcoming 2018), and co-editor of *Rediscovering Victorian Women Sensation Writers* (Routledge, 2014). Anne-Marie has published articles on Braddon, Wilkie Collins, Ellen Wood and Amelia Edwards, including essays for Blackwell's *A Companion to Sensation Fiction* and *The Cambridge Companion to Sensation Fiction*.

Charlotte Boyce is a Senior Lecturer in English Literature at the University of Portsmouth. Her research covers a variety of Victorian and neo-Victorian topics, including food and consumption, visual culture and celebrity culture. She is the co-author of *A History of Food in Literature from the Fourteenth Century to the Present* (Routledge, 2017) and *Victorian Celebrity Culture and Tennyson's Circle* (Palgrave Macmillan, 2013).

Alice Crossley is a Senior Lecturer in English Literature at the University of Lincoln, where she is also Programme Leader for English. She writes about gender, youth and age in the Victorian novel, and is completing a monograph for Routledge on *Male Adolescence in Mid-Victorian Fiction*, focusing on the work of George Meredith, William Makepeace Thackeray and Anthony Trollope (Routledge, forthcoming 2018). She has published articles and chapters on masculinity, aging and age difference, dandyism, serialisation and the Victorian valentine. In 2017 she edited a special summer issue of *Nineteenth-Century Gender Studies* on Age and Gender (*NCGS Journal*, 13: 2), and co-edited (with Dr Richard Salmon) a volume of essays on *Thackeray in Time: History, Memory, and Modernity* (Routledge, 2016). Alice is part of the Executive Committee of the British Association for Victorian Studies (BAVS), and was co-organiser of the 2017 BAVS conference in Lincoln.

Ruth Heholt is Senior Lecturer in English at Falmouth University. She has published on ghosts, the gothic, masculinity and crime fiction. She works on Victorian literature and culture as well as contemporary texts. She is founding editor of *Revenant: Critical and Creative Studies of the Supernatural* a peer reviewed online journal (www.revenantjournal.com). She has published a critical edition of Catherine Crowe's 1847 novel *The Story of Lilly Dawson* (Victorian Secrets Press, 2015) and is co-editor of the collection, *Haunted Landscapes: Super-Nature and the Environment* (Rowman Littlefield, 2016). She is working on a monograph on Catherine Crowe and has edited the collection: *Gothic Britain*, with William Hughes (University of Wales Press, forthcoming 2018).

Tara MacDonald is an Assistant Professor of English Literature at the University of Idaho. She is the author of *The New Man, Masculinity, and Marriage in the Victorian Novel* (Routledge, 2015) and co-editor, with Anne-Marie Beller, of *Rediscovering Victorian Women Sensation Writers* (Routledge, 2014). She has published widely on Victorian masculinity, sensation fiction, and neo-Victorian fiction.

Meredith Miller is Senior Lecturer in English and Writing at Falmouth University. She has published widely on gender, sexuality and the popular novel. Her most recent academic monograph is *Feminine Subjects in Masculine Fiction: Modernity, Will and Desire, 1870–1910* (Palgrave, 2013). She is also a published author of fiction.

Joanne Ella Parsons is an Associate Lecturer at Bath Spa University. Her PhD is entitled *Food and the Male Body: Narratives of Consumption in the Nineteenth-Century Novel*. She has previously co-edited a special issue of *Nineteenth-Century Contexts*, in which she published an essay on the fat male body in R. S. Surtees' Jorrocks novels. Joanne is the editor of the *Wilkie Collins Journal* and the assistant editor of *Revenant*. She was the co-founder, with Dr Sarah Chaney, of the *Damaging the Body* series of events.

Ryan Sweet is a Wellcome Trust/LHRI ISSF Early Career Research Fellow in the School of English at the University of Leeds. He is currently working on an academic monograph on Victorian cultural and literary representations of prostheses, and a new project that explores the entangled histories of disability and animality. His publications include an article in *Victorian Review* and a chapter in Claire L. Jones' edited collection *Rethinking Modern Histories of Prostheses in Anglo-American Commodity Cultures, 1850–1960* (Manchester

University Press, 2017). He also has a chapter forthcoming in *Literature and Medicine in the Nineteenth Century* (ed. Andrew Mangham, Cambridge University Press). Alongside his research, Ryan is the managing editor of the interdisciplinary peer-reviewed journal *Literature and History* and a contributor to the digital reader *Nineteenth-Century Disability: Cultures and Contexts*.

Alison Younger is Senior Lecturer in English at the University of Sunderland. Her primary research interests lie in Irish and Scottish literatures (particularly Celtic gothic), consumer culture, advertising and literature and monster theory. She has published in the fields of contemporary critical theory, Irish cultural history, advertising and commodity culture, in *Blackwood's Magazine* and on gothic literatures. She has co-edited a number of scholarly collections and is currently researching the role and behaviours of the gothic gentleman in the nineteenth century.

Index

abulia, 227
aesthete, 66, 123, 142, 172–88
alcohol, 49–51, 54–5, 57, 60, 92, 194
animals, 28, 222–3
appetite, 51–2, 59, 194–211, 215–30
asylums, 48, 53, 56–8, 60, 154, 220, 225

Ballantyne, Robert Michael, 93
  The Madman and the Pirate, 87–8, 94, 96
  Why Did I Not Become a Sailor, 94–6, 98–9
Barrie, J. M., *Peter Pan*, 87, 96, 101–2
Bessant, Walter, *The Revolt of Man*, 78
body, the
  bodily fragility, 32–3, 79, 113
  body as metaphor, 12–13
  displayed bodies, 5–10, 34–5, 42, 66–7, 69–71, 76, 229–30
  objectified bodies, 4–6, 9, 66–71, 75–9, 159, 229
  othered bodies, 2, 4, 6, 9, 13, 144, 152, 159, 236, 243–7
  visible bodies, 2–8, 34, 159

bodybuilding, 65–6, 70
Bohemians, 69–70, 182, 184, 188
Braddon, Mary Elizabeth, 234–6
  'Garibaldi', 234–8, 239–40, 244–4, 248–9
  'Olivia', 234–8, 239–49
Broughton, Rhoda, 148
  Twilight Stories, 151, 154–5, 159–62
Brown, Hugh Stowell, 46
bullying, 26, 29, 32, 33–7, 50

Carlyle, 141, 172, 187, 196–7, 199
Chartism, 203
Christianity, 12, 31, 100, 139, 157, 206
class, 2, 12, 14–16, 18–19, 26–7, 32, 46, 48–51, 59, 72–3, 97–8, 100, 108, 117, 130, 133, 136–8, 140, 150, 165, 171–2, 175, 177–9, 188, 193–211, 242, 246
Cockney School, 109
Coleridge, Samuel Taylor, 116
Collins, Wilkie
  The Law and the Lady, 100
  The Woman in White, 215–30

Colney Hatch Asylum, 47,
    53–6
colonial, 2, 4, 6–9, 12–14, 157,
    159, 184, 239
Connelly, John, 59
consumption, 108–12, 114–15,
    117–19, 122
Contagious Diseases Acts, 66,
    71–3, 75
corporal punishment, 26,
    29–33
corpulence, 215–30
criminality, 186, 215–30, 238
Crowe, Catherine, 148, 165
    The Night Side of Nature,
    150–1, 153–4, 159–60, 162
Cruikshank, George, *The
    Bottle*, 50–1

dandy, 78, 128, 130–1, 140–4,
    172, 179
decadence, 111, 120–1, 123,
    131–2, 134, 138, 142, 144,
    172–3, 181–2
degenerate, 18, 66, 76, 129–
    31, 133–4, 139–40, 172–3,
    175–6, 181–2, 186–7
degeneration, 66, 72, 76, 131,
    133, 181–7
deviance, 68, 130
Dickens, Charles, 29–30
    David Copperfield, 27–33,
    39, 40, 42, 97
    Our Mutual Friend, 92, 101
    Pickwick Papers, 215
diet, 47–9, 193–211, 215–30
disability studies, 89, 91,
    95, 98
discipline, 46–8, 57, 60, 66,
    129, 194–5, 197–211,
    216
disease, 40–1, 48, 51–4, 58–9,
    66, 71–3, 75, 79, 102, 109,
    111, 114, 123, 140, 172,
    183–4, 186, 208, 227,
    238–9
Disraeli, Benjamin, *Coningsby;
    or, the New Generation*,
    36–7
Dowie, Muriel, Ménie, 67
    Gallia, 67–81
Du Maurier, George, 172–88

east, the, 110, 116, 219,
    245–7
eating, 193–211, 215–30
economics, 49, 68 89, 100,
    121, 136, 140, 151, 171,
    178, 193, 196–8, 200–2,
    225, 237
effeminacy, 47, 58–9, 61, 65,
    129, 139–41, 157, 176,
    178, 245
Eliot, George, 108
    Daniel Deronda, 112–18,
    121, 125
emotions, 46–7, 49, 51–3,
    55–61, 110, 217–18
eugenics, 66–8, 73, 80
excess, 47, 59–60, 110,
    219, 222
exercise, 5–6, 65–6, 70

Fanon, Frantz, 3–5
Farrar, Frederick W., *Eric, or
    Little by Little*, 26, 41–2
fashion, 71, 128, 130, 132,
    135, 137–44, 175
fatherhood, 68–9, 81
fighting, 34–5, 56
food, 34, 48–9, 193–211,
    215–30

Gaskell, Elizabeth
    Mary Barton, 193–211
    North and South, 193–4

gentlemen, 35, 49, 116, 120, 129–38, 140, 143–4, 173, 175, 195
ghosts, 124, 148–66
Gissing, George, *The Odd Women*, 75–6
Gothic, the, 123–4, 128, 131, 143–4
Grand, Sarah, 65–6
The Beth Book, 76

Haggard, H. Rider, *King Solomon's Mines*, 6–11
heredity, 111, 113–14, 116–17
Homme com il faut, 136–8
homosexuality, 1, 38, 124–5, 131–3, 165
Hughes, Thomas, *Tom Brown's Schooldays*, 26, 37–42
hunger, 194–211
Hunt, Leigh, 108–9
hysteria, 58

illness, 51, 58, 76–7, 102, 108–25, 206, 240
Italy, 219, 234–49

James, Henry, 108
The Portrait of a Lady, 109, 112, 118–25
The Wings of a Dove, 109
Johnson, Captain Charles, *A General History of the Pyrates*, 90

Keats, John, 108–12

Labouchère Amendment, 131
Lambert, Daniel, 217
landscape, 8–11
Leech, John, 172
Lockheart, John Gibson, 108–9, 125

macaronis, 138–40
madness, 47, 51–61, 94, 208, 238
  General Paralysis of the Insane, 53, 58–9
manliness, 2, 12, 14, 18–19, 26–7, 30–1, 35, 37–8, 40, 42, 46–53, 56, 59–61, 66–7, 79, 129, 131–2, 139–41, 143–4, 157–8, 162, 166, 172–3, 176, 178, 194–8, 207–8, 216, 222, 234–6, 245
marriage, 67–9, 79, 224–5
Martineau, Harriet, *The Crofton Boys*, 39
masculinity studies, 13–14
masturbation, 40–2, 48, 52, 55, 134
medicine, 40–1, 51–60, 72, 76, 128, 182, 184–208, 215
Melville, Herman, *Moby Dick*, 88, 95
Meredith, George
  The Adventures of Harry Richmond, 27, 32
  The Egoist, 30–1
military, the, 153–4, 157, 159–60, 236, 238–40
money *see* economics
morality, 12, 27, 48, 52–7, 60, 67, 76, 89, 94–5, 129–31, 134, 136, 140, 142, 144, 149, 157–8, 162, 171, 176, 178–9, 181–2, 184, 186–8, 193, 196–8, 200, 218–19, 222, 230, 234, 241
  moral treatment of the insane, 56–7, 60
motherhood, 74–5, 77
muscles, 53–5, 65–6, 69–70, 164
Muscular Christianity, 12, 26, 131, 139, 157, 172, 177

Napoleon, 218
national identity, 12, 16, 18,
    65–6, 71, 73, 81, 108, 110,
    112–14, 116–21, 123–5,
    129–30, 133, 135, 137,
    140, 144, 157, 173, 181–2,
    184–5, 196, 235–6,
    238–43, 245, 247–9
nerves, 115–16, 153, 220, 228
Nesbit, Edith, 148, 151–2
  'From the Dead', 155–64
  'John Charrington's
    Wedding', 162–5
New Man, 66–9, 73, 76,
    78, 81
New Woman, 66–9, 72–5, 78

opera singers, 219, 240, 242,
    244–5

Paris morgue, 229–30
postcolonial, 2, 13–14, 159,
    239
posture, 175–81
prosthetics, 87–102
  narrative prosthesis, 95–6
prostitutes, 72–3
Punch, 171–88

race, 1–4, 6–15, 65–7, 81,
    113–14, 116–19, 125,
    137–8, 247
reproduction, 68, 75, 77

Sandow, Eugen, 5–6, 65–6, 81
scales, 216
school, 12, 25–42
  schoolmasters, 29–31, 33
science, 5, 66, 76, 79, 113,
    128–9, 150–1, 216,
    224–5
self, the, 3, 9, 11

self-control, 47–51, 53, 55,
    57–8, 197
self-denial, 194–5, 197, 200–6
sensibility, 108, 111, 113,
    115–16
sex, 49, 51, 54, 59–60, 68,
    72, 77
sexuality, 59, 110, 218–19,
    241
Shelley, Percy, Bysshe, 109–11
Smiles, Samuel, *Self Help*,
    48, 134
Smith, Albert, *Natural History
    of the Gent*, 135–6
social purity movement, 72–3
spiritualism, 152, 158
sport, 5, 12, 26, 36, 40, 48,
    135, 137, 140–1
Stevenson, Robert Louis, 101–2
  *The Strange Case of Dr Jekyll
    and Mr Hyde*, 76, 128,
    131–6, 138
  Treasure Island, 88–93, 96,
    98–102
Stoker, Bram, *Dracula*, 76, 138
strength, 52, 54, 65
Symonds, John Addington, 39

temperance, 49–51, 54, 59
Thackeray, William Makepeace,
    26, 31–2, 34, 40
  *Doctor Birch and His Young
    Friends*, 27, 35
  Irish Sketch Book, 31
  Men's Wives, 34
  'Mr and Mrs Frank Berry',
    27, 34–5, 42
  'The Snobs of England, by
    one of themselves', 173
  Vanity Fair, 35, 36, 215
tuberculosis, 108–12, 114–15,
    121–3, 125

Tuke, Harrington, 59
Tuke, Samuel, 56–7, 60
  Description of the Retreat, 52

vegetarianism, 49
violence, 25–37, 51, 56, 95–6, 98, 134, 223
virtue, 46–7, 49, 66, 108

weight management, 216, 227
Wilde, Oscar, 173, 175, 179, 183
  The Picture of Dorian Gray, 131, 138, 141–4

Yonge, Charlotte, *The Heir of Redcylffe*, 34

EU representative:
Easy Access System Europe
Mustamäe tee 50, 10621 Tallinn, Estonia
Gpsr.requests@easproject.com

www.ingramcontent.com/pod-product-compliance
Lightning Source LLC
Chambersburg PA
CBHW061709300426
44115CB00014B/2622